KU-207-464

Theory and the Practice of Education

Volume I
Theory, values and the classroom teacher

Theory and the Practice of Education

Volume II

Academic disciplines, educational policy and the education of teachers

edited by

ANTHONY HARTNETT

Lecturer in the Sociology of Education, School of Education,
University of Liverpool

and

MICHAEL NAISH

Lecturer in the Philosophy of Education, School of Education,
University of Liverpool

HEINEMANN EDUCATIONAL BOOKS LTD

Heinemann Educational Books Ltd
LONDON EDINBURGH MELBOURNE AUCKLAND TORONTO
HONG KONG SINGAPORE KUALA LUMPUR
IBADAN NAIROBI JOHANNESBURG
LUSAKA NEW DELHI

ω 5766 73.33 · 5.78

ISBN 0 435 80413 8

© Selection, arrangement, introductions
to the readings and some issues arising
from the readings
Anthony Hartnett and Michael Naish 1976

© Reading 4, Michael Naish, Anthony Hartnett
and Douglas Finlayson 1976

First published 1976

Published by
Heinemann Education Books Ltd
48 Charles Street, London WIX 8AH

Photoset and printed by
Interprint (Malta) Ltd

Contents

Contents of Volume 1

Contents of Volume II

Index

Preface

This book arose out of our work at the School of Education, in the University of Liverpool, where between us we were teaching the philosophy of education, and the sociology of education, to three groups of students: experienced teachers attending full-time or part-time in-service courses for advanced diplomas; experienced teachers studying for the Master of Education degree; and graduates on a one-year, full-time, initial training course. During the course of our work, we came to reflect more and more on the issues that teaching such courses raised for our students, and for us.

Our students appeared to have diverse, and often incompatible views, both about what theory was in education, and about what it could offer them. They could, speculatively, be divided into the following groups, depending on their view of theory.

(*i*) Those who believed that all theory was irrelevant to good practice. For these students all that mattered was diverse experience in schools.

(*ii*) Those who thought that theory could resolve value disputes and problems about what roughly might be called educational ends, namely the aims, purposes, and point of education.

(*iii*) Those who did not see theory as impinging upon questions of ends, but solely on those of means. Theory, on this account, enabled people to be more effective in doing whatever they thought worth doing. Thus a teacher of science might see theory as telling him how to teach effectively, or more effectively, or how to use what is often called educational technology (visual aids and so on), where it is taken for granted that science should be taught, and that its nature is understood. Heads and aspiring heads might see theory as telling them how to run their schools more effectively, where some account of what education is, and of what is educationally valuable, is assumed. Students in this group, in particular, were inclined, when discussing theory, to deploy pairs of terms such as relevant and irrelevant, constructive and destructive, positive and negative, practical and academic, or practical and theoretical. In these pairs were embodied, it seemed to us, a number of implicit and unexamined views about the roles of teachers and others in the educational system; about our roles; and about education itself.

(*iv*) Those who saw theory as a source or corpus of officially approved views about what ought to go on in schools.

None of these views about theory seemed to us to be adequately grounded, and we were led to reflect on the whole problem of the relationships between theoretical activities (such as philosophy and sociology) and practical activities (such as teaching). We came to the conclusion that the connexion between theory and practice, which students of education are often expected to make for themselves, ought not to be left peripheral to or outside a course, but ought to be its central point. This book is a consequence of this conviction. We also decided that more light might be cast upon the problems of theory and practice in education if philosophy and sociology were together used to examine them.

The format of the book

Given these points, the question then arose about the sort of book which would best suit our purposes. We did not want to write a textbook, partly because we wished to include views other than our own. Nor did we feel that a book of readings, with a short introduction, would adequately cover the issues we wished to raise. All too frequently readers of such books are left to discover why the readings were included, how they relate to each other, and what sort of issues they give rise to.

Eventually, we decided on a compromise between a textbook, and a book of readings. Volume I consists of seven readings, and is in two sections. Volume II consists of the remaining six readings. Each reading is given an introduction in which we pick out the main points it makes *for our purposes*, and we say (where this is necessary) why it has been included in the book, and how it relates to education. Following the readings in each section of Volume I, and following those in Volume II, there are discussions entitled 'Some issues arising from the readings'. These discussions are meant to raise issues that might be further followed up, rather than to be considered contributions to the literature. Although each volume is self-contained and can be read without the other, the two volumes together are intended to constitute a unified argument about the role, and particularly about some of the limitations, of theory in education.

There is a final point about the format of this book and this concerns what might be taken to be our lavishness with footnotes and references to literature. Footnotes enable us to raise issues arising from points we make, without at the same time breaking the flow of the discussion. Citing literature enables us to indicate where points that we merely mention are more fully discussed. It is also a way of inviting students to look up things for themselves, and to see that very few things in philosophy and sociology are undisputed. This seems to us something that is very important to learn. Further, the amount and range of literature called upon in the philosophy and sociology of education seems to us lamentably small. The same references appear again and again, even though there is a considerable body of work in the main disciplines that remains unexploited. One useful exercise (in the sociology of knowledge) would be to see who cites whom, and what communality of viewpoint this indicates. One reason, therefore, for our citing such literature as we do is simply to bring it to people's notice and to indicate that the frontiers of the philosophy and sociology of education can be much wider than some discussions presuppose.

Using the book

The articles and discussions vary in difficulty. We found this hard to avoid, partly because of the nature of the issues themselves, partly because we did not wish to pass off as relatively simple issues those which were not, partly because we have preferred to choose readings for the quality of their discussion even if this meant excluding those which were of a lesser quality but which might be thought, on a conventional assessment, to be open to a more immediate understanding. In any case different readers, depending on their experience and background, are likely to find different parts of the book easy or difficult. One way into the readings and discussions may be: (*i*) to read our introductions to the readings and then the readings themselves; (*ii*) to re-read the introductions in the case of the more difficult articles; (*iii*) to look at the section entitled 'Some issues arising from the readings'. Introductory material to the area under discussion can often be found among our references to the literature.

The role of theory: our position

Our views about what theory can offer those who work in schools and elsewhere in the educational system, and about what we think the consequences of these views are for the way education should be conducted are, we hope, reasonably explicit in what we have ourselves written in this book, and in the quotations at the front of Volume I. Our view on the place of theory is, briefly, one of what might be called a moderate scepticism, relative both to the claims for theory often made by those professionally engaged in the education of teachers, and to the claims that (to judge from the use they put it to) a number of policy makers, and others administering or otherwise working in the educational system, are currently prepared to make for it. In particular, it needs to be said that neither sociology nor philosophy is likely to make the often intractable problems faced by teachers, policy makers, and others any easier to solve. The contrary might often be true. For what these disciplines might do is to narrow the area of what is unquestioned in education. They might make teachers, policy-makers, and others more aware of their own values, more critical of what might be called 'official views', more aware of the values of those they teach, and more aware of what is not known, and so of what they do not know. Because it is important, in our view, that teachers and others have, as far as possible, a reasonably grounded and realistic view about what theory can offer (both in their own interests, and in those of the children and students with whose well-being they are concerned) this book is intended very much more as a discussion of the limitations of theory, than as a justification of philosophy and sociology in the education of teachers, though we do discuss this issue towards the end of the book. But to the extent to which the issues raised in this book are of importance to teachers, it might be said to be at least a contribution towards how philosophy and sociology are to be justified in the education to teachers, without being designed as one.

A possible criticism

One complaint that might be raised against this book is that it is neither sociological nor philosophical, but occupies a sort of no-man's-land beyond the trenches of academic and intellectual respectability. It needs to be emphasized that this book is concerned with a problem, or series of problems, centred on theory and practice, which we believe can be illuminated by the *joint use* of philosophy and sociology. Though we have been concerned to identify the sorts of question with which we had to deal (normative, conceptual, logical, empirical, etc.), it has been a matter of comparative indifference to us whether, on some conventional categorization, they are to be described, in particular cases, as philosophical or as sociological. Even so, parts of the book can be reasonably held to be more philosophical or sociological than others. In some parts the distinction may be harder to draw, and we do not regard this as a defect. But even where the distinction can be fairly sharply drawn, the responsibility for what is said there is joint. The choice of articles is joint, each read the work of the other as the book went through its numerous drafts, and we did not feel precluded from making comments or writing on topics that might reasonably be held to have fallen under the other's discipline, when we felt that this could be profitably done. Whether or not the journey to this no-man's-land has been worth while, we leave for the reader to judge.

Possible readership

We stated at the beginning of this preface that this book arose from our teaching with a number of different groups of students at Liverpool, and we hope that the book will appeal to those who are similarly placed and to others – that is, to experienced teachers on in-service courses who are studying philosophy and sociology of education; students studying for Masters degrees in education; students undergoing initial training in university departments of education, polytechnics, and colleges of education; as well as those who are professionally concerned with the training and education of teachers. Some parts of the book raise issues about how decisions may be made at the level of educational policy. Those who are interested in this area, whether as participants, researchers, or spectators may also find something of use.

To
Elizabeth,
Isobel,
and Vera

Acknowledgements

A book of this sort consists of a large number of intellectual debts, many of which have been unconsciously incurred. We would, however, like to mention some of the people whom we know have influenced its final form, and contents.

We would like to thank those who have taught us in the recent past, especially Basil Bernstein, Brian Davies, Mrs Pamela Huby, and Michael Young.

We are indebted to Alan Blyth, Douglas Finlayson, Steve Ferguson, Derek Meakin, Hazel Sumner, Norton Tempest and David Thomas, and to other of our colleagues in the School of Education, including those involved in the Schools Council Project, 'History, Geography, and Social Science 8–13'. They have provided us with ideas, references, and stimulation. What they said at coffee, they may well now find in our book.

It can be inferred from the Preface that perhaps our greatest debt is to the students who have attended our courses, especially those who took the Diploma in the Advanced Study of Education, the Diploma in Special Education, and the Master of Education degree, between 1969 and 1973. They have been confused and baffled by our early attempts to deal with some of the issues discussed in this book. We can only hope that the interest they have shown, the questions they have asked, and the criticisms they have made, have been taken adequate note of, and that now the issues seem a little clearer.

We would like to thank the children, staff, and headteachers of two primary schools – Cherryfield County Primary School and St Francis Xavier's Primary School – where we made some videotape recordings. We are also indebted to the director and staff of the Audio-visual Aids and Programmed Learning Unit of the University of Liverpool, who enabled us to make the recordings. It was during filming at these schools that we developed some of the ideas and issues with which the book deals.

It has been our delight to use one of the best education libraries in the country. We owe a great debt to John Vaughan (the tutor-librarian), to his assistant Geoffrey Smith, and to the library staff in general. They have helped us with inter-library loans, with the purchase of books, with the photo-copying of material, and have given us a great deal of useful advice. Their tireless co-operation made this book possible.

We would like to thank those who have read part, or all, of the various drafts that this book has been through: David Aspin, Olive Banks, Alan Blyth, Leon Boucher, Brian Davies, Ray Derricot, Douglas Finlayson, F. H. Hilliard, Liz Hindess, Derek Meakin, Peter Renshaw, and Norton Tempest. They all took a great deal of care, often at busy times of the year, to make detailed and helpful comments. We would like to thank, too, Joan Carr who read the entire manuscript, and who kept a sharp eye on our English. We owe a great debt to Mrs Kath Moore, who, as if by magic, transformed our illegible, cut-up, corrected, manuscripts into clear, accurate, double-spaced typescripts. Without her help, neither of us would have been able to read what the other had written.

We are grateful to the copyright holders for permission to reproduce material included in the *Readings* Sections. Full details are given at the beginning of each reading.

We would, finally, like to thank Paul Richardson and Philippa Stratton, of Heinemann Educational Books, who waited for our vague ideas to be turned into a book, and who gave us encouragement and advice while they waited.

SCHOOL OF EDUCATION
UNIVERSITY OF LIVERPOOL
NOVEMBER 1975

Introduction to the readings

Preliminary comments

The readings in Volume I Section 1 enabled us to indicate one or two elementary ways in which theory and practice could be distinguished, and in 'Some issues arising from the readings' we looked at the distinctions in more detail and raised other related matters. Some of the main points of our discussions were as follows.

(*i*) Education gives rise to complex and often intractable value disputes. These arise partly from the nature of education itself; partly because at least some of the specific practical moral problems that face teachers, administrators, and others, may have more than one justifiable solution; partly because people may be unable to accept that solutions are justified when they are; and partly because the status of relevant empirical data may be in dispute.

(*ii*) Because practical problems in education have to be solved under 'bounded rationality', the scale of justifiable change in education is limited; feedback from the implementation of decisions is very important; and the solution of one practical problem may well give rise to a further practical problem or be only a partial solution.

(*iii*) Both for considerations depending upon contingent factors (for example, the paucity of relevant knowledge) and for what can be called, loosely, considerations of logic, it is unreasonable to expect that solutions to practical problems can be simply read off from empirical or other theoretical statements, or to expect that the acquisition and intelligent exercise of skills (for example, of the classroom teacher) can depend in any complete way upon theory (in the sense of prescriptions, maxims, rules of thumb, etc.).

(*iv*) If the suggestions contained in (*i*)–(*iii*) are true, then the help educational theory can offer to teachers and others is and will always be limited.

In Volume I Section 2, empirical evidence was provided about the activities that classroom teachers undertake, about the social contexts in which they work, and about the kind of knowledge available to guide them in solving their practical problems. Some of the main points of the discussion in 'Some issues arising from the readings' in Section 2 were as follows:

(*i*) There is a disparity between the actual tasks that some teachers perform, and the high expectations which are held about education.

(*ii*) There are various constraints of which teachers have to take cognizance when they make judgements about what to do. Those noted included, the physical plant available; interactional factors within the school; and time.

(*iii*) Value issues and disputes are inextricably bound up with teachers' roles. Specific examples were provided of these (for example, in the reading by Dumont and Wax) and general comments were made about the difficulties involved in categorizing children; about making judgements about the superiority of one form of culture over another; and about related matters.

(*iv*) Educational processes are complex, and their outcomes may be difficult to investigate.

(*v*) There is a dilemma arising from the high expectations held about education, and the lack of knowledge about how to achieve them. The research by Gross et al. was taken as a case study of change in schools.

The issues discussed in Volume II arise from those of Volume I. Volume II, therefore, continues the discussion of theory and practice. The questions raised in it concern the contribution of academic or (as they are also called) theoretical disciplines, particularly philosophy and sociology to (*i*) solving and justifying solutions to practical problems in education, and (*ii*) teacher education. The answers given to the questions raised under (*ii*) are likely to be related to on those given to the questions raised under (*i*).

We interpret the relationship between theory and practice in this part of the book as the relationship between academic disciplines (theory) and practical problems (practice). It seemed important to look at this relationship for a number of reasons. The first was that in what are intended to be justifications of educational policies and practices, appeals to theoretical work appear to be more frequent now than in the past, or at least they are now more explicit.[1] The second was that in recent years academic disciplines, particularly philosophy and sociology, have played, in England at any rate, an increasing part in teacher education.

[1] Cf. the use of psychology and sociology by advocates of comprehensive schools, or of psychology by advocates of discovery methods, or of sociology by advocates of educational priority areas. Consider also the theoretical underpinning that, it is hoped, philosophy might give the work of the Farmington Trust Research Unit in Moral Education, or that linguistics might give to recent foreign language projects. See 'Some issues arising from the readings' in Volume II, pp. 164–70. It is worth adding here that we use the term 'theoretical work' to mean 'work from academic (or theoretical) disciplines.' For a discussion which suggests that such work might perhaps consist in part of *practical* judgements, if only of a general kind, see Volume II pp. 147–51. For the term 'practical judgement', see Volume I Section I.

The third was that, on occasions, the theoretical work seemed not to have survived the journey from the academic world to that of education. What the work was taken to be in education was often different from, and even inconsistent with, what it was taken to be in the discipline from which it came. It seemed worth asking why this was.

The readings in Volume II consist of six articles which can usefully be read in pairs. The first two articles (one by Nagel, and one by Burns) are concerned with the academic disciplines of philosophy and sociology respectively. These discussions are not meant to embody definitive accounts of the disciplines. The second two articles (one by Smith and Stockman, and one by Naish, Hartnett, and Finlayson) are concerned with public explanations and justifications of policy – Smith and Stockman with them as they appear in government reports, and Naish et al. with them as they appear in what are called 'educational documents', which may, but need not, be such reports. Both these articles raise issues about the role of philosophy and sociology in education. The final two articles (one by McNamara, and one by Scheffler) discuss, respectively, the role of sociology and of theoretical studies in general in the education of teachers.

Volume II concludes with 'Some issues arising from the readings'. A brief summary of these is given on page 139.

Introduction to readings by Ernest Nagel and Tom Burns

Ernest Nagel, 'Philosophy in educational research'[2]

In this article Nagel is concerned with two general issues. The first concerns the nature of philosophy. The second concerns 'the role of philosophy in the study of educational problems'.

After commenting on the ambiguity of the word 'philosophy', Nagel begins the first part of his article by rejecting conceptions of philosophy which assign to it special procedures for discovering 'the basic kinds and structures of reality' or for establishing 'propositions about human values'. He suggests that the task of philosophy is to offer 'a *critique* of cognitive claims'. He indicates what he means by this phrase and offers a three-fold classification of the problems of philosophy so conceived.

In the second part he divides educational research problems into two

[2]Chapter 5 of *Educational Research: Phi Delta Kappa First Annual Symposium*, ed F. W. Banghart (USA, 1960), p. 71–84. Nagel's article can be usefully read in conjunction with R. S. Peters and J. White, 'The philosopher's contribution to educational research', *Educational Philosophy and Theory*, Vol. 1 (1968), pp. 1–15. See also M. Brodbeck, 'The philosophy of science and educational research', *Review of Educational Research*, Vol. 27 (1957), pp. 427–40; M. Scriven, 'The philosophy of science in educational research', *Review of Educational Research*, Vol. 30 (1960), pp. 422–9; E. Nagel, 'Philosophy of science and educational theory', *Studies in Philosophy and Education*, Vol. 7 (Fall 1969), pp. 5–27.

kinds. The first are empirical in a narrow sense. The second concern
educational objectives and policies and involve both factual and moral
issues. Of the first kind, he suggests that a philosophical critique might
produce a more sophisticated understanding both of scientific method
and of various research techniques than is sometimes seen in educational research.[3] Of the second kind, he suggests that philosophy might
offer a critique of some of the 'conceptions of human nature underlying
proposed educational objectives';[4] that philosophy can raise issues concerning the feasibility or desirability of various educational programmes;[5]
and that, finally, philosophy might help to articulate a central educational
objective – that of promoting 'intellectual habits that place a premium
on responsibly based thought'.[6]

Tom Burns, 'Sociological explanation'[7]

In this article Burns makes two important points, among others, about
sociology. Firstly that 'both as description and as explanation, sociology
is always a critical activity'. Sociological investigation can be characterized as a 'critical, assumption-testing' activity. He suggests that 'the role
of educational sociology is to examine, to question, to raise doubts about,
to criticize the assumptions on which current policy, current theory, and
current practice are based'. Secondly, Burns argues that the areas which

[3] Some of Nagel's comments at this point are echoed by Scriven, op. cit. (1960),
pp. 426–7. See also D. P. Ausubel, 'Learning by discovery: rationale and mystique',
The Bulletin of the National Association of the Secondary School Principals, Vol. 45 (1961),
pp. 18–58 (see particularly p. 56).
[4] Nagel's discussion can usefully be read with P. H. Hirst and R. S. Peters, *The Logic of
Education* (Routledge & Kegan Paul, 1970), Chapter 3.
[5] A number of issues raised in Volume I of this book are relevant here. See, for
example, the discussion of practical reasoning (p. 94); Emmet's discussion of un-
intended consequences (p. 60); and the discussion of educational expectations (p. 190).
[6] Compare Nagel's comments with R. F. Dearden's discussion of 'personal autonomy
based on reason' in Chapters 3 and 4 of R. F. Dearden, *The Philosophy of Primary
Education* (Routledge & Kegan Paul, 1968). See also the references to P. H. Hirst in
the bibliography of Dearden's book.
[7] Inaugural lecture as Professor of Sociology at the University of Edinburgh. Reprinted in *British Journal of Sociology* (December, 1967), pp. 353–69. This article can be
usefully read in conjunction with the following: P. Winch, *The Idea of a Social Science*
(Routledge & Kegan Paul, 1958); K. Popper, *The Logic of Scientific Discovery* (Hutchinson,
1959); H. L. Zetterberg, *On Theory and Verification in Sociology* (Totowa, N. J.:
Bedminster Press, 1963); A. V. Cicourel, *Method and Measurement in Sociology* (New
York: Free Press, 1964); T. S. Kuhn, *The Structure of Scientific Revolutions* (Chicago:
The University of Chicago Press, 2nd edn, 1970); Imre Lakatos and Alan Musgrave, eds.,
Criticism and the Growth of Knowledge (Cambridge University Press, 1970); Barny G.
Glaser and Anselm L. Strauss, *The Discovery of Grounded Theory* (Weidenfeld & Nicolson,
1968). For other useful discussions see: Robert W. Friedrichs, *A Sociology of Sociology*
(New York: The Free Press, 1970), and the bibliography in that volume pp. 375–418;
M. Brodbeck, ed., *Readings in the Philosophy of the Social Sciences* (New York: Collier-
Macmillan, 1968); Keith Dixon, *Sociological Theory: Pretence and Possibility* (Routledge &
Kegan Paul, 1973).

sociology studies are marked out, and defined for it, in that it 'operates upon previously organized bodies of knowledge'. Included in these are 'scientific and academic knowledge' and 'systems of beliefs, and codes of accepted practice'. He gives examples from sociological research which demonstrate these and other points.

Introduction to readings by Gilbert Smith and Norman Stockman, and by Michael Naish, Anthony Hartnett and Douglas Finlayson

Preliminary comments

Before we turn to the specific introductions to the two articles, we indicate a few reasons why issues about government reports and educational documents are raised in Volume II.

(*i*) Government reports and educational documents are likely to use theoretical work from academic disciplines to justify the practical and other judgements they make. They raise issues, therefore, about the relationship between theory and practice, as this is interpreted in Volume II of this book.[8]

(*ii*) The policies, proposed and actual, of which explanations and justifications are offered in reports and documents, may greatly affect the organisation, structure, and size of schools, teaching methods, and curricular materials. Teachers, therefore, (and children) have an interest in the quality of the argument by which policies are defended and in knowing what grounds there are for believing that a policy, overall, is beneficial.

(*iii*) Though Smith and Stockman and Naish et al. discuss reports and documents concerned for the most part with policy, the issues raised by them are relevant to decisions taken at lower levels of the educational system.

(*iv*) Smith and Stockman indicate how value judgements and empirical statements are likely to enter into reports. See, for example, their discussion (pp. 44–49) about diagnosis, policy objectives, and technical recommendations. They make a number of comments about the role of research and social science in reports.

(*v*) Both Smith and Stockman and Naish et al. (the latter in detail) indicate some ways in which the quality of the argument in reports and documents might be assessed.

(*vi*) Both give rise to issues about how claims made in documents might be inadequately supported and about how theoretical work might be misused in justifications of policies.

(*vii*) Both indicate ways in which philosophy and sociology, individually and together, might be used to examine reports and documents, and

[8] See pp. 2–3.

so to examine proposed solutions to various practical problems in education. A complete examination of such reports and documents requires
other disciplines too. It can be seen from Naish et al. that, in education,
psychology is required, as well as the history of education and comparative education. The examination of documents and reports suggests
ways in which interdisciplinary study might be undertaken in education,
both as part of the education of teachers and at the level of research.

(*viii*) In general the two articles raise issues about the role of philosophy, sociology, research, and academic disciplines in (*a*) policy-making
in education and (*b*) the study of reports and documents which either
contain, or purport to contain, explanations and justifications of policies.

It is worth noting that the relationship between academic disciplines,
and government reports and educational documents, can also be seen
as the relationship between two kinds of theory, because such reports and
documents might themselves be called theory. In so far as they contain
normative judgements about educational policy and practice, they can
be understood as educational theory, in P. H. Hirst's use of that term.[9]
The book by T. Burgess,[10] for example, discussed in Naish et al., can be
seen as a defence of what Hirst takes to be a (practical) educational
principle in educational theory, namely that 'all secondary education
ought to be given in comprehensive schools'.[11]

The readings by Nagel and Burns are very relevant to the issues raised
by Smith and Stockman, and Naish et al.

Gilbert Smith and Norman Stockman, 'Some suggestions for a sociological approach to the study of government reports'[12]

The central claims of the article by Smith and Stockman are as follows.
(*i*) Government reports are 'forms of socially generated knowledge'.

[9]See P. H. Hirst, 'Educational theory', in J. W. Tibble, ed., *The Study of Education* (Routledge & Kegan Paul, 1966), pp. 29–58.
[10]T. Burgess, *Inside Comprehensive Schools* (HMSO, 1970).
[11]P. H. Hirst, in J. W. Tibble, op. cit. (1966), p. 50. Where reports and documents
are seen as theory, a further question might be asked about theory and practice, and
that is about the relationship of the reports and documents (theory) to what in fact
goes on in schools and in the educational system (practice).
[12]*The Sociological Review*, Vol. 20 (1972), pp. 59–77. For three articles which, though
they adopt a different perspective, can usefully be read in conjunction with that of
Smith and Stockman, see: P. W. Musgrave, 'A model for the analysis of the development of the English educational system from 1860', in P. W. Musgrave, ed., *Sociology,
History, and Education* (Methuen, 1970), pp. 14–29; M. B. Katz, 'From Bryce to Newsom: assumptions of British educational reports, 1895–1963', *International Review of
Education*, Vol. 2 (1965), pp. 287–302; Gerald Grant, 'Shaping social policy: the
politics of the Coleman Report', *Teachers College Record*, Vol. 75, No. 1 (September,
1973), pp. 17–54. See also section 8 in Anthony Hartnett, ed., *The Sociology of Education: An Introductory Guide to the Literature*, Library Publication No. 3, School of Education, University of Liverpool, (1975).

(*ii*) They make assertions and can be assessed as such. (*iii*) Questions in the sociology of knowledge can be raised about such reports. (*iv*) An assessment of the validity of the 'knowledge'[13] contained in such reports must precede the formulation of sociological questions about the contents of the reports, because rational and irrational 'knowledge' need to be explained differently. (*v*) Criteria of rationality drawn from social science, among other areas, can be used to assess causal and other empirical claims made in the reports.[14]

After some introductory comments, Smith and Stockman argue against a current tendency to treat, for the purposes of sociological inquiry, all 'knowledge' as equally valid. They raise some complex issues about rationality, particularly about the extent to which its criteria are 'universal' or 'context-dependent'. They distinguish, and note the relationship between, rationality and truth, and say that the concept of truth and criteria of rationality derived from it have application only 'in contexts in which people are trying to make assertions'. They go on to state *à propos* of the relationship of the criteria of rationality to contexts, that different forms of activity require different forms of assessment, and that where there is difficulty in identifying the form of activity in question, there will also be difficulty in deciding upon the appropriate criteria for assessment. They say that Government 'Committees of Enquiry are a case in point' because some of their members may, for example, see themselves as engaged in a scientific enterprise, others in a political one, but that even so it is possible to determine what criteria are relevant to assessing a committee's activities, because these take place 'within a context of assertion'.[15] They bring three sorts of consideration to support this view.

Firstly, they say that in essence government reports consist of three components each of which consists of or presupposes descriptions (which can be true or false) of the world and causal relationships within it. These three are as follows.

[13]The inverted commas indicate that in the sociology of knowledge, the word 'knowledge' is, in many cases, likely to be a courtesy term only. It is often used there not only of knowledge or of what might reasonably be taken to be such, but of beliefs in general. In the usual meaning of 'knowledge', phrases such as 'invalid and valid knowledge' and 'rational and irrational knowledge' are not permissible.

[14]For example, psychology, sociology, among other disciplines, are relevant to an analysis of Chapters 2 and 3 of the Plowden Report. What disciplines are in fact relevant to what reports will depend on the subject matter in question. Almost any discipline might be relevant to one report or another.

[15]The uncertainty about the nature of a committee's activity may result from the diversity of those who serve on them. Among the members of the Plowden Committee, for example, were professors of logic, social administration, child health, and education, the editor of a weekly journal, a director of a publishing house, and headteachers, teachers and parents. It may be thought that, by including different sorts of people, diverse functions (for example, undertaking or commissioning research, taking and assessing verbal evidence, undertaking political persuasion) can all be carried out adequately by one committee.

(*i*) 'An account of how the world works' (called the 'diagnosis'). The Plowden Report's description of the English primary-school system is cited as an example of a diagnosis.[16] In some cases the diagnosis may be implicit in a committee's terms of reference.[17]

(*ii*) 'An account of how the world should be' (called the 'policy objectives'). These involve value and empirical issues, and Smith and Stockman make a number of points about the relationship between facts, values, and policy: (*a*) the 'statement of policy objectives assumes that it is possible to achieve the desired state of affairs',[18] (*b*) the policy recommended in any particular report may depend 'upon marshalling various opinions as to what states of affairs are desirable', and finding out what people consider desirable is an empirical matter;[19] (*c*) any committee's policy objectives are likely to involve assumptions about other areas of social policy.[20]

(*iii*) The third component of a report consists of recommendations as to how the policy objectives can be achieved. These 'technical recommendations' are in essence 'conditional predictions based upon factual assertions'.[21]

Secondly, Smith and Stockman say that committees undertake activities which are normally undertaken only by those 'who are attempting to make true assertions about the real world'. They collect, for example, what 'they refer to as "evidence"' and 'conduct " research".'[22]

Thirdly, they say that historical considerations support the view that committees' activities take place in a 'context of assertion'.

Given these points, Smith and Stockman conclude that the criteria for assessing the validity of the knowledge contained in a report are to be drawn from science. The rest of their article is concerned with the application of social scientific criteria (to which they limit themselves) to government reports.

---

[16]See in particular, Part Four of the report.

[17]This point is important. A diagnosis can be taken to be a definition of the situation in which action has to take place. When such a definition is included in a committee's terms of reference, its adequacy might go unexamined and the committee be precluded from coming to certain sorts of recommendations. The issue, that is to say, is to some extent prejudged. Compare the apparently implicit assumption of the Seebohm Report about organizational variables, mentioned by Smith and Stockman on page 46.

[18]Cf. Chapter 4, 'Objectives', of The Newsom Report.

[19]Consider, for example, the empirical issues raised by the view expressed in the James Report (Paragraph 6.3, p. 67) that 'the present pattern of training, despite its merits, has been the cause of widespread misgiving'.

[20]Much may depend on these assumptions, particularly in education, where government policies on, for example, housing, wages, family benefits, and employment may be as important as what a particular committee recommends ought to take place *in classrooms*.

[21]For some examples of such recommendations see the Plowden Report, Chapter 5, 'Educational Priority Areas'.

[22]Cf. The James Report, Appendices 1–5, pp. 80–95.

They suggest social science can extract the causal models from a report. If these are inconsistent, then the report will need to be explained on an assumption of irrationality and only then will reference to competing pressure groups, for example, become relevant.[23] If these models are consistent but not well grounded, then the deviation from social scientific rationality needs to be explained and this might be done, for example, by reference to the pressures of a government bureaucracy.[24] They say that sociologists can ask why a committee did in fact conform to the standards of scientific rationality but that, because explaining rationality and irrationality are different tasks, questions about a report's rationality are prior to an explanation of its content.

Smith and Stockman illustrate some of their points from the Seebohm Report. They extract a causal model from it and suggest: (*i*) the assertions advanced in it are in general inadequately supported; (*ii*) some of these assertions, even when they are initially posed in tentative form, are later assumed to be better grounded than they are; (*iii*) evidence submitted by witnesses was not independently assessed; (*iv*) the heading under which evidence was submitted made it unlikely that the committee's view about the causal role of organizational variables could be refuted. Given this, they conclude that what needs to be explained is the report's deviation from 'perfect rationality'.

The application of Smith and Stockman's article to the study of educational reports should not be hard to see.

Michael Naish, Anthony Hartnett and Douglas Finlayson, 'Ideological documents in education: some suggestions towards a definition'[25]

What is required by way of introduction to this article is at the beginning of the article itself. All we do here, therefore, is to make a brief comment on its relation to the article by Smith and Stockman.

The central part of the article by Naish et al. consists of a set of indices constituting a critical apparatus which can be used to examine reports and documents. It is argued that the indices can be taken as indicators of discussions that are less than fully rational and, further, as indicators of discussions that are ideological. To this extent the article is meant to be a contribution to the study of ideology, particularly in education.[26] In their article Smith and Stockman argue that sociological

---

[23] For a discussion of inconsistency see p. 50.

[24] For discussion of inadequately grounded assertions see p. 53.

[25] Published for the first time in this volume.

[26] Smith and Stockman draw attention to a link between irrationality and ideology (pp. 41–2).

questions, particularly in the field of the sociology of knowledge, can be asked about reports and, we might add, about educational documents. One such question is 'Why did the report say what it did?' But, they go on to say, in order to answer this and other related questions, questions first need to be raised about the rationality of the claims made in reports. For on how these are answered depends what needs to be explained. A distinction needs to be made between, in their words, 'rational and "irrational" knowledge'. The article by Naish et al. picks up this point and offers some help in making such a distinction.[27]

Introduction to readings by D. R. McNamara and Israel Scheffler

D. R. McNamara, 'Sociology of education and the education of teachers'[28]

This article is concerned with 'the place of the sociology of education in the professional training of teachers'.

McNamara begins with a discussion of the development of sociology and of sociology of education in Britain in recent years, and distinguishes 'sociology of education' from 'educational sociology'. The former is concerned with advancing understanding, irrespective of its practical bearing. The latter is 'the applied branch of the subject where the concern is with solving practical problems which are likely to arise for the educationalist'. McNamara goes on to bring a number of arguments against educational sociology (as that was normally understood in colleges of education) and against a conception of sociology of education proposed for such colleges by W. Taylor. Firstly he suggests that a weakness of courses in educational sociology is that they often contain implicit value positions and ideologies.[29] Secondly he argues, in opposition to Taylor, that sociology of education is not a science[30] and that, therefore, it has no necessary place in the education syllabi of colleges of education. Thirdly he argues that there may well not be enough relevant and distinctively sociological research to justify courses in the subject for teachers.[31] Finally, he puts forward proposals for a kind of sociology of education which might be of value to classroom teachers.

---

[27] It was not designed to pick up the discussion by Smith and Stockman. That it did so was fortunate but fortuitous. The article by Naish et al. had gone through several drafts before Smith and Stockman was published.

[28] *British Journal of Educational Studies*, Vol. 20 (1972), pp. 137–47.

[29] So, of course, might 'purer' sociological courses, but the value positions they contain may be harder for the unpractised eye to detect.

[30] See also 'Some issues arising from the readings', pp. 157–64.

[31] For a suggestion that definitions of 'sociological' (and of 'philosophical') are likely to be disputed, see 'Some issues arising from the readings', pp. 140–45.

Israel Scheffler, 'University scholarship and the education of teachers'[32]

In this article, Scheffler sets out to justify, against the arguments of an opponent identified as a 'sceptic', the inclusion of theoretical disciplines in the education of teachers.

He begins by saying that there is no 'distinctive science of education' but there are rather 'multiple modes of analysing educational problems' and that teachers should relate their work to them.[33] A sceptic might argue, however, that because knowledge of theoretical disciplines is not 'necessary for effective teaching', they should be excluded from the education of teachers, or alternatively that they should be included only in so far as they advance 'the technology of education'. To this Scheffler replies, firstly, that justification can be not simply a matter of necessity but of desirability and, secondly, that the sceptic will find it difficult to predict which bits of theory will effect such an advance. But to meet fully the sceptic's second point in particular, Scheffler argues that the sceptic implicitly conceives of a teacher's role as analogous to that of an industrial technician and that this is 'radically wrong, both normatively and descriptively'. He goes on to suggest that a teacher, on a proper conception of his role, needs to have insight into and to be able to reflect critically upon 'his own principles and allegiances'. To the objection that concepts such as 'insight' are not operational, Scheffler replies that if his own argument is sound, then doubts arise about the adequacy of a justification depending solely upon operational terms; and, further, that the sceptic himself has recourse to non-operational terms when he admits that a teacher should have a wider grasp of his subject than is required for the current lesson or course. Given this, Scheffler suggests that whatever improves a teacher's grasp of his subject or of the social or philosophical aspects of his work (it is here particularly that 'theoretical studies of education are relevant') can contribute to the education of teachers. Such a contribution, Scheffler notes, should not be seen in terms of 'the ordinary notion of a subject' but of an unrestricted one.

Scheffler goes on to argue that the notion of 'effective teaching' on which the sceptic's case largely depends cannot bear the weight the

---

[32] *The Record*, Vol. 70 (1968–69), pp. 1–12.

[33] Cf. I. Scheffler, 'Is education a discipline?', in *The Discipline of Education*, ed. J. Walton and J. L. Kuethe (Madison, Wisconsin: University of Wisconsin Press, 1963), p. 47. In this sense of 'discipline' there is, Scheffler argues (p. 48), neither a discipline of education, nor of engineering, nor of medicine. None of these has its own special science underlying it. Each rather calls upon a number of different intellectual disciplines which gives rise to different sorts of question. R. S. Peters, in the same volume (p. 17) states that education is 'a focus or a meeting place of disciplines'. This is compatible with P. H. Hirst's view. See his 'Educational theory' in *The Study of Education*, ed. J. W. Tibble (Routledge & Kegan Paul, 1966), pp. 29–58.

sceptic gives it;[34] and that, more fundamentally, it implies too narrow a view of the teacher's role. He suggests that in a free society teachers cannot be 'mere agents of others, of the state, of the military, of the media, of the experts and the bureaucrats' but 'need to determine their own agency through a critical and continual evaluation of the purposes, the consequences, and the social context of their calling'. Given this wider role, the theoretical study of education, though it may not 'directly enhance craft', gives rise to questions which teachers need to face. Scheffler concludes with some comments on the role of the university in linking the preparation of teachers with such questions.

[34]For some comments on the notion of effective teaching and on Scheffler's account of teaching see J. Cooper, 'Criteria for successful teaching: or an apple for teacher', *Philosophy of Education Society of Great Britain, Proceedings of the Annual Conference* (1966), pp. 5–18.

Readings

8 Philosophy in educational research   ERNEST NAGEL
(F. W. Banghart, ed., *Educational Research: Phi Delta Kappa First Annual Symposium*, Indiana, 1960, Chapter 5)

The word 'philosophy' is notoriously ambiguous. Indeed, even the more definite label 'philosophy of science' in its current usage does not designate a precisely delimited area of study, but on the contrary covers a variety of concerns between which there is often only a tenuous connection. Nevertheless, the task widely assumed to be distinctive of philosophy since its beginnings in Western thought has been to assess and systematically relate from some integrating perspective the diversity of human knowledge and experience. Although as will soon be evident I have serious reservations about the way this unifying function has frequently been performed by philosophers, the general spirit of this view of the office of philosophy inspires the present paper. On the other hand, my familiarity with the substantive materials of educational research is at best peripheral; and I offer these reflections of the philosophy of educational research with the acute sense that I have ventured on territory upon which it would be far wiser for me not to tread. But in any event, I must first take some space to indicate a bit more fully how I envisage the task of philosophy in general and of the philosophy of science in particular, as an essential preliminary to a brief outline of what seems to me a possible role of philosophy in the study of educational problems.

I

According to an ancient and still influential tradition, philosophy is the fundamental, because most general, science of existence. Its major objective is to discover the basic kinds and structures of reality, and to establish by way of an infallible insight into the nature of things the necessary principles that constitute the intellectual foundations of all knowledge of specialized subject matters. This conception of the aim and method of philosophy has been increasingly on the defensive since the rise of modern science, and especially since developments within pure mathematics and physics have undermined the authority of appeals to allegedly self-evident truth for validating claims to knowledge. Nevertheless, this conception of philosophy has been enjoying a flourishing renaissance in recent years, a revival not without a following among students of education. Moreover, even before this revival, many thinkers who have neglected these ancient pretensions of philosophy concerning matters belonging to the province of the positive sciences, have continued to advance analogous claims for the competence of philosophy to establish the ultimate moral norms and objectives of both individual and social behavior.

The prospects for this conception of philosophy seem to me hopeless, though because of lack of time I must be dogmatic in stating my dissent. I do not believe, in the first place, that truth-claims about the occurrence of events and processes, or about relations of dependence between events, can be established by a logic of procedure other than the one used in a relatively crude fashion in ordinary affairs and employed in a more or less refined manner in the various positive sciences. Insofar as philosophers profess to base their cognitive claims about the nature of things on the methods of empirical science, they are themselves empirical scientists; and their claims must be judged by the same logical standards that are operative in specialized areas of inquiry – standards which, by and large, are not even approximately satisfied by such claims made by exponents of *philosophia perennis*. The supposition that philosophy can supply the foundational principles upon which genuine knowledge of any sector of the world must rest therefore seems to me thoroughly mistaken, and to be belied by the actual history of thought. Nor do I believe, in the second place, that the cognitive issues generated in assessing moral choices or the worth of proposed human ideals can be resolved by invoking a different logical method from the one employed in the positive sciences. In my view, therefore, philosophy does not possess a distinctive procedure for certifying propositions about human values, and philosophers *qua* philosophers are not in a privileged position to make warranted pronouncements about human nature and the proper goals of human effort.

But if the notion of philosophy as the master architectonic science is a blunder, as I think it is, is there a viable alternative to it? I believe there is. For although there does not seem to me to be any *subject matter* that is distinctively and inherently philosophical, there is a large if vaguely demarcated class of *questions*, many of which arise in connection with every specialized subject matter, that are generally regarded as being characteristically philosophical. They are so regarded not simply because they happen to be discussed for the most part by those who are philosophers by profession, since in point of fact such questions are frequently pursued by thinkers in almost every domain of professional activity. The questions are held to be philosophical because they deal with *foundational* problems and more specifically with *foundational problems of knowledge* – with the analysis of ideas central to some particular area of thought as well as with the general conditions under which discourse is meaningful; with the grounds of beliefs dominating some department of inquiry as well as with the logic implicit in evaluating the worth of evidence; or with the relations of one branch of knowledge to some other branch as well as with the general principles presupposed in integrating the conclusions of specialized inquiries into a unifying perspective upon the diverse materials of human experience. For example, one is tackling a philosophical question in this sense when one attempts to clarify such notions as that of cause or energy in physics, growth or adaptation in biology, instinct or purpose in psychology, democracy or property in political science, and responsibility or self-development in moral theory. Again, one is raising a philosophical question when one asks whether the law of effect in psychology has the status of an empirical generalization or that of a definitional truth, what is the rationale for punishing those guilty of criminal offenses, and in what respects the logic employed in supporting the contention that litigants at law should receive treatment irrespective of their race is similar to or differs from the logic used to warrant the claim that blue-eyed human parents have blue-eyed children. Once more, it is a philosophical problem to determine in what way admitted facts of psychology are contingent upon the findings of physics and biology, or to assess the bearing of current knowledge in the natural and social sciences upon some proposed ideal for human conduct.

It will be evident that on this conception of the role of philosophy, its task is not to add to our knowledge of the *primary subject matters* explored by the various branches of substantive inquiry, neither in the form of propositions about individual happenings nor in the form of general statements about the regularities with which things happen. On this conception the task of philosophy is to be a *critique* of cognitive claims, with the intent, in part, to purge our ideas and beliefs of unclarities and dubious assumptions, in part to make us self-conscious about the nature and grounds of our intellectual commitments, and in part to enlarge the angle of our vision by suggesting alternative ways to unreflectively habitual ones for organizing and bringing into mutual relations various detailed portions of our knowledge. It will also be evident, however, that on this conception of philosophy, competent philosophical inquiry requires both considerable familiarity with the substantive content and the procedures of specific inquiries, as well as some mastery of techniques of logical analysis. That is why, although in my opinion much of the best work in the philosophy of science has been done by philosophically minded scientists, most practising scientists neither give serious consideration to philosophical questions nor are they able to discuss such questions in a mature manner. That is also why philosophers who have developed some sensitivity to logical issues and some skills in resolving them as part of their professional training are often particularly well-equipped to deal with at least certain types of problems in the philosophy of science.

In my view, therefore, philosophy can serve as an integrating discipline, even if not quite in the traditional sense, by articulating, assessing, and thereby perhaps helping to reorganize the logical organization of our knowledge, and the logical principles employed in establishing cognitive claims. At any rate, this is the central concern of the philosophy of science, despite the fact that philosophical discussions of science often appear to deal with a miscellany of unrelated themes. There are many ways of classifying these themes, especially when the word 'science' is used broadly, as I propose to use it here, not only for the various conventional divisions of inquiry into natural and social phenomena, but for any areas of reflective thought, including the domain of moral deliberation, in which cognitive claims stated in propositional form can be significantly made. However, without pretending to offer an exhaustive listing of major problems that are considered in the philosophy of science – indeed, I am deliberately excluding from this account questions in the sociology of knowledge which deal with certain factual matters concerning the mutual relations of science and society, and which are sometimes subsumed under the philosophy of science – I have found the following three-fold classification useful for indicating the office of philosophy as a critique of discursive thought.

1. Problems relating to the evaluation of evidence. Under this heading belong, among other things, analyses of the requirements for significant observation and experiment, of the various canons for estimating the probative force of evidential statements, of the nature and rationale of probable inference, and of principles for judging the competence of decisions between alternative policies.

2. Problems relating to the explication of concepts. This rubric covers such matters as the examination of varieties of definitional procedures, of the criteria for the empirical significance of statements, of the logic of classification and measurement, and of the logical requirements for generalizing the applicability of ideas.

3. Problems relating to the construction of systematic bodies of knowledge. Under this label are included discussions of the types and functions of general statements, of patterns of explanation and prediction, of the role of analogies and models in the expansion of knowledge, and of the logical conditions for assimilating different branches of inquiry into a common intellectual framework.

These groups of problems are in general not independent of one another, even though it is often the case that some thinkers are more attracted to one group, or are better equipped to deal with some of the specific questions subsumed under it, than to another group. Moreover, each of these convenient divisions also contains not only discussions of the general problems I have mentioned, but also discussions of special forms of these problems in the context of some concrete branch of inquiry. But I hope I have said enough to suggest that the philosophy of science, or philosophy as a critique of reflective thought, can play a significant role in every domain in which a quest for responsibly grounded knowledge is actively pursued.

II

I must now indicate in what way philosophy so construed may be pertinent to the enterprise of educational research. If I can judge from the small fraction of its literature with which I am familiar, educational research is addressed to two roughly distinguishable sets of problems. The first group of questions are empirical or factual in the narrow sense of these words. They deal with such matters as the testing of traditional or proposed techniques of instruction and learning, the development of reliable measures for various types of ability and achievement, the effectiveness of some designated course of study and training for achieving a stated aim, or the optimal structure of various administrative units in the organization of educational institutions. The second set of problems is often regarded as the distinctively philosophical or foundational sector of educational research. These problems are in the main concerned with formulating, analysing, and to some extent justifying less inclusive educational objectives and policies, in part in the light of various biological, psychological, and sociological assumptions about human capacities, in part under the influence of more or less explicitly avowed moral and social ideals. Although these problems raise some issues that can be resolved only by reference to ostensible matters of fact, so that those issues can in principle be settled in an admittedly objective manner, these problems also involve questions concerning the comparative worth of alternate and frequently incompatible human aspirations and moral standards. In consequence, this area of educational research is faced by most of the difficulties that confront those who attempt to supply a rational basis for moral choice and value judgements.

1. Insofar as educational research is a branch of positive science, a philosophical critique can contribute to its development in a fashion quite analogous to the way such a critique functions in other positive inquiries. I do not feel qualified to cite chapter and verse in this connection. But at the risk of appearing presumptuous, I do want to mention some pertinent though elementary considerations in the logic of science, greater familiarity with which on the part of those engaged in positive educational research is eminently desirable.

(*a*) In the first place, the simplicistic Baconian conception of science still seems to dominate much empirical research in this area, so that the assiduous collection of data, uninformed by a clearly formulated and consciously entertained controlling hypothesis, is often taken to be the paradigm of sound inquiry. This state of affairs is not improved by the circumstance that unacknowledged assumptions may enter critically into the interpretations which the investigator places upon his data. Although no one can be explicitly aware of all the tacit assumptions one is making in the conduct of any inquiry, it is well to realize that one is always operating within some framework of presuppositions, and to be habitually on the lookout for those that are highly questionable. This point seems to me especially important in a domain, such as the study of human behaviour, in which theoretical notions are frequently taken for granted that are still not firmly established. The rather prominent fluctuations of fads and fashions in educational practice, though presumably each is based on the findings of allegedly 'scientific' research, provide some evidence that many of those findings are not the conclusions of a critically conducted inquiry.

(b) It is also my impression, in the second place, that although research techniques are often employed in this domain with undoubted mechanical expertness, those who use them do not always possess a mature understanding of their intellectual tools. For example, they are in general not sensitive to the limitations of various types of quantitative scales currently in use, and are sometimes not aware of even such fundamental points as that the relative magnitudes of numerical differences on an ordinal scale are without significance. Similarly, they apply many statistical formulas in drawing inferences from data, without much thought to the fact that while those formulas may be valid within the framework of theoretical assumptions in which the formulas are derived, these assumptions may not always be realized with a sufficient degree of approximation to warrant the inferences. Moreover, there is often only a dim conception of the nature of controlled experiment, so that general propositions are asserted on the basis of ostensibly confirmatory data that do not provide competent support for those conclusions. In any event, there is a frequent neglect of the fundamental canon of experimental reasoning that the mere agreement of factual data with a given hypothesis does not constitute cogent evidence for the latter, if those data are also compatible with equally plausible competing hypotheses.

2. But I must turn to the second group of problems in educational research.

(a) I introduce my first point with the obvious reminder that since proposed educational objectives and practices may in part be based on allegedly warranted conclusions of some other branch of inquiry, some consideration deserves to be given to the question whether those conclusions are indeed solidly grounded. Now the physical sciences, and to a lesser extent the biological ones, have been operating during a fairly long period with standards of workmanship that have yielded intellectual products which have proved to be generally reliable; and there is therefore a reasonable presumption that the conclusions accepted from these sciences are firmly grounded. However, this cannot be said about psychology, a major source of many of the assumptions upon which educational objectives and practices are supported. For although there are currently differing 'schools' of psychology, there are today no comparable 'schools' of physics. Accordingly, so long as there are such schools, so long as competently trained students disagree in their interpretations of psychological data because of their adherence to differing psychological theories, educational objectives and practices based (even if only partially) on such disputed matters may often be only the expressions of partisan commitments in a warfare of psychological schools. Moreover, there are reasons for suspecting that some of these current schools, such as variant forms of psychoanalysis or of behaviorism, are in turn elaborations of antecedently adopted general assumptions (or 'philosophies') about the 'real' nature of man – assumptions which may be too vague to be capable of either proof or disproof by experiment, but which may nonetheless significantly color the selection and formulation of observed data. There is a manifest circularity in advocating a conception of human nature on the ground that the conception is in conformity with the facts of psychology, if those facts are themselves the products of an interpretation of empirical data that is controlled by such antecedent assumptions about the nature of man. It is evident that a philosophy of educational objectives erected on the foundations of such a conception of human nature has an empirical backing that may be largely specious, and may in fact only serve as window dressing for a conception that is wholly an a priori construction.

The point I am therefore concerned to make is that a philosophical critique of the ostensibly empirical assumptions upon which conceptions of human nature underlying proposed educational objectives are based can render a vital service to educational research. An indispensable prerequisite for such a critique in the present connection is competent familiarity with the special discipline (which is not necessarily psychology) into whose province the assumptions under discussion fall. But a no less essential requirement is logical maturity, combined with a sensitivity to shifts in meaning that words may undergo as they are moved from one context of usage to another. I have already said something about logical maturity, and will therefore illustrate only the second part of this latter requirement. Consider, for example, the transformations in the meaning of the word 'development' when it is transplanted from biological to psychological to moral contexts, as in the following sequence: 'development of an embryo', 'development of an idea', 'development of human individuality.' In the first of these phrases, the word is used in an exclusively descriptive or nonevaluative sense, and refers to some series of definite stages in the 'natural' formation of increasingly more complex organic structures. In the second phrase, the word is again used in an essentially nonevaluative fashion, to designate some sequential elaboration of a notion, whether in the direction of its explicit formulation, the derivation of some of its logical consequences, or its extended application to various types of problems. In the third phrase, the word is employed in an unmistakable approbative or evaluative sense, though without any clear indication of the direction of the changes that ostensibly merit commendation. However, despite these alterations in meaning, there is a considerable carry-over to other contexts of the sense of the word as used in the biological domain. There is thus a temptation, to which some thinkers have indeed succumbed, to assume, for example, that the development of human individuality is a biological rather than a distinctive moral notion, and to believe that the word 'development' when employed in discussions of educational ideals is as nonevaluative as when it is employed in biology. More generally, the occurrence of an expression in a variety of contexts with somewhat altered though apparently 'continuous' meanings is often a sign that some analogy whose terms are borrowed from one domain is being exploited in some other area. But while analogies may have great heuristic value, their use may also conceal crucial differences between the allegedly analogous traits of different subject matters, and may therefore be misleading. To call attention to analogies that may control the discussion of educational objectives, to make explicit the tacit assumptions employed in this domain, to examine their credentials, is one important task that a philosophical critique can undertake.

(b) A second though related task that such a critique can perform is to reveal elements of a sterile utopianism and of an ineffective sentimentalism that may present in actual or proposed educational ideals, by examining, on the one hand, current assumptions about the relations of means to ends, and on the other hand the coherence of envisaged ideals of educational practice with the acknowledged facts about the human materials of education. Educational objectives are often defended by reference to biological and psychological information concerning human capacities, without serious consideration of the nature of the social institutions in which those capacities will presumably manifest themselves. In consequence, specific educational ends may be proposed, as if those ends could be realized irrespective of what social mechanisms other than the schools are in operation or what objectives other than educational ones are being pursued in the society under discussion. Thus, even a relatively definite educational ideal such as universal literacy will in practice have a different specific content, according to the composition of the community in which that ideal is adopted and according to the uses to which literacy is put because of the institutional arrangements of the community. Moreover, the assumption is commonly made that objectives can be chosen in a principled manner, independently of the means through which those objectives may be realized. However, this assumption rests on a serious error of oversight, of neglecting the elementary point that the consequences produced by two different means are never precisely the same, and that the *total* ends achieved through the use of distinct means are not identical. For example, there undoubtedly are different ways of teaching children how to read, and one of these ways may be regarded as the preferable one because its adoption leads to a more rapid acquisition of reading skills than do the alternative ways. However, even if maximum speed of acquiring such skills is a desideratum, the method of teaching that achieves this result is not necessarily the most desirable one. For the use of that method may have other consequences as well (e.g., it may generate a tendency to misspell, or a questionably sound habit of reading all texts at the same rate). Such possible 'side-effects' must not be ignored, for they are obviously included in the total end achieved through the use of that method. We are therefore foolishly utopian if we think that ends can be properly adjudicated without consideration of means for attaining them.

But inversely, educational objectives need to be examined for their compatibility with what is presumably known about the capacities and the aspirations of those for whom the objectives are being proposed. I must content myself with but one example of what I have in mind. Some contemporary thinkers maintain that in a society whole-heartedly dedicated to democratic ideals, all schools inclusive of college should seek to generate a sense of common heritage by requiring all students to follow a *uniform* course of study in the sciences and the humanities. According to these thinkers, schools betray the democratic ideal when they are organized to provide one type of instruction for those likely to enter one of the so-called professions, and a different course of instruction for those headed for more 'practically' oriented careers; and an identical 'liberal' education is therefore recommended as a right and a duty for all citizens of a democratic society. For the purposes of the present discussion, I will take for granted the desirability of a widespread familiarity with the heritage of thought and artistic expression that is our portion as members of a liberal civilization; and I agree that it would be undemocratic to deny equal educational *opportunities* to those possessing the *requisite and comparable aptitudes* for preparing themselves for desired careers. But I also think it is muddled if well-intentioned sentimentalism to argue that a genuinely democratic ideal demands a system of public education which gives the *same* training to everyone, irrespective of individual differences in capacity and aspiration, and that this ideal is compromised when provision is made in courses of study even in elementary and secondary schools for those to whom a stress on various 'practical' subjects is more congruous with their abilities and ambitions than is an exclusive emphasis on the purely theoretical content of the sciences and humanities. A uniform requirement with respect to the content of instruction leads to a debasing of that content if, as no one seriously disputes, there are important differences in the individual capacities of students. Moreover, if a democratic society is directed toward the moral ideal that all men be given equal opportunities for realizing their distinctive talents, uniformity in respect to the content of education for everyone contributes to the defeat of that ideal, since it can impede students from preparing themselves for careers congruent with their individual gifts.

(c) Thus far I have been stressing the purgative role of philosophic criticism. However, as has been often and justly noted, we cannot live on disinfectants alone; and although I do not believe that philosophers have special prerogatives in matters concerned with values, neither are philosophers necessarily disqualified for discussing them. My concluding remarks are therefore intended to suggest briefly a positive contribution that philosophy can make to the articulation of what in my judgement is an important educational objective.

I must prepare the ground for my suggestion by mentioning the familiar fact that in almost every field of inquiry specialization is increasing at an accelerated rate, and that in consequence there is some basis for the frequently expressed alarm that the incapacity for communicating with one another which was finally exhibited by the ancient builders of the tower of Babel is a fate that also threatens ourselves. Moreover, partly as a consequence of this increasing specialization and of the attendant difficulties that a nonspecialist experiences in trying to understand current scientific theories, and partly because responsibility for many of our current ills is frequently laid at the door of modern science, there is a widespread conviction that the sciences are not humanistic disciplines. Despite the many admittedly beneficial contributions that technologies based on scientific theories have been making to the enhancement of human life, the traditional hostility between the sciences and the humanities has become intensified.

It would take many volumes to fill in with some degree of adequacy this thumbnail sketch, and to examine the complex issues that are generated by the situation it describes. The only one of these problems I have time to mention is that of finding some integrating perspective from which to view the various compartmentalized scientific inquiries, and thereby of achieving a just appreciation of the significance of the scientific enterprise in the economy of human concerns. It is to this problem that I want to address myself briefly. It seems to me that there are just two major ways in which a unified view of science and of the knowledge it achieves can be obtained. The first is to find comprehensive substantive principles, with the help of which the innumerable items of information amassed in specialized inquiries can be exhibited as details in an intelligible pattern of relations. For example, Newton affected such a unification of the then current knowledge of mechanical phenoma through the introduction of his axioms of motion and theory of gravitation. In my opinion, however, a comparable unification for the entire range of our present knowledge is not likely to occur in the foreseeable future. But in any event, a unification of this sort is something that must await further scientific advances; and as I have already indicated, philosophy can contribute little if anything to achieve that objective.

The second way for integrating knowledge is to exhibit the findings of the sciences as well as the warranted cognitive claims made in other contexts of human concern as the products of a common intellectual method. If there is a logic of inquiry that is canonical for investigations into all subject matters (as I believe there is, though I can assert this here only dogmatically), and since in point of fact philosophers are often particularly concerned with articulating its features and examining its credentials, philosophy can render an important service in such a task of integration. But I hasten to add that it is a task which philosophers cannot undertake unaided.

My suggestion pertinent to the present context therefore is that philosophers can play a constructive role in the detailed formulation of a central educational objective. That objective, when stated in general terms, is to replace intellectual habits which tend to make men accept and retain unexamined beliefs by intellectual habits that place a premium on responsibly based thought. However, if this general objective is to be realized, the character of cogent reasoning must be set forth clearly, not simply in the abstract but in the context of teaching the concrete materials of various specialized domains of inquiry. In short, I believe that a supreme educational objective can be realized only if both the sciences and the humanities are presented to students not simply as miscellaneous bodies of useful and enlightened information, but as the fruits of a characteristically human method of intelligence. For organizing such presentations, there is needed expert familiarity with the accredited outcome of educational research, and expert familiarity with the relevant distinctions and principles of logic. By participating in such a cooperative reorganization of the content of instruction, philosophy can make what I think is an invaluable contribution to educational practice and theory. In this way, philosophical criticism can be of constructive aid in exhibiting the unity of the logical foundations of our knowledge, and in showing that the various sciences, like the disciplines traditionally designated as the humanities, are the interrelated products of a single, intellectually liberating and humanistic enterprise.

9 Sociological explanation   TOM BURNS*
(*British Journal of Sociology*, Vol. 18, No. 4, 1967, pp. 353–69)

Having to give an inaugural lecture is a rather daunting affair though, I am sure, a salutary one. Luckily, there is always tradition to sustain one

*Tom Burns B.A., Professor of Sociology, University of Edinburgh (Inaugural lecture).

and to afford some guidance. There are, one finds, models, or types, of inaugural lectures. I cannot claim to be a connoisseur, but, judging from a small and heavily biased sample, they seem to fall into three groups. There are those, to begin with, which announce new departures for a subject, new horizons, recent territorial acquisitions in teaching or research, perhaps a reformed constitution: they are, in short, manifestos– delivered, of course, modestly, even diffidently sometimes, and with proper deference to neighbours and previous tenants, but manifestos nevertheless; muted manifestos. The second kind defines itself more precisely. There is hardly a single field of scholarship or science in which the contribution of Scotland, of this University itself, has not been extensive and weighty – even, at times, momentous; very few branches of learning in which it is not possible to point to a noble and inspiring tradition of intellectual endeavour. There is special propriety on the occasion of an inaugural lecture, then, in recalling – invoking – the achievements of predecessors, of the giants on whose shoulders we presume to stand; there is a special propriety in setting oneself the aim, not unduly modest, either, of continuing or reviving the traditions they formed. And for those who invest in this kind of inaugural, there is the very large bonus to collect from the rich deposits of portable quotations which lie embedded in so much of Scottish intellectual history, with its unique rewarding blend of wit and sententiousness, of high thinking and low living. Inaugurals of this kind are known to the trade as Scotch, or Upper Library, jobs.

Third, and last, is the guided tour through the main thoroughfares of a new and unfamiliar subject. Less striking in its appeal than the first, less elegant in manner than the second, more pedestrian by definition of course than either, the guided tour runs the twin hazards of losing half one's audience by boring them with what is already distressingly familiar stuff, and the other half by hurrying them through the more complicated or remote precincts.

These risks I have to ask you to face with me, however, because this is the form and pattern I want to adopt for this lecture. I do so not because sociology is new or unfamiliar – for me to think so would be presumptuous – but because it has seemed to me a subject more than usually susceptible to misconception and misconstruction.

There is, I shall argue, a special reason for this. All branches of knowledge, scientific and other, are concerned with description as well as with explanation, have their substantive content as well as their methodology, are fact-finding, diagnostic or taxonomic activities as well as theoretical and model-building activities. It is indeed by their descriptive activities, their substantive area of study, that specialist studies are known to the non-specialist public. Sociology is no exception, and it is because of this, I believe, that the misconceptions have arisen. For the misconceptions, such as they are, relate to what is publicly known about the descriptive activities of sociology.

The title I have chosen for this lecture, therefore, while not deliberately misleading, is rather elliptical. I shall have to deal with sociology in its descriptive aspects, and, moreover, to try to show how both as description and as explanation sociology is always a critical activity. In considering sociological explanation, furthermore, I shall not seek either to present you with a review of the methods of research used in sociology or of customary procedures in analysing research data – which would be very tedious and exceedingly inappropriate. I shall also steer very clear of the ground which has been ploughed so heavily in recent years by British and American philosophers. My references will be to empirical sociology rather than to what is commonly designated by sociologists as social theory. My object is to try to point out by example and to explain as best I can what is distinctive about sociology in its approach to its subject matter. And I shall do this cumulatively, adding items to the account as we go.

Let me begin by taking it as common and undisputed ground that we tend to live more and more in a world of organized, departmentalized, bodies of knowledge; and that this is not a matter merely of the exigencies of university curricula, or of the shortness of life and the accumulation of knowledge which forces increasing specialization on us. Intellectual life, scholarship and science are subject increasingly to the principles which govern the division of labour in the rest of civilized existence. We have become acutely aware of the cultural divisions which can grow up as a consequence, and, in time, as reinforcement, of specialization, and there is an increasing number of enthusiastic or conscience-stricken attempts to bridge the gaps. But there are other consequences which we are perhaps less conscious of. Among them is the odd tendency for the world in which we live, the environment of physical matter, of natural circumstance, and of events, to shape itself and to become organized after the same pattern of specialisms, and in their terms. History is, of course, both the past and the study of the past – of course; more particularly it is the body of recorded and ascertainable facts about the past which is regarded by historians as relevant to historical studies. Law has the same familiar and entirely undeceptive ambiguity in common usage; it is both the body of law and the study of law. And it is difficult to think of a time or a possible circumstance in which it might have made sense in either case to regard the subject matter in any different way from the study of it. But it also makes equal sense to talk of chemistry and physics in the same way; and there was certainly a time when even quite civilized people did not. For us there is a chemical world and a physical world: the chemistry of aircraft engines or their physics, the chemistry or the physics of the human body, are terms in general currency. More significantly, during the past few generations new disciplines have acted on the world and on circumstances in the same fashion. Instead of enumerating all the particulars of forms of livelihood, standard of living, division of labour, system of exchange, modes and rates of capital formation, range of products, and so on, it is meaningful, acceptable, and common usage to speak of 'the economy'.

There is a specific reference here to those actions, events and objects which are the relevant objects of study to economists. And the reference is really quite specific. It is not uncommon, for instance, to find in accounts and explanations of movements in prices, or of fluctuations in consumption, allusions to 'non-economic' variables, so-called, which nevertheless do effect changes in 'the economy'. Psychology has acted as an organizing principle in a similar fashion, so that the special attributes of individual attainment, emotional response, mental experience and development which have become appropriate for psychological study now make up a recognized and recognizable sector of the world as we experience it. One can speak meaningfully of the psychology of a person and mean something different from what we mean when we speak of 'a person'.

In all these instances, a science or a discipline has come to achieve so established a recognition as a map of a segment or a set of elements in the world of common experience that it serves as a handy way of discriminating the world of common experience itself. It is one of the ways in which the world becomes a manageable place to live in. Most of us, after all, do seem to think most easily of the world itself as a map. But the process by which economics maps into 'the economy' or by which chemistry maps into 'the chemistry' of our bodies tends for the most part to be taken for granted or completely elided.

Organizing our experience of the world in this fashion, convenient, customary and unexceptionable as it is for the layman, is often unwelcome and embarrassing to the specialist himself. Every decade produces its fresh crop of new specialisms which transcend the boundaries of disciplines almost as soon as they are firmly established in the public mind. But the point of this excursion into the higher generalities is to underline what I am sure you have run ahead of me to perceive, namely, that there is no segment or set of elements in the world of common experience which is organized in this way by sociology. One cannot speak of the sociology of Scotland as one can of the Scottish economy, nor of the sociology of children as one can of child psychology. Interestingly enough, substantive fields of sociology, many of them at least, go by titles like the sociology of education, the sociology of law, the sociology of politics, the sociology of medicine. In all these cases, the substantive area of study is defined by another discipline. The mapping has been done by it, not by sociology.

It is for this reason that this guided tour is taking place under the advertised announcement of 'sociological explanation'. For the substantive areas of sociological studies are composed out of the way in which sociology operates upon previously organized bodies of knowledge, not, let me hasten to add, only and merely upon bodies of scientific and academic knowledge but also upon systems of belief, and codes of accepted practice. Sociology operates in and upon these fields in quite specific directions and in quite specific ways. It does so by questioning assumptions which seem to be made by people, and especially by people in authority in education, law, politics, and so forth, about the behaviour of people. These assumptions are sometimes explicit in the form of expressed statements, more often implicit in the form of preference orderings or concealed value-judgements, but they are all formulated within what I can best call the territorial boundaries of each system of organized knowledge and practice; they are assumptions to the effect that the human behaviour visible to the educationist, the lawyer, the politician and so on, is ordered sufficiently for their purposes according to the principles and the vocabulary of ideas developed within the educational system, the law, political science, and so on. Let me try to make this rather opaque pronouncement clearer by instances of what I mean.

I can begin by what will be for many of you very familiar ground. The 1944 Education Act for England and Wales, like the later Scottish Act, was designed to provide for more education at the secondary level, for different kinds of secondary education, and altogether to ensure that opportunities for educational and thus occupational and social advancement would be equally accessible to all children. There is no reason at all to question the sincerity of those who framed and later administered the Act. Indeed, the strength of the point I wish to make lies in the very genuineness of the attempt to reduce to vanishing point the inequities which had been built into the educational system maintained by the state. Within the perfectly valid frame of reference adopted by legislators, administrators and their advisers, the system of selection for secondary education was as psychologically sophisticated and as fair as one could possibly expect. Certainly, so far as I know, no fairer system of selection has since been devised. Yet a series of studies carried out during the 1950s by the London School of Economics demonstrated conclusively that equality of opportunity had certainly not been achieved. These studies were not, of course, concerned in the least with the techniques of selection themselves, the apparatus of tests, their administration, the impartiality of teachers and educationists – anything but. The enquiries were directed towards bringing to light considerations and factors affecting educational performance which, familiar as they are to all of us now, had simply not been taken into account in the design of the new educational system; it is not that the structure of families and their material and social circumstances were thought of as not affecting the school life and career of the child – of course they were. But those factors had not been treated as affecting attainment in the ways and to the extent they were now shown to do.

During the 1960s the considerations or assumptions treated as external to the frame of reference of education, or disregarded entirely, have been added to by educational sociologists. Educational performance is now being related to organizational features of the school system, to the institutional character of the class-room situation, to the particular difficulties and anomalies of the teacher's role, and the structure of the teaching profession. Those later researches, like the earlier, are directed towards eliciting considerations and determining factors which, previously lying outside the technical scope of the educational system, are nevertheless relevant to the educational process and should henceforward be taken into account. There is an important sense, therefore, in which educational sociology is tributary to the theory and practice of education.

I suggested that the clear definition of the boundary of a field of scholarship or science and the coherence and homogeneity of the kind of facts regarded as lying within it – the fact that we can talk about education as a body of knowledge, and as an administrative system, and as a developmental process of a special kind – that all this comes from the existence of a publicly accepted frame of reference and a particular coinage of ideas and beliefs which is in good currency. The frame of reference changes, of course, and so does the body of ideas, aspirations and values accepted as good currency. The main tradition of sociological writing in the field of education – a tradition which stretches through the work of Durkheim (himself, incidentally, a Professor of Education), Weber, and Mannheim (who also, when he came to this country, occupied a chair of Education) – this main tradition bears on the way in which ideas and beliefs about the purpose, the appropriate administration, and the nature of education have changed in response to changing and emerging needs in society. The actual 'causes of change' as Ginsberg said, 'are motivated acts, but the motives themselves are shaped by changes in conditions.'[1] And these changes occur at an accelerating pace under industrialism, which throws new burdens on educational institutions – the progressive burdens of mass instruction, promotion of scientific and technological progress, occupational recruitment and now, it seems, social selection – for, in the case of the great majority of people in this country, the place they are going to occupy in the social system and the class structure is settled before they are twenty years old.

'Under conditions of advanced industrialism', as Mrs Floud and Dr Halsey have said, 'the economy becomes increasingly dominated by the institutions of research and technological innovation. . . . So that the educational system comes to occupy a strategic place as a central determinant of the economic, political, social and cultural character of society.'[2] On this larger scale, as well as in the study of educational opportunity and educability, the role of educational sociology is to examine, to question, to raise doubts about, to criticize the assumptions on which current policy, current theory, and current practice are based.

The essentially critical function of sociology at this level is just as

[1] Morris Ginsberg, *Social Change, Brit. J. Sociol.*, IX, 1958, p. 213.
[2] Jean Floud and A. H. Halsey, 'The Sociology of Education', *Current Sociology*, Vol 7, no. 3 (1958), p. 169.

clearly present in political sociology. I have to insist on this critical function in the case of this field of studies, because the rendering of the purpose of sociological explanation in this context that I want to put forward is not widely current. In particular, it is very different from that advanced by Martin Lipset and Reinhard Bendix, who are individually two of the most distinguished contributors to this field of sociology, and who, in combination, carry a very formidable – a papal – weight of authority. They write: 'Like political science, political sociology is concerned with the distribution and exercise of power in society. Unlike political science, it is not concerned with the institutional provisions for that distribution and exercise, but takes these as given. Thus political science starts with the state and examines how it affects society, while political sociology starts with society and examines how it affects the state: i.e., the formal institutions for the distribution and exercise of power.'[3]

We all, as academic teachers and students, deal in over-simplifications and learn to live with those of other people. But this attempt to dichotomize the study of political science and political sociology by polarizing them, so to speak, on different points of origin is more than a pardonable oversimplification. It seems to me false as to the facts, possibly with regard to political science, certainly with regard to political sociology, which began with the attempt to measure the extent to which political institutions of a particular kind – namely, political party machines – can and do influence the behaviour of people in society. It is categorically false; the two kinds of study do not occupy two halves of the same football pitch or defend two goals, one labelled 'state' and the other labelled 'society', and advance towards the other; they are different kinds of games, played on different pitches. And the statement is, I believe, false as to the relationship between the two studies. Political sociology is not just the study of the same substantive field as political science but from a different angle of approach. It is tributary to – or, if you like, parasitic upon – political science, in the same way as educational sociology is upon education – parasitic, in the sense in which criticism is parasitic.

There are several fairly distinct divisions of activity in political sociology. The best known is the study of voting behaviour which effectively begins, despite Andre Seigfried's notable work completed before the first world war, with Lazarsfeld, Berelson and Gaudet's panel study of the American presidential election of 1940.[4] What Lazarsfeld and his research team did was to interview a sample of 3,000 electors in a part of Ohio at the beginning of the election campaign, and to interview sections

---

[3] Reinhard Bendix and Seymore M. Lipset, 'Political Sociology', *Current Sociology*, Vol. 7, no. 3 (1958), p. 169.
[4] Paul F. Lazarsfeld, B. Berelson and H. Gaudet, *The People's Choice*, 2nd edition (Columbia University Press, 1948).

of the main sample at regular intervals up to the presidential election in November. The research design was concerned specifically with estimating the actual influence exerted on voting by the campaigns of the two parties throughout the whole six months preceding the election. From this, and subsequent studies in America, Britain and elsewhere, we have gained an increasingly vivid and detailed picture of how much voting is a matter of habit, how little rational choice seems to enter in, how far political allegiances are formed virtually in childhood, how few voters change that allegiance in normal election circumstances. We are getting to know more about the influence of demographic factors and about the curiously overlooked part played by religious affiliation in certain countries. None of this work, or of other work on party organization or pressure groups, on the nature and social function of ideology contributes anything to the solution of the major issues of political principle or of political organization. It is not an approach to the field of study of political science from another point of departure. But it does affect very much the terms in which these issues are to be debated, and the limits of the considerations which must henceforward be regarded as pertinent to political studies. W. G. Runciman has remarked that 'Lazarsfeld's work has placed an important limit on the scope of *a priori* theorizing about democracy; and it has done so by producing sociological evidence directly relevant to the tenets of political theory. It is not evidence which necessarily supports a left-wing or a right-wing view; but it is important precisely because any theory of democracy, whether left or right, must take account of it.'[5] I would, while supporting this, also say that the importance of the sociological work in this field lies not in its limiting the scope of *a priori* theorizing but in extending it – of pointing to considerations which political studies must take into account beyond those which were previously seen as 'politically relevant'.

There are two corollaries to which I think I can now point as proceeding from what I have said so far. The first I have already suggested – which is that the relationship of sociology to these and other fields of substantive study is tributary. Sociologists, more than most scientists perhaps, admit the force of the injuction to forget their past, since much of what of value there is in it has been incorporated and has taken root in other disciplines. Secondly, while the direction and purpose of sociological kinds of explanation has been to amend and supplement the kinds of evidence and consideration lying within substantive areas of organized knowledge mapped by other established disciplines, the outlines of what might turn out to be a substantive area peculiar to sociology are perhaps becoming perceptible. In the cases I have mentioned, sociology has not only pointed to uniformities and variations in performance and in choice which are inexplicable

[5] W. G. Runciman, 'Sociological Evidence and Political Theory' in Peter Laslett and W. G. Runciman (eds.), *Philosophy, Politics and Society* (Blackwell, 1962), pp. 42–3.

in terms of the existing rationale of education or of politics, but has identified the external factors in terms of unwitting regularities among groups and categories of individuals, of latent controls and limitations of action, of conventions and observances which hardly can be said to rise to the surface of articulate expression. We are, in fact, dealing with the institutional framework of social behaviour, the implicit, unthinking and unarticulated code of norms which govern or influence individual conduct. Vilhelm Aubert's study of the judiciary in Norway,[6] when it was first published, evoked violent reactions among the legal profession precisely because it pointed to the fact that, in giving sentence, judges appeared to be following a tacit code which contravened the explicit code of equality before the law. We are, in this country, aware of the embarrassing variations in the practices followed in different magistrates courts in giving sentence – the large discrepancies in the penalties exacted for identical infringements of the law in apparently very similar circumstances. These variations have been the subject of a good deal of discussion and criticism in recent years, and, indeed, investigations have been undertaken to establish just how far the inconsistencies range. But the presumption in this connection, so far as this country is concerned is, I believe, that the inconsistencies are just that – that the natural range of variation which must occur because of differences in temperament, idiosyncratic interpretation of the law, uncontrollable prejudice against persons, and so on, is perhaps wider than it should be. What Aubert did was to scrutinize and compare the sentences and the utterances of judges (senior as well as junior) in giving sentence, relate those to the recorded circumstances of the cases on which sentence was pronounced, and demonstrate that the variation in sentencing behaviour correlated extremely closely with the social class of the accused person. Not an astonishing conclusion, perhaps, but interesting. Interesting, because the correlation bespeaks a rule, a normative principle influencing the sentences given, which is certainly external to the principles which overtly apply to the behaviour of judges, and even contravenes those principles. Other studies, notably the Chicago studies of the conduct of arbitration cases by lawyers, point to the existence of rather more complicated normative principles which seem, in the same latent, unwitting fashion, to distort or contravene the principles of action which prevail, and which are – I must emphasize – honestly maintained, within the system of law itself.

I have, so far, kept to what I have thought might be more familiar ground for this explanation of sociological explanation, largely because I hoped in doing so to make clear the way in which sociological explanation is shaped by its special purposes. I want now to discuss rather more

---

[6] Vilhelm Aubert, *Sociology of Law*, Chapter 6, 'Law Courts and the Class Structure' (Oslo Institute for Social Research, 1964, mimeographed).

closely the essentially critical, assumption-testing nature of sociological investigation. I can, I think, bring most light to bear by recounting some research experience of my own in industrial organizations.

Most empirical studies of organizations depend a good deal on interviews with managers. One begins these interviews conventionally with questions about the particular job one's respondent does, and how it fits in with other people's and with other departments. The next step is to examine the discrepancies between the picture one gets from different respondents of the organization in which they all work. There always are discrepancies, of course. But the question presented by these inconsistencies is not 'Which version is right?' but 'How do these differences arise? How is it that these different versions of the same set of circumstances and actions have arisen in the minds of people who have to co-operate with each other in the very circumstances they view so differently?' The need to account for these differences marks the first stage beyond narrative description.

Some years ago, at the outset of one such enquiry, I encountered a major difficulty even before reaching this first stage, when comparison becomes feasible. The firm was in a very rapidly expanding and technologically advanced industry. A whole series of interviews with managers followed a rather disconcerting pattern. After listening to my account of myself and of what I was interested in finding out, they would say, in answer to my first question, 'Well, to make all this clear, I'd better start from the beginning', and then proceed to give me an account of their careers in the firm. This account would be lucid, well-organized, and informative, but would stop short at some time beforehand – when, in fact, they had arrived at their present position. I would then ask again what they were in fact doing now, what the different functions were that they carried out, whom they saw in connection with them, and so on. After a pause, they would then go on to explain, equally lucidly, how they and their department would operate when the present crisis was past, or the very big job they were rushing through was completed or when the re-organization I had doubtless heard about had been carried through, and they could all settle down to work to a plan. After a succession of such interviews I was fairly certain that I had encountered the sociologist's poor substitute for the natural scientist's 'discovery' – the feeling that what had looked like good, common-sense ground (and what could be more common sense than that managers know what jobs they are supposed to be doing?) was turning into rather liquid assumptions.

Luckily, the managers who had provided me with this experience found my reaction, when I was sure enough of myself to tell them, as interesting as I did, and agreed, four of them in one department, to carry out an experiment. This consisted merely in each keeping a detailed record over a period of five weeks of how he spent his working time, whom he met, what problems he was concerned with, whether he issued instructions, whether he gave, exchanged, or received information, and so on.

I should like to dwell on this account of the genesis of a particular piece of research a little. Like any other kind of enquiry which has a history and an establishment, sociology seems at any one time to be pursuing not so much the right kind of knowledge as the right kind of questions, not definitive information but fresh hypotheses. Anyone who has done research in any field will testify to the truth of Agnes Arber's remark that the difficulty in most scientific work lies in framing the questions rather than in finding the answers. What is not so often insisted upon is that the questions do not suggest themselves or rise at the bidding of the specialist student with a little time on his hands. They arise from doubt. Doubt, in turn, arises from the existence of an alternative where none was previously suggested; it arises from a discrepancy between facts, or between accepted interpretations, or between intended and achieved results. In this particular case, it arose from doubt as to whether what everybody regarded as an abnormal departure from the pattern of activities as they should be was not in fact the normal condition of things.

Let me go on to say a little more about the research project which followed. The four people who carried this through did so in quite exemplary manner, swamped me with thousands of record forms and launched a research project which kept me, and a hundred other managers in a number of different industrial concerns, fully occupied at intervals over the next two years. There is one aspect of the results of this first, pilot, study which I want to mention here. I extracted all the record forms on which the departmental manager and one or other of his subordinates had recorded meeting each other. There were 240 of these. In 165 of them, the departmental manager had noted that he was giving a subordinate instructions or decisions; when one turned to the records made by the subordinates of the same episodes, only 84 of them indicated that they were receiving instructions or decisions. In fact, then, half the time, what the manager thought he was giving as instructions or decisions was being treated as advice or simply information.

This result, which I talked over at some length with the people who had done the recording, is open to a number of interpretations, all of them throwing some light, I think, not only on what we may call the pathology of the systems of bureaucratic authority on which so much of organized life in society depends, but on the way in which people living in a world in which equality is their prescriptive right as citizens yet accommodate themselves to the working necessities of subordination and inferior status. But for my present purpose, what I want to underline is the way in which the rules of the game which was actually being played between these four people – all of them young, intelligent, hard-working, ambitious – were in fact unrecognized by them. There were many other ways which the same suggestion made itself felt – that organizations are made to work very often by the unwitting observance by their members of rules of the game which are not only different from the formal articulated body of rules but are not realized in anything like explicit form by the players themselves. The management of this department, for example, when they were asked at the end of this five-week period – when they had been composing almost minute-by-minute records of their activities – how much of their time was spent on all matters directly related to production, gave roughly well over half of their combined time as the answer. And in this they were, they thought, being conservative; after all, they *were* running a production department. In fact, they spent less than a third. In other companies, estimates of how the whole management group's times was spent – given after each individual member had spent several weeks in unusually close attention to just this – were even more wildly out. These results, incidentally, have inclined me to attach rather less than full objective validity to the figures published in one of the appendices to the Robbins Report (which are based on an enquiry conducted by postal questionnaire) into the way in which university staff distribute their time among their various activities.

I have used a miniature, perhaps trivial, illustration to demonstrate the widespread and pervasive tendency for human action to proceed in a *context* of thought and belief and intention very largely at variance with the manifest import of the actions themselves. In his 1961, Trevelyan lectures, E. H. Carr argues that what the historian is called upon to do is to investigate what lies behind the act. It was, he went on to suggest, a serious error to assume, as Collingwood had, that this meant the investigation of the thought and purposes of the individual actor. These may, said Carr, be quite irrelevant. 'The relations of individuals to one another in society and the social forces which act through them produce from the actions of individuals results often at variance with, and sometimes opposite to, the results they themselves intended.'[7]

Sociology also has been described – by Karl Popper among others – as concerned, in the way E. H. Carr suggests, with the unanticipated consequences of human action. There are innumerable examples of this in the field of administrative action and planning. I can take one from near home. In 1954, a group of professional people working in Pilton, a large Edinburgh ward which is almost wholly made up of municipal housing estates, asked the Department of Social Study to carry out a survey which would help clarify some of what they saw as the social problems of the area. Most of these, at the time, had to do with juvenile delinquency and with a whole series of related difficulties to do with the unruliness of children and adolescents and their hostility to ordinary controls. As part of the preliminaries to the survey, which was carried out by graduate students in the department, I looked at the make-up of the population of the ward – which, even at that time, numbered some 28,000 people – about the same size population as Stirling. There were three noteworthy

[7]E. H. Carr, *What is History?* (Penguin Books, 1964), p. 52.

features. First, there was marked preponderance of young people. Virtually one in four of the population was between 10 and 20 years old; this compared with one in eight for Edinburgh as a whole, and one in eleven for the Central wards. In some parts of Pilton, this disproportionate number of children was even higher – in one section, over half the population was composed of school children and older teenagers. There was also a corresponding numerical deficiency of people between 25 and 35 years old – the most active section of the mature adult population, and there were very few old people.

Now it seemed to me then, and I still believe, that the implications of this state of affairs are quite obvious. The social control and social education of children is immeasurably more difficult in a population with mature adults so heavily out-numbered. The mere thickness on the ground of young children and adolescents will tend to make them a much more powerful force in any community than normally, will reinforce any resistance to adult control from inside or outside a community, and will tend to make adults look for their own entertainment and recreation away from the area. The incidence of unacceptable forms of individual and group activity among children and adolescents will appear to be much higher than in other districts of the City. The forms of activity at any given time, and the choice of companionships open to the individual child will be much more diverse than usual. Child and adolescent society will tend, therefore, to be more self-sufficient.

I think it is reasonable to conclude that the 'youth problem' of Pilton at the time was largely demographic in character. And the population structure which produced a kind of dislocation in the normal system of relationships between adult and children and, in the behaviour of children, was the direct consequence of a housing policy which, in Edinburgh as everywhere else, filled large housing estates built in the 1930s with young families. From ten to fifteen years later, the population of course consisted largely of the middle-aged and the adolescent, and there appeared the sudden growth of delinquency rates in suburban areas which was a notable feature of so many English and Scottish cities. It is as though society played confidence tricks on itself.

On a larger scale, society seems to play not confidence tricks so much as self-confidence tricks on itself. These are a familiar element in social history. It took an immense amount of painstaking effort over many years to prove that a third of the working class population of London was living in poverty; more years of work still, by Rowntree, to prove that the vast majority of families are able to afford less food, clothing and warmth than on the most spartan of reckonings constituted bare subsistence level, had not been plunged into distress through some moral obliquity or defect of character, but through pressure of circumstances which they had no possible means of controlling. The astonishing feature of the *Our Towns* report on the condition of children evacuated from city slums in

1940 was not the squalor and unseemliness of the children but the blank ignorance of all other sections of society about them and the circumstances of urban life which had produced them. Within the last few weeks, Professor Townsend's survey of the millions of families in Britain living at or below the subsistence level represented by national assistance has come, again, as a shock. The results of Harrington's survey of the incidence of poverty in the United States three years ago came as a shock. Now, they are the stock in trade of the week-end political speaker.

The traditional role of descriptive sociology, in this country and elsewhere, has largely been to point our what is immediately obvious to everybody as soon as the task of collecting and presenting the facts has been done. In this, sociology performs its familiar tributary function, this time in the formation and development of public opinion and common knowledge. In its other, more specialized, task of searching for explanations of behaviour, sociology often seems even more directly concerned with the obvious. A little while ago, I said that if one could point to a substantive area which constituted the field of study for sociology, it would be the institutional norms which seem to govern action in the sense of providing navigational rules for decision and action, or limits and constants which the behaviour of people seems to observe. But there exists already an enormous fund of knowledge – common knowledge based on common experience and common sense – about the characteristic patterns of behaviour which can be observed among different groups of people and in different kinds of situation. Many years ago, Paul Lazarsfeld wrote a lengthy review of the first two volumes to be published on the studies conducted during the Second World War into the morale of American troops and the reactions of conscripted men to army life. He lists a number of conclusions, and suggests that most people would dismiss them as familiar, or as so obvious that there was no point at all in examining them. For example: better educated men show more psycho-neurotic symptoms during training than those with less education – (the mental stability of the intellectual compared with the psychological resilience or impassivity of the ordinary man has often been commented upon). Second, men from rural backgrounds were usually in better spirits during their army life than men brought up in the City. Third, troops from the Southern States were better able to stand up to the climate in the hot Pacific Islands than Northerners. Fourth, white privates were more eager for promotion than Negroes. One can add a fifth, equally obvious: officers and men in units where promotion was most frequent and rapid were more satisfied with their present positions and prospects than were people in units where there were least chances of promotion.

'We have in these examples', Lazarsfeld remarks, 'a sample list of the simplest kind of interrelationships which provide the bricks from which an empirical social science can be built. But why, since they are so obvious, is so much money and energy given to establish such findings? Would it not be wiser to take them for granted and proceed directly to a more sophisticated type of analysis? This might be so except for one interesting point about the list. Every one of these statements is the direct opposite of what was actually found. Poorly educated soldiers were more neurotic than those with higher education; Southerners showed no greater ability than Northerners to adjust to a tropical climate; Negroes were more eager for promotion than whites; and so on.'[8]

In this last instance, as in all the others, sociology defines itself as a critical activity. The purpose of sociology is to achieve an understanding of social behaviour and social institutions which is different from that current among the people through whose conduct the institutions exist; an understanding which is not merely different but new and better. The practice of sociology is criticism. It exists to criticize claims about the value of achievement and to question assumptions about the meaning of conduct. It is the business of sociologists to conduct a critical debate with the public about its equipment of social institutions.

This purpose of critical understanding is more important now than it has ever been. Sociology, like other social sciences, is the creature of the new human situation which industrialism has brought about. It emerged, tentatively at first, as the need grew to understand, mitigate and possibly even control the transformations which individual lives and the social order continually undergo. As it has developed, it has become clothed with more and more of the objectivity and methodology of the natural sciences, and has become infused with more of their spirit of enquiry and discovery as ends in themselves; but like other social sciences, its character has nevertheless remained basically ideographic. All the social sciences are, I believe, governed by the need to understand and to represent in adequate terms the nature of individual personality and mental experience, or the relationship of individuals to each other, or the varieties of economic and political institutions and relationships, or the social order itself.

The new impetus which has been given in our generation to the pace of scientific and technological development and to industrial and economic change all over the world gives a new urgency to these studies.

In many ways, the pressing need to know more about human behaviour in all contexts – a need which has found increasingly popular expression during this century – is a manifestation of the disparity between man's understanding and control of nature and his insight into and command over his own conduct and his own affairs. Traditional wisdom, the oversight of the 'intelligent amateur', and the accumulation of experience over a lifetime, which served earlier generations are now insufficient when we are so promptly confronted with the direct and the indirect, the projected and the unanticipated, consequences of discoveries and decisions. Earlier generations, however fast they saw their world chang-

---

[8] Paul F. Lazarsfeld, 'The American Soldier – an Expository Review', *Public Opinion Quarterly* (1949), p. 380.

ing, were at least persuaded that certain traditional institutions and values were immutable, and even that the passage of time alone might solve major difficulties and problems.

Time, indeed, was seen in the nineteenth century as on the side of man. Now, it seems, time is against us. More accurately, perhaps, if more prosaically, the difference lies in the sheer multiplicity and technical difficulty of the factors entering into the decision-making process. The point here is that we are in a fundamentally different situation from that obtaining when piecemeal changes could be made in social, economic or political systems as and when it seemed best, and when institutions could be discarded or replaced without much regard being paid to the social fabric of which they formed part. Decisions, planning and action in scientific, educational, economic and social affairs must now take cognizance of an ever-increasing span of considerations if they are both to be effective and not do more harm than good. Similar circumstances obtain for public and private corporations; and the concurrent growth of studies of decision-making in economics, sociology and psychology is again a manifestation of the way in which development in the social sciences reflects the emergent needs of society.

It is not fortuitous that all societies, whatever their political character or stage of economic development, have realized the need for some form of planning. 'Planning', in fact, is a word of dubious relevance to what is happening, if it is read in its traditional sense of producing a design which future actions, at set times, will convert into a finished construction in complete accordance with it. It is much more a matter of deciding the direction and the goals of activity, of setting the upper and lower constraints to the amounts and to the kinds of activity which are pertinent to the achievement of the goals. This new connotation places much more emphasis on selecting the sets of relevant variables and on understanding and controlling them and the factors which affect them. Planning, in short, has become a complicated process of social cybernetics, into which psychological, social, geographic, economic and educational factors enter, and a process which has to be implemented in terms of organizational and administrative expertise compared with which our existing procedures are but primitive craft skills.

The demands which present social needs are putting on the social sciences are already enormous. I am convinced that a far greater volume of demands and needs is present in latent form, or is building up. These demands are being expressed in a bewildering variety of forms. They are altogether out of proportion to the present capabilities and resources of the social sciences. If they are to come within measurable distance of an adequate response to the need which society has of them, positive and substantial efforts must be made to foster their development. These efforts are now, I believe, visible in a number of countries in Europe. They appear to be imminent in Britain.

I began this lecture by observing that sociology was not a new discipline. This is true, but it is, in one sense at least, new to this University. It has been born at a time when the demands on it, as on other social sciences, are growing, and at a time also when the character of the discipline itself is changing out of recognition. Sociology in Edinburgh looks forward to a strenuous but, I hope, an adventurous and lusty infancy.

10 Some suggestions for a sociological approach to the study of government reports[9] GILBERT SMITH and NORMAN STOCKMAN

(The Sociological Review, Vol. 20, No. 1, February 1972, pp. 59–77)

'.... You would be surprised at the number of years it took me to see clearly what some of the problems were which had to be solved .... Looking back, I think it was more difficult see what the problems were than to solve them, so far as I have succeeded in doing, and this seems to me rather curious.' (Darwin)[10]

There has been no distinctly sociological approach to the study of Reports of Royal Commissions and Government Committes of Enquiry.[11] Since such Reports have, in the past, tended to fall predominantly within the compass of social scientists with a practical interest in social policy and social administration, the sociologist with more theoretical interests has received little guidance in deciding what are important sociological questions to ask about a Report and what method of analysis might prove most fruitful. Much methodological debate has taken Darwin's comment to heart and has devoted considerable attention to the nature of the assumptions upon which a well-formulated problem depends.[12] It is

[9]Colleagues in the Department of Sociology, University of Aberdeen offered helpful comments in the preparation of this paper. We are particularly grateful to Mr. Gordon Horobin. Smith acknowledges support from the Nuffield Provincial Hospitals Trust.
[10]Charles Darwin, quoted in Robert K. Merton: 'Notes on Problem-Finding in Sociology', R. K. Merton et al. (eds.): *Sociology Today*, Harper and Row, New York, 1965, Vol. I, p. ix.
[11]We shall adopt the shorthand of using 'Committee' to refer to both Royal Commissions and Government Committees of Enquiry, and 'Report' to refer to the output of all such bodies.
There are a limited number of sociological articles which comment on particular Reports. See, for example, Marjorie McIntosh: 'The Report of the Royal Commission on Local Government in Greater London', *Brit. J. Sociol.*, XII, 1961, pp. 236–248; O. R. McGregor: 'The Morton Commission: A Social and Historical Commentary', *Brit. J. Sociol.*, VII, 1956, pp. 171–191; and Tessa Blackstone: 'The Plowden Report', *Brit. J. Sociol.*, XVIII, 1967, pp. 291–302. None of these, however, derives from a general sociological framework.
[12]See Mario Bunge: *Scientific Research*, Springer-Verlag, Berlin, 1967, Vol. I, p. 179.

with this question that out paper is concerned. Our aim is to suggest one way in which the formulation of sociological problems concerning government Reports may be grounded on well-founded assumptions. One basic question which the sociologist is led to ask can be posed in the very general form 'why did the Report say what it did?' We suggest that if these Reports are viewed as forms of socially-generated 'knowledge', and if their study is located in the sociology of knowledge, then a more rigorous statement of this question can be attempted. This leads us to an issue central to the sociology of knowledge itself.

There is a tendency within the sociology of knowledge to consider the social processes generating 'knowledge' in isolation from questions concerning its validity. For instance a recent contribution from Berger and Luckmann asserts:

> 'The sociology of knowledge must concern itself with whatever passes for knowledge in a society regardless of the ultimate validity or invalidity (by whatever criteria) of such knowledge.'[13]

In stating this Berger and Luckmann are not only expanding the range of the sociology of knowledge to include the study of common-sense beliefs of everyday life, but are also arguing that sociologists cannot pronounce on the validity or otherwise of these beliefs:

> 'The philosopher ... is professionally obligated to take nothing for granted, and to obtain maximum clarity as to the ultimate status of what the man in the street believes to be "reality" and 'knowledge" ... (T)he philosopher is driven ... to differentiate between valid and invalid assertions about the world. This the sociologist cannot possibly do.'[14]

It is our contention that this current tendency in the sociology of knowledge (to treat all knowledge as if it were of equivalent intrinsic status) is itself a mistake. Valid and invalid knowledge are problematic in different ways. In particular, social science can justifiably pronounce some statement about society as valid or invalid in terms of standards that are generally accepted by the scientific community of the day.[15] Thus we can empirically, as well as logically, distinguish between knowledge about society which is scientifically based and that which is not. We are arguing that only by analysing the validity of knowledge can a social scientist formulate precisely problems for sociological analysis in this field.

[13] Peter L. Berger and Thomas Luckmann: *The Social Construction of Reality*, Allen Lane, The Penguin Press, London, 1967, p. 15. cf. Gerard de Gré: '... gnosio-sociology never raises the question of the material truth or logical validity of the ideas or of the thought-systems that provide its subject matter.' 'The Sociology of Knowledge and the Problem of Truth', in James E. Curtis and John W. Petras: *The Sociology of Knowledge*, Duckworth, London, 1970, p. 665.
[14] Berger and Luckmann: op. cit., p. 14.
[15] We realise, of course, that particular standards may not be accepted by the scientific community of the day. The significance of this point for our later argument is dealt with below.

In this paper, then, we wish to argue that in the study of Government Committee of Enquiry Reports or the Reports of Royal Commissions, a similar separation of questions concerning the social processes generating a Report and questions concerning the validity of the 'knowledge' contained within it, would be equally confusing. We shall try to show that the attempt to explain why a Report said what it does, as an exercise in the sociology of knowledge, involves asking questions about both the social scientific status of the Report, and its evidence and research. Furthermore, we suggest that by answering a series of questions about the Report's evidence, research, arguments and conclusions, the sociologist is able to pose well-formulated questions, within the sociology of knowledge, about Government Reports.

The question of rationality

The point we are making is related to that made by MacIntyre in his paper 'A Mistake About Causality in Social Science'. He concludes his argument thus:

> 'To explain actions within it (the social system) we have to identify the rules and their connection with reasonable or unreasonable, true or false beliefs. Thus we cannot explain actions by means of beliefs and not raise questions of truth or falsity, reason or unreason. For an explanation of why someone did something will be quite different if the agent's beliefs are true from what it will be if they are false, since there will be something quite different to explain. Thus in any society we shall only be able to identify what is going on if we have identified and assessed the established methods of reasoning and criticism in that society. And this will bring us into the sharpest conflict with any school of sociological thought which holds that questions of truth or reasonableness of beliefs either ought not to be or cannot be raised by sociologists.'[16]

If this argument is applied to the sociological study of Government Reports, then an assessment of the 'reasonableness' or rationality of their evidence, research, and the arguments leading from evidence and research to conclusions and recommendations becomes a pre-requisite to the decision as to what it is about a Report that requires explanation. Our application of this argument here attempts to forestall the raising of questions prior to the adequate investigation of the assumptions on which they are based. For example, a sociologist may be convinced that Reports merely reflect the ideology of a ruling class and base his analysis of all Reports in these terms. But if the notion of 'ideology' minimally refers to a social situation in which some group's beliefs about the work-

[16] Alasdair MacIntyre: 'A Mistake about Causality in Social Science', in Peter Laslett and W. G. Runciman (eds.): *Philosophy, Politics and Society* (2nd Series), Blackwell, Oxford, 1964, p. 62.

ing of their society can be said to be false or distorted, then clearly this analysis will be based on assumptions – about the beliefs embodied in Reports – which could themselves be false. The concept of ideology, defined in this way, would be applicable only if the Committee's beliefs had deviated in some way from relevant standards of 'truth or reasonableness'.

In order to follow through this suggestion, it is necessary to be able to identify the relevant standards. Lukes has set out in schematic form some ways in which a belief or a set of beliefs may be said to be irrational.[17] The criteria for making such judgements he divides into two types: 'universal' criteria and 'context-dependent' criteria. There has been considerable debate in recent years over whether there are any criteria of rationality that are universally applicable, and if so, which; or whether all criteria of rationality are relative to the particular society or even social contexts in which they are meaningful. Winch has been one of the major protagonists of this latter view, arguing that judgements of rationality or even logicality can only be made within, and not between, 'forms of life' or 'modes of social life'.[18] In a later paper he argued, against Evans-Pritchard, that it was wrong to measure Azande witchcraft beliefs against standards drawn from Western science. Furthermore he insists that even rules of logic vary between societies, except possibly 'certain formal requirements centering round the demand for consistency', though even here these 'tell us nothing about what in particular is to count as consistency'.[19] Both MacIntyre and Lukes have entered the lists in opposition to Winch. MacIntyre has stated that 'it seems quite clear that the concept of ideology can find application in a society where the concept is not available to the members of the society, and furthermore that the application of this concept implies that criteria beyond those available in the society may be invoked to judge its rationality.'[20] Lukes has begun to identify what such universal criteria might be, and roots part of his argument in the possession of a language by any social group. He summarises his argument thus: 'I conclude that if (a group) has a language in which it expresses its beliefs, it must, minimally, possess criteria of truth (as correspondence to a common and independent reality) and logic – which are not and cannot be context-dependent.'[21]

It would be impossible in a paper such as this to go into all the argu-

[17] Steven Lukes: 'Some Problems about Rationality', *Archiv. europ. sociol.*, 8, 1967, pp. 247–264.

[18] Peter Winch: *The Idea of a Social Science*, Routledge and Kegan Paul, London, 1958, p. 100.

[19] Peter Winch: 'Understanding a Primitive Society', *American Philosophical Quarterly*, 1, 1964, pp. 307–324.

[20] Alasdair MacIntyre: 'The Idea of a Social Science', *Aristotelian Society Supplementary Volume*, LXI, 1967, p. 101.

[21] Steven Lukes: 'On the Social Determination of Truth', in Robin Horton and Ruth Finnegan (eds.), *Modes of Thought*, Faber & Faber, 1973, pp. 230–248.

ments for and against these two positions. At this point we believe that the balance of argument lies heavily on the side supported by Mac-Intyre and Lukes. However, in one particular it is necessary to probe a little deeper, since it bears on our later argument. Lukes's statement of a simple correspondence theory of truth as a universal criterion is, in fact, over-simplified. While it may be the case, as Dummett argues, that philosophers have abandoned the search for a criterion of truth and, in so doing, have given up the correspondence theory, we all remain realists at heart, as Dummett also argues; that is, we cling to the beliefs that 'A statement is true only if there is something in the world *in virtue of which* it is true.'[22] Thus far we may be with Lukes. However, in order to transform this universal criterion into a tool that may be used in the sociology of knowledge, we need to formulate a relationship between criteria of truth and criteria of rationality. Rationality and truth are not equivalent concepts. It is not irrational to believe that which only much later is discovered to be false, so long as at the time the belief was reasonable. However, there is a relationship. Earlier in his paper Dummett argues that 'it is part of the concept of truth that we aim at making true statements'.[23] Truth and falsehood are not simply ways of sorting propositions; we do not fully understand the concept of truth unless we realise that, when making assertions, we try to assert true propositions and not false ones. Thus criteria of truth, even if they be universal, are only applicable in contexts in which people are trying to make assertions, and by uttering or writing empirical sentences are to be taken as trying to express true propositions (as opposed, for example, to making conversation in order to pass the time of day). Hence, in order to use criteria of truth to generate criteria of rationality, we must be able to identify contexts as what one might call 'contexts of assertion'.

This leads us to a consideration of context-dependent criteria of rationality. These are criteria which are only relevant to particular 'modes of social life' or forms of activity. The main difficulty with these criteria is deciding on the limits of different forms of activity. For, given that it would be wrong to apply to one form of activity (say portrait painting) the criteria of reasonableness specific to some other form of activity (say statistical inference), the problem arises of deciding where the boundaries of forms of activity in any society lie. Lukes suggests that one of the ways in which beliefs may be irrational is 'if the ways in which they come to be held or the manner in which they are held are seen as deficient in some respects'.[24]

---

[22] Michael Dummett: 'Truth', *Proceedings of the Aristotelian Society*, 59, 1958–9, pp. 141–162, reprinted in P. F. Strawson (ed.): *Philosophical Logic*, Oxford University Press, 1967; the quotation is found on p. 63.
[23] Dummett: loc. cit., p. 50.
[24] Lukes: op. cit., 1967, p. 259.

But the criteria applicable to the way in which a belief comes to be held are themselves context dependent. Different criteria are appropriate to arriving at say, theological beliefs from scientific beliefs or from political beliefs, yet the boundaries between theology, science and politics may be difficult for the sociologist to establish. Furthermore, in any given society which recognizes these different forms of activities, there may even be debate and dispute as to where these boundaries lie.

Committees of Enquiry are a case in point. The criteria applicable to the investigation of these Committees may be in dispute because it is not clear what form of activity is involved. While some may view it as a scientific enterprise, where the relevant criteria are those drawn from the canons of scientific methodology, some may hold it to be a legal enterprise in which the relevant criteria are those drawn from the procedures for weighing evidence. Yet others may view the task as that of reconciling the claims of competing pressure groups. Here the criteria would be political. No doubt this list could be extended.

However, what we wish to suggest is that we need not simply conclude that since the form of activity involved in Committees of Enquiry is in dispute, it is impossible to decide what criteria of rationality would be relevant to assessing their activities. We try to show that, by examining the nature of such Committees' tasks and of their Reports, it is possible to see their Reports as consisting of a large number of assertions, and the propositions asserted as consisting of those, the judgement of the truth or falsehood of which would be a province of the social sciences.[25] If this is the case, the criteria of rationality which would become relevant in assessing to what extent the Committee's beliefs were reasonably or unreasonably held, would be those drawn from social science itself. Such an assessment is central to the task of explanation since valid and invalid 'knowledge' are problematic in different ways.

The components of a report

With this discussion in mind, the first task is that of examining the nature of the statements made in a Government Report in order to determine what criteria, and therefore what forms of activity, are relevant to assessing their validity. In essence a Report consists of an account of how the world is and how it works, an account of how the world should be,

---

[25] We are aware that in the case of any particular Report it may be impossible to view it as consisting entirely of such assertions. But, as we shall argue, there are good *prima facie* reasons for assuming that a Report does consist of assertions of this kind and for treating other kinds of statements as exceptions, the criteria of rationality for which must be established empirically.

In this paper we are concerned only with those statements the validity of which the sociologist is competent to judge. We would, however, argue that the sociologist of knowledge shall depend upon other scientists to determine the validity or otherwise of statements within their field of competence.

and a series of recommendations as to how this desired state may be achieved. We shall refer to the first set of statements as the Committee's 'diagnosis', to the second set as the 'policy objectives' and to the third set as the 'technical recommendations'.

Each of these sets of statements consists of or presupposes factual assertions about the social world or implies causal relationships between states of affairs. In the case of the diagnosis it is immediately apparent that a series of descriptive and causal statements is involved. For example the diagnosis component of the Plowden Report is a description of the English primary school system. It may be, of course, that the diagnosis presented by a Committee was already implicit within its terms of reference. For example the Roskill Commission was set up,

> 'To enquire into the timing of the need for a four-runway airport to cater for the growth of traffic at existing airports serving the London area, to consider the various sites, and to recommend which site should be selected.'[26]

This embodies a whole series of assumptions both about the future rôle of air transport and the focus of communication structures in Britain on London and the south-east region. However, even armed with such terms of reference, a Committee invariably elaborates this descriptive account.

The technical recommendations are related to the diagnosis in the following way. Since the diagnosis involves not only a static description but also and necessarily the analysis of the way in which the elements of that description are causally related, the technical recommendations are derived from an application of this causal model to achieving the desired objective. Thus in essence the technical recommendations take the form of conditional predictions based on factual assertions.

It is not quite so clear that the policy objectives are exclusively statements in the form of factual assertions. It is often thought that the formation of policy objectives is a purely evaluative task. Even here, however, matters of fact are relevant. First, the statement of policy objectives assumes that it is possible to achieve the desired state of affairs. Just as physical laws will place constraints on the construction of a bridge or an aeroplane, so social scientific laws may suggest that particular combinations of social variables are most unlikely. For instance, many, although by no means all, sociologists believe that industrial society must inevitably be stratified.[27] Similarly, demographic constraints may place limitations on policy objectives.[28] Secondly, if the formation of

---

[26] Quoted in Peter Hall: 'Roskill's Airport: The First Days', *New Society*, 1968, p. 939.

[27] See the debate over the functionalist theory of stratification which followed the publication of Kingsley Davis and Wilbert E. Moore: 'Some Principles of Stratification', *American Sociological Review*, 10, 1945, pp. 242–249.

[28] For example the alternative policies on university expansion available to the Robbins Committee were constrained by demographic factors such as the size of age groups. Committee on Higher Education: *Higher Education* (Robbins Report), H.M.S.O., London, 1963, Cmnd. 2154, para. 152.

policy depends upon marshalling various opinions as to what states of affairs are desirable, then again a number of questions of fact are involved since in forming its policy objectives the Committee will, implicitly or explicitly, have made certain factual assumptions. For example, it may have assumed that individual witnesses really were representative of the interests they purported to represent, that there really was a consensus of opinion *within* the groups the Committee treated as unitary, and so on. Thirdly, since the Committee's policy objectives will have implications for other aspects of social policy, the formation of a Committee's policy objectives does involve assumptions about the congruence of these objectives and those of other policy-making bodies. Thus here again factual assumptions as to the compatability of various states of society will be involved. The formation of policy objectives, then, is at least in part an empirical matter. But unlike the prior diagnosis and technical recommendations, other forms of activity will be pertinent too. Factual assumptions are involved, however, in that they set the logical limits within which a Committee works. And, as with the diagnosis, a Committee here too may be given policy objectives within its terms of reference. The Seebohm Committee, for example, had the following terms of reference:

'To review the organisation and responsibilities of the Local Authority Personal Social Services in England and Wales and to consider what changes are desirable to secure an effective family service.'[29]

These suggest not only that the existing social services are in some way deficient but also that the situation can be rectified by service provision based upon the family unit.

Hence the diagnosis, technical recommendations and, in major part, the policy objectives components of a Report consist of or presuppose a series of empirical statements. This gives us a *prima facie* case, on logical grounds, for assuming that the series of statements which is a Report, is intended by the Committee to be a set of true assertions. The Committee's enterprise is therefore conducted within what we have previously referred to as a 'context of assertion'.

This logical case is supported by the fact that a Committee also generally reports that it engaged in a series of activities which are normally engaged in only by people who are attempting to make true assertions about the real world. First, Committees invariably claim to have collected material which they refer to as 'evidence'. They do this both by soliciting written evidence from groups and individuals, by inviting particular witnesses to give oral evidence and, on occasion, by undertaking visits of observation. The written evidence is usually submitted in response to a letter of enquiry which sets out a limited number of head-

[29] *Report of the Committee on Local Authority and Allied Personal Social Services* (Seebohm Report), H.M.S.O., London, 1968, Cmnd. 3703, para. 1.

ings on which information and opinions are required.[30] This type of written evidence is often quite extensive. The Robbins Committee, for instance, collected 'over 4,000 documents of written evidence',[31] and the Morton Commission on Marriage and Divorce reports that it received 'over two thousand letters, statements and other written material'.[32] The oral evidence is then invited from selected persons and organizations and may be either new material or an elaboration of previous written submissions. On occasion, too, Committees will report that they have been willing to consider unsolicited evidence that was submitted to them.

Secondly, Committees often conduct 'research' which may either be done by outside academic teams or by the Government Social Survey. One of the best examples of a Committee at work in this way is the Donovan Commission. Its report comments:

> 'The Commission was particularly concerned as part of its programme of research to obtain information about industrial relations at workshop level, and especially about the rôle played by shop stewards. With this object arrangements were made by the Government Social Survey Department to conduct interviews on the basis of a series of questionnaires. . . .'[33]

A Committee may also claim that its account of the desired state of affairs is similarly based upon the 'evidence' it collects and the 'research' it conducts. However it may treat its conception of the desirable as not in need of such support. As early as its first paragraph the Plowden Report, for example, accepts 'equality of opportunity' as an undisputed objective:

> 'The purpose to be achieved, and the test by which its success can be recognised, he (Sir Henry Hadow) defined in 1931 in these words 'What a wise and good parent will desire for his own children, a nation must desire for all children.' Of course, equality of opportunity, even when it means weighting the scales to reduce inequalities, still results in unequal achievements. But coupled with a commitment to the highest educational standards, it is the touchstone to apply.'[34]

The research programme the Committee set up was then deliberately designed with this objective in mind.[35] Since, as we have explained,

---

[30]These letters and lists of headings are usually available appended to the Report. See, for example, Central Advisory Council for Education (England): *Children and their Primary Schools* (Plowden Report), H.M.S.O., London, 1967, Vol. 1, Annex A; and Seebohm Report, Appendix A.

[31]Robbins Report, Annex, para. 19.

[32]*Report of the Royal Commission on Marriage and Divorce* (Morton Report), H.M.S.O., London, 1956, Cmnd. 9678, Appendix IC.

[33]*Report of the Royal Commission on Trade Unions and Employers' Associations* (Donovan Report), H.M.S.O., London, 1968. Cmnd. 3623, para. 12.

[34]Plowden Report, Vol. 1, para 1.

[35]*Ibid.*, Vol. 2, p. 91.

a Report's technical recommendations are derived from an application of the causal model (based on the set of empirical statements within the diagnosis) to achieve the desired policy objectives, the 'research' that a Committee claims to have conducted and the 'evidence' it says it collected, are also relevant to its technical recommendations.

That a Committee conducts its affairs within a context of assertion is demonstrable not only by such matters of logic (namely that the series of statements which is a Report, is and presupposes a description of the world) and by the fact that, in general, a Committee is at pains to point out the time and effort it spent in engaging in a series of activities that are usually undertaken only by those who are concerned rationally to make factual assertions or uphold causal models. It is also demonstrable by reference to historical evidence that this is in part how Government Enquiries have developed. The relationship between the work of Committees and social science goes back to the nineteenth century. Two trends have had both personnel and ideas in common. The first was that towards the statistical description of social facts exhibited in 'the establishment of the Statistical Office of the Board of Trade and the Register General's Office in 1837, and the founding of the Statistical Section of the British Association in 1833, and of Statistical Societies in all the major cities, beginning with Manchester and London in 1833 and 1834.'[36] The second was that towards Benthamite 'factual enlightenment' in the process of administration, exhibited in the Reports of the Poor Law Commissioners and of later Royal Commissions. The growth of official statistics and their use by Government Committees, the setting up of the Government Social Survey in 1941 – which came to be a link between departmental Committee enquiries and academic social sciences[37] – and, as demonstrated above, the increasingly academic nature of much of the research commissioned by Committees,[38] all suggests that the work of Committees continues to be seen as an empirical exercise within a context of assertion.

In short then, we have tried to establish that the Report of a Committee consists of and relies on a series of assertions of empirical propositions. We have arrived at this conclusion by examining, first, the nature of the statements within a Report, second, the activities in which Committees appear to find it appropriate to describe themselves as having engaged, and third, certain aspects of the historical development of British Govern-

[36] Harold Perkin: *The Origins of Modern British Society, 1780–1880*, Routledge and Kegan Paul, London, 1969, p. 326.

[37] C. A. Moser: *Survey Methods in Social Investigation*, Heinemann, London, 1958, p. 24.

[38] Of which perhaps the best recent example was the research done for the Robbins Committee, about which the Report stated: 'In this way there has been gathered together a mass of material which, apart from its relevance to the Report, must be regarded as valuable in its own right.' Robbins Report, para. 11.

ment Committees of Enquiry. The importance of this conclusion is that, if it is correct, it allows us to formulate appropriate criteria for assessing the validity of the 'knowledge' presented in a Report. If, as we have argued, a Report embodies both factual statements and the elements of causal models which are intended to be accurate, then the appropriate criteria will be those relevant in assessing the accuracy of such statements and the evidence on which they are based. These criteria will be drawn from science.[39] That is, the 'research', 'evidence' and terms of reference, and the way in which these are used by the Committee in constructing its diagnosis and technical recommendations, are appropriately assessed by the application of criteria that are scientific. While these criteria may be drawn from whichever branch of science is appropriate, in the rest of this paper we shall be concerned only with criteria drawn from social science. This use of scientific criteria may well conflict with the Committee's own definition of its task. It might for example regard itself as a political instrument for the promotion of particular policies, as a mechanism for reconciling the claims of competing pressure groups, or even in religious or humanitarian terms. To assess the reasonableness of the Committee's beliefs defined in these terms it would be necessary to use different and context-dependent criteria. But just as we have argued that a sociologist who wished to use the notion of ideology in his analysis of Committee Reports would have assumed that the Committee's beliefs could not be justified on rational scientific grounds, so an over-hasty use of the Committee's own definition of its task would involve making the same assumption. Thus the examination of a Report in terms of scientific standards is prior to a formulation of the problems that have to be solved and the nature of the explanatory concepts required to solve them. As we have argued, rational and irrational 'knowledge' are problematic in different ways.

Problem generation: illustration

It follows that a full sociological analysis of a Committee Report should begin with a systematic application of relevant social scientific criteria to the empirical statements and causal models in the Report and to the evidence and research on which they are based. In this section we illustrate our proposed approach to the study of Government Reports. As we have argued above, the exact formulation of problems concerning a Report will depend upon an assessment of the scientific rationality of

[39] For the purposes of our analysis, we assume that there will be agreement within the scientific community as to what these criteria are. Clearly this will not always be the case but this should present no particular problem. Scientist have to cope with the fact of academic dissensions and are forced to resolve these problems in their work while nevertheless remaining scientific. How scientists do this is an important question in the sociology of science beyond the scope of this paper.

the knowledge contained in the Report. An examination of the diagnosis will show how quite different problems are generated within the sociology of knowledge. This is the component of a Report in which a Committee develops its account of the workings of that part of the social world under its purview.

Apart from the very general picture implicit (as we have already mentioned) within the terms of reference, the members will themselves come to the Committee with their own conceptions. These will be either of a 'common-sense', or more or less specialised nature. These are the basis for initial deliberation. In addition, consideration of evidence and possibly research will eventually result in that part of the Report that describes the Committee's final account of the world as they see it. The Committee may not, of course, adhere to a single, well-integrated account throughout its Report. It is even possible that viewed as a whole, the descriptions embodied within a Report may be internally contradictory. The sociologist may systematize the Committee's account by extracting causal models from its Report and any inconsistency will be clearly evident in the terms of this model.

The question of consistency immediately demonstrates how alternative sociological problems may arise. Where the account is found to be internally consistent there will be no deviation from normal logical criteria. Only if there are inconsistencies will the sociologist proceed to an explanation of the Report based on an assumption of its irrationality. Having established the validity of this assumption, the sociologist's use of variables which refer to the social processes generating the Report *then* become relevant. Inconsistency may have arisen, for example, through the activities of competing pressure groups advancing differing accounts. It may, on the other hand, have arisen through compromise within the Committee. This suggests that the application of a small-group model would be fruitful. Or it may have arisen because different individual members of the Committee have been influential in drafting different sections of the Report.

If the model appears to be consistent, the problem then arises of ascertaining whether or not the Committee had good grounds for believing it to be an accurate model. We have already argued that since this component of a Committee's Report is subject to scientific criteria, we would have expected the Committee either to have tested their model against existing research findings, or, if these were not available, to have commissioned relevant research of their own. If the Committee failed to test its model in this way, or if its tests were inadequate in terms of the standards of the scientific community of the day, the sociological problem is to explain deviation from social science rationality. It may be, for example, that although the Committee was aware of the need for research, its activities in this respect were thwarted by the government bureaucracy of which it was a part. Or, on the other hand, it may have been that the Committee's account merely reflected the ideology of the ruling class. If this were the case the Committee might not even see the *necessity* of supporting its account with the findings of social scientific research.

We are not arguing here that no sociological problems arise if the Committee does conform to social scientific standards in supporting its causal model. While we earlier assumed that a Committee's logically consistent reasoning was unproblematic, there may be no prior assumption that their grounds for believing their account to be accurate will be adequate in scientific terms. Thus sociologists may sensibly ask why it was that a Committee managed to conform to the standards of scientific rationality; but, as we have argued, explaining rationality and irrationality are very different tasks.

We have shown, then, that questions concerning a Committee's rationality are theoretically prior to the explanation of the content of its Report within the sociology of knowledge. The illustrations of our proposed approach have demonstrated that attempts to introduce at an earlier state variables referring to social processes generating a Report would be attempts to answer questions that are prematurely raised.

A simple example: The Seebohm Report

Having briefly illustrated our argument in general terms, discussion of a part of one specific Report will give some indication of how this approach may be applied. The Report we have selected is that of the Committee on Local Authority and Allied Personal Social Services.[40] The terms of reference of this Committee, sitting under the chairmanship of Frederick Seebohm, have already been quoted. It made the recommendations which later formed the basis of the *Local Authority Social Services Act (1970).*[41]

This Committee began by specifying what it regarded as the major deficiences in existing social service provision. In order to make its technical recommendations as to how to remedy these deficiences, the Committee elaborated its diagnosis by outlining the causes that it thought were responsible for each of these deficiences in turn. This section (Chapter 5) of the Seebohm Report has been systematised by Smith as a causal model (Figure 1).[42] Only a study of the evidence on which this model is based allows us to formulate precisely problems in the sociology of knowledge as to why the Committee did in fact put forward this account.

The statements in the Report from which the causal model was ex-

[40] Seebohm Report.
[41] *Local Authority Social Services Act (1970)*, H.M.S.O., London, 1970.
[42] Gilbert Smith: 'Some Research Implications of the Seebohm Report', *Brit. J. Sociol.*, XXII, 1971, pp. 295–310.

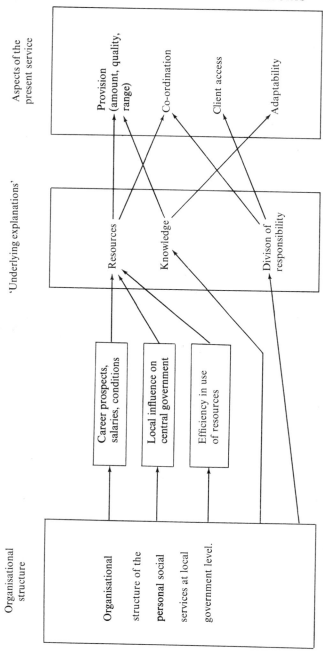

FIGURE I

tracted take the form of a series of causal assertions.[43] The crucial aspect of these assertions is that, in general, insufficient evidence is advanced to support them. For instance, we are offered no grounds at all for believing that,

> 'Changes in Committee responsibility and departmental organisation at the Local Government level may enable the personal social services to obtain extra resources. The most powerful Local Authority Committees and departments are in a strong position to influence decisions on the distribution and use of ratepayers' money and Exchequer grants.'[44]

The same is true of the assertion that,

> 'Changes in administrative structure, particularly those affecting the provision of field work training, could allow facilities to be better used and ensure wider provision of a more useful generic training.'[45]

Some of these statements, it is true, are posed in a tentative form, but they are nevertheless subsequently employed as the basis for the argument leading to the final recommendations and are thus treated as if they were rather more firmly substantiated than in fact they are. It is also true that evidence is sometimes employed to support the statements of a causal relationship. For instance, in arguing that,

> 'The degree of shortage affects the quantity, range and quality of services'[46]

the Committee reports,

> 'Most of those submitting evidence thought that shortage of resources was fundamental to the present problems. For example, of 25 London Borough Councils, most of which are comparatively well-staffed in the personal social services, 18 mentioned shortage of trained manpower as one of the main obstacles which prevented them from developing their services as they would have wished.'[47]

No attempt is made, however, to provide independent assessment of the opinion of such witnesses, as would have been required by social scientific standards. Furthermore the headings under which witnesses were requested to submit their evidence made it extremely unlikely that the Committee's assumption that organisational variables had causal primacy could be refuted. Thus that 'evidence' which the Committee does present

[43] *Ibid.*
[44] Seebohm Report, para. 91.
[45] *Ibid.*, para. 93.
[46] *Ibid.*, para. 88.
[47] *Ibid.*

is clearly inadequate in social scientific terms.[48] Indeed the adequate
testing of such a causal model would be a very complicated procedure.[49]

Thus we now have some basis for formulating what it is about this
part of the Seebohm Report that requires sociological explanation. Since
it is clear that the causal model in the diagnosis of the Seebohm Report
was not advanced on grounds that are rational in terms of the criteria of
social science, what is problematic about this Report may be phrased not
in terms of such generalities as, 'What groups influenced the production
of the Report?', but rather in terms of such specific questions as, 'How is
it that the Committee's *prima facie* case for organisational change rests
on scientifically untested causal assertions?' The importance of this conclusion lies in our earlier argument that the explanation of irrationally
held beliefs poses problems which are different from that of those which
are held on rational grounds. To summarise this simple example, the
process of generating this specific sociological problem can be set out in
diagrammatic form (Figure II).

First are posed some of the questions that we have argued the sociologist would ask of a Report in order to decide what it is that he wishes
to explain. Then are set out the answers to these questions arrived at by
assuming 'perfect rationality'.[50] Finally we give the answers that emerge
from our examination of the Report of the Seebohm Committee. It is the
deviation from perfect rationality that arises in answer to the fourth
question that allows us to pose specific questions within the sociology

FIGURE II

	Does the Report propose a description of the world?	Does description embody a causal model?	Is this causal model consistent?	Is this causal model adequately supported?
'Perfect rationality' assumption	Yes	Yes	Yes	Yes
The Seebohm Report	Yes	Yes	Yes	No

[48] Whereas in this particular example (the Seebohm Report) it is possible to form an
assessment of rationality on the basis of published material alone, this will not necessarily
always be the case. The researcher operating within the framework proposed here might
need, even at this early stage, to examine aspects of a Committee's work on which no or
insufficient data have been published.

[49] See, for example, Hubert M. Blalock, Jr.: *Causal Inference in Non-Experimental
Research*, University of North Carolina Press, Chapel Hill, 1961. Also his *Theory Construction*, Prentice-Hall, Englewood Cliffs, 1969.

[50] For the idea of the 'perfect rationality' assumption, see Q. Gibson: *The Logic of Social
Enquiry*, Routledge and Kegan Paul, London, 1960, p. 164.

of knowledge about this part of the Report. The answering of such questions, once formulated, is an empirical task. It is only at this point that such variables as the characteristics of individual Committee members, the pressures of competing groups, and so on become relevant.

Conclusion

In this paper we have viewed the Reports of both Royal Commissions and Government Committees of Inquiry as particular forms of socially-generated knowledge, and the study of them as part of the sociology of knowledge. However, within the sociology of knowledge we have adopted a particular standpoint. It is one that is in opposition to those, such as Berger and Luckmann, who argue that questions of the validity or invalidity of knowledge are not the sociologist's concern. Indeed, questions of this kind have become central to our proposed mode of analysis of these Reports.

We have argued that in order to specify precisely sociological problems concerning a Report, it is necessary to assess the validity of the knowledge contained in the Report. We then argued in some detail that the criteria on which this assessment should be based are those of social scientific rationality. These criteria were then used to illustrate the way in which problems may be generated within the sociology of knowledge.

11 Ideological documents in education: some suggestions towards a definition   MICHAEL NAISH, ANTHONY HARTNETT and DOUGLAS FINLAYSON[51]

Introduction

The purpose of this paper is to provide a number of criteria by which documents containing ideological discussions of educational practice and policy might be identified. In the introduction we make some general points about ideology and our approach to it, and comment on the choice of documents which we have used to illustrate our discussion in the second section. In this section 'The Critical Apparatus' we give the criteria, or as we call them the 'indices', by which ideological documents are to be identified. The indices are grouped under three dimensions. In the concluding section we attempt to show that the indices offered can be reasonably held to provide a way of identifying ideological documents. We then discuss the use and limitations of the indices, the origins of ideological documents and the problem of justifying the use of such documents.

[51] Specially written for this book.

THE CONCEPT OF IDEOLOOGY: AN APPROACH[52]

This paper arose from attempts to investigate a number of problems about ideologies and their role in education. But it quickly became apparent, in a survey of some of the relevant literature, that the terms 'ideology', 'ideological', 'ideologized' and other derivative and related terms, were used in a number of different senses, and that though they were used with reasonably clear (if different) senses on some occasions, on others they were not. It followed that if the terms were to be usefully employed, some choice of meaning had to be specified and, further, that because a number of meanings were already available (clear and not so clear) and none offered any obvious binding paradigm, some freedom of stipulation was open to us.

We felt, however, that any stipulation that was likely to be useful for our purposes, would need to take into account a number of general features of the uses of 'ideology' and of its cognates, about which there was reasonably widespread, though not universal, agreement. These features were as follows. Firstly, ideologies in general embody views about what should or should not be done, about what is good and bad, about what is right or wrong, etc., in life in general or in a particular area of life.[53] They are, that is, prescriptive, and contain what were called, in Volume I, 'practical judgements'.[54] These purport to offer answers to practical problems of various sorts. Secondly, they contain what are meant to be, at least, empirical claims, many of which are offered in support of the practical judgements. They contain, therefore, what were called in Volume I 'theoretical statements'.[55] The third feature is that to call a set of statements, a set of beliefs, or a discussion, 'ideological' is, in general, though not always, to make an adverse comment on it. 'Ideology', that is to say, is commonly a dyslogistic term. To call a set of statements or a discussion 'an ideology' or 'ideological' is often to impugn their rationality in one way or other. A discussion might be said to be 'ideological' for example on the grounds that the central claims contained in it are inadequately supported, or that they simply reflect an individual's or a group's interests, or that they are covertly vacuous, though they appear to be substantive.

It can be seen from the first two features that, like many non-ideological documents, one purpose for which ideological documents are likely to be composed is to persuade people of the truth of certain views, especially

---

[52] Support for some of the claims we make here can be seen in the third section of this paper.

[53] This point is seen in the social science literature where 'ideology' is often used of ideas, or systems of ideas, which relate to social action and which are used to support particular social structures.

[54] See Vol. I pp. 94–121.

[55] See Vol. I pp. 94–119.

those concerning practical matters. Ideological documents are likely to seek to persuade their readers, depending on their position, skills, and aptitudes, either to carry out the practice or policy advocated, or to support it in some other way, perhaps by political action or by lobbying, or even merely not to hinder its implementation. Further, such documents purport to, and may have been intended to, contain reasons justifying the claims (theoretical or practical) that they make. They, like non-ideological documents, are likely to be addressed to audiences whose co-operation must be, or alternatively must appear to be, won rather than forced. But though both may seem to offer a rationally argued case, ideological documents will not do so and will seek to win the support of their audiences by other means.[56]

Rational and non-rational arguments[57]

On this account, what is ideological is distinguished from what is not ideological, not by subject matter, but by the nature of the argument put forward. Ideological and non-ideological cases for policies might in fact co-exist. There might be, for example, both ideological and non-ideological cases for comprehensive schools, or for grammar schools. To show that a case made out for a particular policy is an ideological one, is not thereby to show that a non-ideological case cannot be made out. Nor does it follow from the connexion of the ideological with the non-rational that the theoretical and practical statements of which ideologies consist are false, since there might be, at a given time, no grounds for

---

[56] The success of ideological documents in persuading people to believe the claims they make will depend in part on the extent to which audiences for them are unable, or unwilling, to distinguish arguments that proceed rationally from those that do not. See pages 113–15 of the conclusions of this paper for further relevant discussion. It is worth noting that whatever other functions an ideological document might have, they seem to depend on their persuasive one. Such documents might be produced, for example, to offer people engaged in activities which they do not know how to justify, or even which cannot be justified, a means of publicly defending what they are doing. They might not themselves *believe* what is contained in the documents. But in so far as the documents are effective in offering a defence, they will need to have some effect on the beliefs of those to whom the defence is made.

[57] There are various ways in which 'rational', 'non-rational', and 'irrational' might be distinguished. For one way see C. L. Stevenson, *Ethics and Language* (New Haven, Connecticut: Yale University Press, 1944), Chapter VI. For the distinction we draw here between 'rational' and 'non-rational' arguments see the discussion on pages 103–5 of this paper. Briefly we take an argument or presentation of a case to be rational when it conforms to the standards given by H. Feigl, 'Education in our age of science', in *Modern Philosophies and Education*, The 54th Yearbook of the National Society for the Study of Education, ed. N. B. Henry (1955), pp. 335–6, and non-rational when it does not. Feigl's standards are given on pp. 104–5 of this paper. For some issues about cross-cultural factors in rationality see Anthony Hartnett and Michael Naish, eds., *Knowledge, Ideology, and Educational Practice* (in preparation).

believing a statement which is, in fact, true. Equally, non-ideological documents need not contain only true statements since there might be, at any given time, grounds for believing a statement which is, in fact, false. What, in our view, is one general criterion of what is ideological is that statements are offered as true or false on inadequate grounds.

But even though this much at least could be extrapolated from some of the literature, there appeared to be no detailed account by which ideological and non-ideological documents could be distinguished. As a consequence, it was difficult to give any precise sense to phrases such as 'the grammar school ideology', 'the comprehensive school ideology', 'the progressive ideology', 'the ideology of streaming' and so on.[58] In any case, it might be argued that there is no such thing as '*the* grammar school ideology' or '*the* comprehensive school ideology' and so on, since in each case a *number* of different defences might be made out, some ideological and others not.

It follows from this that 'ideology' and 'ideological' might be profitably used of specific (attempted) defences and justifications of particular policies and practices, and not of some abstract defence whose existence might be, at best, metaphysical. The most accessible concrete examples of specific defences and justifications were written ones, found in books, pamphlets, reports and articles. We refer to these as 'documents', and as 'educational documents' when they are concerned with educational policies and practices. In the sense that we give to 'ideology' and 'ideological', therefore, the terms do not refer, for example, to the belief system of individuals,[59] nor to beliefs which members of a group share, and which are necessary for membership of the group.[60] Documents might thus be ideological, on our account, whether or not any individual or group has or has not believed them, or ever will. The empirical questions about why ideological documents are produced, whether they are believed by anyone, and what effects they have, are all irrelevant to their identific-

---

[58]Sometimes in phrases like this, 'ideology' is not used dyslogistically, but neutrally to describe a set of evaluative and linked theoretical claims. For one such use see P. Corbett, *Ideologies* (Hutchinson, 1965), pp. 11–12. One disadvantage of this, particularly if the intention to use 'ideology' neutrally is not made explicit, is that people tend to infer that the evaluative and other claims so described are not justified, or even justifiable. They may or may not be. It is worth noting that claims are not shown to be unjustified or unjustifiable, nor do they become so, simply by being called 'ideologies' or 'ideological', even when those terms are used dyslogistically. For a discussion of some of the meanings of 'ideology' see N. Harris, *Beliefs in Society* (Penguin Books, 1971), Chapter 1 and, Arne Naess, Jens A. Christopherson, Kjell Kvaló, *Democracy, Ideology and Objectivity* (Oslo: Oslo University Press, 1956).

[59]There are some disadvantages in linking accounts of 'ideology' to what is believed. Firstly, it is likely to become a matter of complex empirical investigation as to whether a set of claims do constitute an ideology, and if so to what extent. Secondly, one set of claims may at one time be an ideology and at another not, depending on how people's beliefs change.

[60]Cf. P. Corbett, op. cit. (1965), p. 12.

ation as ideological in the way the term is defined here, though these might be very important in other accounts of the concept.[61]

The important thing, then, is to provide a means of distinguishing ideological and non-ideological documents, and this depends on providing a means of distinguishing cases, defences, and justifications that rely on rational argument from those that do not. However, there is no one obvious and simple criterion which might be an infallible sign of what is and is not rational. Arguments may fail to be rational in a number of ways. The words 'rational' and 'non-rational' (and 'irrational' even) can be used to describe a variety of virtues and vices in thought and conduct, to adapt some words of Feigl.[62] Further, rationality admits of degrees. People may be less or more rational, either *in toto* or in some matters as opposed to others, and a case might be argued entirely, or partly, or to a small degree only, in a rational way.

Two things follow from this. The first is that a number of detailed and specific indices[63] are needed, which would be indicators of a less than fully rational discussion. The second is that a particular document might be allowed to be less or more ideological, depending on the extent to which the discussion in it could be cited under the indices.[64] Given these two points, 'ideological' might be imagined to be at one end of a continuum, at the other end of which stood 'rational', and the more a document scored on the indices the nearer the ideological end of the continuum it would be placed. The indices we offer are given in the second section of this paper, which contains what we call 'the critical apparatus'.

The indices and the dimensions

The sixteen indices given in the critical apparatus can be said to be indicators both of discussions that are less than fully rational, and also of those that might be reasonably described as 'ideological'. The account of rationality that we use here is one suggested by six general criteria

[61] See Volume II pp. 99–117 for some further comments on these points.

[62] H. Feigl, op. cit. (1955), p. 335.

[63] We take this term from A. Edel. See A. Edel, 'Reflections on the concept of ideology', *Praxis* Vol. 4 (1967), p. 572 and A. Edel, 'Education and the concept of ideology', *Proceedings of the 24th Annual Meeting of the Philosophy of Education Society of America* (1968), p. 81. Edel's notion of an index is different from ours to some extent, but the discussions in his articles are relevant to the points made particularly in this and the preceeding paragraphs. We use 'indices' instead of 'criteria' since the latter term has a number of specifically philosophical uses with which we are not concerned. For a discussion of general relevance, see A. Kaplan, 'Definition and specification of meaning', *Journal of Philosophy*, Vol. XLIII (1946), pp. 281–8.

[64] The notions of 'less' and 'more' ideological here apply to an individual document. For difficulties in comparing the extent to which *different* documents are ideological, see pages 107–9.

of rationality of thought and conduct that are offered by Feigl.[65] Details of each index, an account of how examples of each index might be identified, and some examples themselves, are given in the critical apparatus.

The indices are grouped under three dimensions. Dimension I contains five indices, and its title, 'Conceptual and logical confusions', suggests in what ways the indices are indicators of discussions that are less than fully rational. The ten indices under Dimension II, called 'Use of evidence', are concerned with the adequacy of the grounds offered for statements in documents and, in particular, with some of the different ways in which assent to a view is invited where, on what is offered in the document, assent cannot reasonably be given. Under the one index in Dimension III, called 'Proponent and target groups', statements are cited which appear to have a role in getting a policy accepted, but not in justifying it. This index suggests a way in which the content of a document might be affected by its writer's view of his audience. The distinction between proponent groups and target groups is made by Krause.[66] The latter consist of those towards whom the ideologies are directed; the former create, develop, or promulgate ideologies. Krause suggests this is done with the purpose of 'politically organising and energising the target group toward behaving in a manner which is stated in the specific text of the message. This behaviour is explicitly or implicitly stated as valuable and desirable as an activity or goal for the target group. Whether it is in fact valuable for the target group is an open question for research.'[67]

CHOICE OF DOCUMENTS

We have taken examples of the indices from the following documents:

(i) T. Burgess, *Inside Comprehensive Schools* (HMSO, 1970), Chapter 1.

(ii) H. A. Rée, *The Essential Grammar School* (Harrap, 1956).

(iii) *Children and their Primary Schools* (HMSO, 1967), Volume one (The Plowden Report).

(iv) *Fight for Education*, a Black Paper, ed C. B. Cox and A. E. Dyson, (Critical Quarterly Society, 1969).

(v) *Black Paper Two*, ed. C. B. Cox and A. E. Dyson (Critical Quarterly Society, 1970).

(vi) Schools' Council, Working Paper 27, '*Cross'd with Adversity*':

[65] See H. Feigl, op. cit. (1955), pp. 335–6 and also Feigl's comments in *Concepts and Structures in the New Social Science Curricula*, ed. L. Morrissett (New York: Holt, Rinehart & Winston, 1967), pp. 141–2. Feigl's criteria are given in detail on pp. 104–5 of this paper.

[66] E. A. Krause, 'Functions of a bureaucratic ideology: "citizen participation"', *Social Problems*, Vol. 16, No. 2 (Fall, 1968), pp. 127–43.

[67] Ibid., p. 132. Krause's distinction between proponent and target groups can be utilized outside the field of ideologies.

the Education of Socially Disadvantaged Children in Secondary Schools (Evans/Methuen Educational, 1970).

In the critical apparatus, these are referred to respectively as, Burgess, Rée, Plowden, *Black Paper One*, *Black Paper Two*, *Working Paper 27*.

A number of points need to be noted about the choice of documents, and the examples of indices we give from them.

Firstly, we are specifically *not* concerned with the merits of the policies advocated in the six documents listed above. It should be noted that the list includes documents advocating traditional and progressive policies (to use the current, and largely useless, jargon).

Secondly, because citations under an index or indices imply that the particular discussion contained in a document is, to some degree or other, less than fully rational, they do give some indication of the quality of the discussion. But from the fact that a document can be cited, even very frequently, under the indices, it does not follow that a rationally argued and cogent case cannot be made out for the policy in question. It might in fact have been made out elsewhere. Frequent citations might, however, throw doubts on a policy, where there were grounds for believing that the case in the document represented the best that could be offered in support of it.

Thirdly, no conclusions about our views on secondary school reorganization should be drawn from the fact that there are more citations from Burgess in the critical apparatus than from any other of the documents. To make even a tentative judgement about the usefulness of the apparatus, it was necessary to discover whether most of the indices were applicable to a *single* discussion. Our work on Burgess showed that they were, and at the same time provided a number of examples suitable for a published version of the apparatus.

Fourthly, the citations in the apparatus by no means exhaust those that can be made from the documents we have used.[68]

We now turn to the critical apparatus itself.[69]

The critical apparatus

Dimension 1   Conceptual and logical confusions
Index 1 Ambiguity

[68] We can say this with some confidence since the second section of this paper (the critical apparatus) is a reduction of a much longer draft. For reasons of space we do not, for the most part, illustrate each index with more than one example. We suggest in footnotes, from time to time, where other examples might be found.

[69] We are extremely grateful to Leon Boucher, of Chester College, for reading several drafts of this paper and for making numerous suggestions about how it could be improved, many of which are now in the text. We are indebted to him, particularly, for the discussion of the evidence from Sweden, and we have usually incorporated word for word the material he supplied. Some of the points made are discussed at greater length in Leon Boucher, *Education in Sweden*, World Education Series (forthcoming).

2 Vacuity
3 Confusions between conceptual, empirical, and normative issues
4 Confusions concerning means and ends
5 Inconsistency

Dimension II   Use of evidence
Index 1 Degrees of assent
        2 Selective use of evidence
        3 Inaccurate account of evidence
        4 Overgeneralization
        5 Irrelevance
        6 Appeals to consensus
        7 Appeals to authorities
        8 Appeals to self-evidence
        9 Appeals to conventional wisdom
      10 Special vocabulary

Dimension III   Proponent and target groups
Index   Proponent and target groups

DIMENSION I – CONCEPTUAL AND LOGICAL CONFUSIONS

Index 1 – Ambiguity

EXPLANATION

A sentence or a phrase or a word may be said to be used ambiguously when it is not clear from its context in which of a number of senses it is to be taken.[70]

EXAMPLE

We cite Burgess' use of 'academic'.

p. 3   They distrusted the more arid aspects of the old academic curriculum.

p. 4   But the grammar schools had traditionally . . . offered an 'academic' education.

p. 4   Selection rested upon three basic assumptions: first, . . . ; second, that only a recognizable minority of children are capable of benefiting from an academic (or as I would say 'secondary') education; and third, . . .

p. 8   . . . academic pupils stay on longer . . .

p. 9   Some of these courses [for 'average' or 'below average' children] were 'unacademic' in the best sense.

p. 9   And those secondary moderns which managed, in spite of all, to

[70] See J. Hospers, *An Introduction to Philosophical Analysis*, 2nd edn (Routledge & Kegan Paul, 1967), pp. 14–15.

build up academic sides and offer courses leading to the General Certificate of Education and other examinations . . .

'Unacademic' (p. 9) is said to have a best sense. It will therefore have at least two others. Given that the meanings of 'unacademic' must each derive from a meaning of 'academic', then 'academic' must have at least three meanings. One meaning of 'academic' is apparently 'secondary' (p. 4), and since it seems unlikely that one of the three meanings of 'unacademic' is 'non-secondary', 'academic' will have at least four senses. In the second quotation from page 9, it is not clear whether offering 'courses leading to the General Certificate of Education and other examinations' is no part of, is some part of, or is the whole of, the meaning of the immediately preceding instance of 'academic'. The quotation might in fact supply a fifth sense. Nor is it clear what the sense of 'academic' is in the quotation from page 3. It might, for example, mean 'secondary' or it might have some other meaning.

It is also worth noting that 'academic' is used apparently in two different senses on one page (p. 4) qualifying the same word, namely 'education'. In the first of the quotations from this page 'academic' seems not to mean 'secondary'. For in this case the quotation would amount to a tautology to the effect that a secondary school offers a secondary education. If however 'academic' here is supposed to have the sense it has either in the quotation from page 3 or even in the one from page 9, why is it printed within inverted commas and they not?

For Burgess, then, 'academic' may be said to have a number of meanings though it is not clear what these all are.[71] Further, it is used ambiguously.

Index 2 – Vacuity

EXPLANATION

The word 'vacuous' here will be used of only those statements which purport to be normative or empirical. It will not be used of those which can be described as 'analytic'.[72] Statements can be said to be vacuous where they lack content – that is to say where it is left more or less entirely open as to what is being described or recommended. The words, phrases, and expressions that give rise to the lack of content can be said themselves to be vacuous. Vacuity, in this sense, can be imagined to be at one end of a continuum at the other end of which is precision, with vagueness[73] situated between.

Vacuous statements are more or less immune to refutation (and to

---

[71] It might be argued that Burgess' use of 'academic' suffers from 'semantic anaemia', that is, that he attaches very little clear meaning to it. For semantic anaemia, see M. Black, *The Labyrinth of Language* (Penguin Books, 1972), pp. 166–70.

[72] See J. Hospers, op. cit. (1967), pp. 160–9 for this term. See also our discussion (pp. 64–6).

[73] See J. Hospers, op. cit. (1967), pp. 67–77 for this term.

confirmation) since it is not possible to discover what, if anything, they are intended specifically to assert.[74] They are, as it were, a conceptual blank cheque which a reader can cash for any sum he pleases. For example, any number of people might agree to some educational innovation or other on the grounds that it was designed to make pupils responsible citizens. Each might have, however, different ideas of what such citizens would be. In so far as these interpretations are incompatible and are left implicit, conflict may go unnoticed. Yet the agreement that has been gained is at most pseudo-agreement in that it is agreement to a form of words and not to any substantive view – normative or empirical.

EXAMPLE
The relevant phrases are italicized.[75]
Black Paper Two
p. 100 The pleasant thing about all this controversy is that nearly everyone is agreed that true education is very much a matter of *catering for individual aspirations and individual needs*: the doubts begin to arise over what are asserted as the best means of achieving this.

Index 3 – Confusions between conceptual, empirical, and normative issues

EXPLANATION

In order to facilitate our discussion here, we need to draw on a number of distinctions between types of statement. These distinctions are taken from philosophy, though their exact nature is there a matter of dispute. We draw the distinctions here at no greater level of sophistication than is needed for our purposes. We distinguish analytic statements, empirical statements, and normative statements.[76]

Analytic statements. Hospers provides an account of analytic statements

[74] E. Best, 'The empty prescription in educational theory', *Universities Quarterly* Vol. 14 (1960), pp. 233–42, calls language of the sort discussed here 'empty'. He suggests that the use of 'empty prescriptions' (p. 237) – that is of vacuous normative statements – arises from their users' lack of confidence that 'a more detailed description of what they seek to produce in education would win general approval' (p. 237). He goes on to say that by the use of such prescriptions 'educational authors have made themselves immune from ... attack, simply because their readers have never had a chance of learning precisely what they are commending.' A. G. N. Flew in 'Indoctrination and doctrines', in *Concepts of Indoctrination*, ed. I. A. Snook (Routledge & Kegan Paul, 1972), pp. 87–8 and J. Passmore in 'The dreariness of aesthetics', in *Aesthetics and Language*, ed. W. Elton (Blackwell, 1954), p. 43, both make points, similar to those of Best, about the vacuity of much discussion of educational policy.
[75] For other examples, see 'a genuine secondary education' (Burgess op. cit. p. 17) and 'perfectly normal, good primary schools alive with experience' (the Plowden Report, Vol. I, paragraph 136).
[76] Cf. C. D. Hardie, 'Description and evaluation in education', *Australian Journal of Higher Education*, Vol. 2 (1965), p. 119; and R. H. Ennis, *Logic in Teaching* (New Jersey: Prentice Hall, 1969), pp. 379–83. For relevant discussions about these distinctions see J. Hospers, *An Introduction to Philosophical Analysis* op. cit. 2nd edn, Chapter 3, and

that is sufficient for our discussion. He says that an analytic statement is one whose truth can be determined solely by an analysis of the meanings of the words in the sentence expressing it.[77] It follows from this, in Atkinson's words, that 'there is no need to refer beyond an analytic statement, to compare it with reality or the facts, in order to see that it is true. It is enough to attend to the meanings of the words with which it is expressed.'[78] An example of such a statement is 'Triangles are three sided'. Analytic statements are said to be logically necessary and the price of this sort of necessity is 'an incapacity to convey extra conceptual information'.[79] They may be said therefore to embody conceptual truths. Statements whose falsity is determined solely by the meanings of the words in the sentence expressing it are called contradictions. They are said to be necessarily false and as such are the negations of analytic statements.

Empirical statements. The truth of these statements cannot be established by an analysis of the meanings of the words in the sentence expressing the statement. Rather, such statements purport to offer information about the world and are confirmed, refuted, shown to be improbable or probable, in terms of our experience of the world. An example of an empirical statement is 'There were more comprehensive schools in the UK in 1972 than there were in 1950.'

Normative statements. We include under this heading all value statements (or judgements) whether to the effect that somebody or something is good, bad, etc., or to the effect that (in a more overtly prescriptive way) something ought, or ought not, to be done. Normative statements need to be distinguished from statements about people's tastes, likes and dislikes, and preferences and, further, from those about what people *believe* to be good, bad, desirable, undesirable, right, wrong, obligatory and so on. Statements about tastes and about what people believe are empirical.[80]

The importance of the distinctions. The general importance of these distinctions is that they enable us to draw attention to the fact that there are at least three different ways in which the truth or falsity of statements might be established. In the case of analytic statements, or of those that

---

(Ftn. 76 cont.)
R. F. Atkinson, *Conduct: an Introduction to Moral Philosophy* (Macmillan, 1969), Chapters 5 and 6. The explanation of this index should also be read in the light of our discussion of ethical naturalism in Vol. I, Section 1, pp. 94–99.
[77] J. Hospers, op. cit. (1967), p. 162.
[78] R. F. Atkinson, op. cit. (1969), p. 66.
[79] Ibid.
[80] Beliefs about what people take to be valuable or obligatory and so on may be the object of empirical study – particularly of the social sciences. But a distinction needs to be made between studying evaluations and making them. See, for example, H. Feigl, 'The difference between knowledge and valuation', *Journal of Social Issues*, Vol. 6, No. 4 (1950), p. 39.

are necessarily false, it is by conceptual considerations. In the case of empirical statements, it is by our experience of the world. How the truth or falsity of normative judgements is to be established is still very much disputed. It is not established by conceptual considerations. Nor are they normally established or refuted in a straightforward way by the production of empirical data, though such data are relevant. For issues arise (a) about what is to be considered as relevant data; (b) about whether such data are all that might reasonably be held to be relevant; and (c) about the relative weightings to be given to the competing considerations (namely, the pros and the cons) that the data will give rise to.[81]

The particular importance of insisting here upon these distinctions between analytic, empirical and normative statements is that they are often confused. Lunsford[82] comments on such a confusion thus – 'When attacking "divisiveness" within the university, administrators sometimes use a style reminiscent of earlier philosophers of moral and social order, intertwining descriptive or analytic statements with normative prescriptions, so that "is" and "ought" become almost indistinguishable to the unpractised eye.' Yet as O'Connor[83] says, normative statements 'should be explicitly formulated, related to practice and recognised for what they are. An undiagnosed value judgement is a source of intellectual muddle.'

One of the reasons for such confusions and for attempts to reduce normative issues to empirical ones may be because empirical questions are not held to be as intractable as some normative ones.[84] It may also be held that empirical statements in general are capable of being established with a greater degree of certainty than normative ones. It may even be, as Bergmann says, that 'the motive power of a value judgement is often greatly increased when it appears within the rationale of those who hold it not under its proper logical flag as a value judgement but in the disguise of a statement of fact.'[85]

Attempts are made also to reduce normative and empirical statements to analytic ones; these attempted reductions which are rarely explicit

[81] For a relevant discussion see Hampshire's article in Vol. I, Section 1, pp. 24–38, and our discussion on pp. 94–103. See also K. Baier, *The Moral Point of View* (New York: Random House, 1965), Chapters 1 and 2.

[82] T. F. Lunsford, 'Authority and ideology in the administered university', *American Behavioural Scientist*, Vol. II (No. 5) (1968), p. 8. See also H. Waitzkin, 'Truth's search for power: the dilemmas of the social sciences', *Social Problems* Vol. 15 (1968), pp. 408–19. Waitzkin comments (p. 413) that 'Because the public statements of social scientists often fail to make the distinction between positive and normative viewpoints, presentation of facts tends to shade off into presentation of value judgements. The public is then left to decide what is fact and what is judgement.'

[83] D. J. O'Connor, *An Introduction to the Philosophy of Education* (Routledge & Kegan Paul, 1957), p. 107. O'Connor states a little earlier that judgements of value 'are inevitable in any system of education, though they are sometimes disguised so that the very proponents of an educational system may be imperfectly aware of the values that guide their practice.'

[84] See the discussion in Vol. I, Section 1, pp. 100–3.

[85] G. Bergmann, 'Ideology', *Ethics*, Vol. LXI (1951), p. 210.

are not always easy to illustrate briefly. Often they are discovered only gradually during the course of a discussion, and then as a result of examining the way that objections to the statements are met. We give one example on page 68 and others can be found in the references below.[86] The apparent gain of such reductions is that the statements offered for assent *seem* to be either empirical or normative, and yet be incapable of being falsified. This is because their truth is held, covertly, to depend on conceptual considerations, and they are held as if they were necessarily true. Such considerations cannot, however, establish the truth of empirical or normative views.[87]

EXAMPLES

We illustrate first the confusion of normative with empirical matters.

Burgess
p. 8   The Swedes suspected that selection was wrong, and arranged an experiment to decide.

Burgess here implies that a normative issue (that selection is wrong) could be settled simply by the production of experimental data, as if it were a scientific issue about, say, whether water expands when heated.[88]

In any case it seems to us irrationally optimistic to expect that any amount of empirical data that we are likely to acquire (let alone that from one experiment, as Burgess describes it) could conclusively establish a normative judgement of the generality of the one cited here from Burgess, given the variety and complexity of institutional, social, and individual factors in education.[89]

[86] See J. Cooper, 'Criteria for successful teaching: or an apple for teacher', *Philosophy of Education Society of Great Britain, Proceedings of the Annual Conference*, Vol. I (1966), pp. 5–18, where, in discussing teaching, both Bantock and Scheffler are accused of promoting 'an ideal under the guise of analysing a concept'; P. Corbett, op. cit., pp. 119–24 and pp. 152–3; B. Mitchell, *Law, Morality, and Religion in a Secular Society* (Oxford University Press, 1970), paperback edition, pp. 14–15; R. Atkinson, *Sexual Morality* (Hutchinson, 1965), pp. 26–9, and pp. 62–70; and Atkinson, op. cit. (1969), p. 63.

[87] For some of the issues raised here, see the discussion in Vol. I pp. 94–99.

[88] See R. Rhees, 'Social engineering', reprinted from *Mind*, Vol. LVI (1947), in R. Rhees, *Without Answers* (Routledge & Kegan Paul, 1969), pp. 50–68. Rhees says (p. 65), 'But the main point is that in social matters the experiments do not decide the issue. . . . It is not like the case in which a scientist learns more about the behaviour of some material.' For another example of this index, see paragraph 522, pages 192–3, of the Plowden Report where there is a discussion of 'the most effective primary school practice, as it has been worked out empirically'.

[89] The sentence cited here from Burgess (p. 8) is also included in the passage cited from Burgess (pp. 7–8) in Dimension II Index 4 – Overgeneralization. The quotation from the Plowden Report in the previous footnote about effective practice might also be cited there. Note R. S. Peters' comments in 'Theory and practice in teacher training', in *Trends in Education*, No. 9 (1968), p. 3. He says that he has 'only one major conviction about methods of teaching – that no overall generalizations about them are possible. Everything depends on what is being taught, to whom, by whom, and to how many.' See also Vol. I, Section 2, pp. 192–6 on this point.

We now give an example of the confusion of conceptual with normative matters.

Plowden

p. 187 para. 505, It is a community in which children learn to live first and foremost as children and not as future adults. ['It' here stands for 'a school']

We owe this example to R. F. Dearden, and we quote some relevant comments of his on it. He writes, 'Another way in which the value divergencies are glossed over, especially in official reports, is to present a value judgement as a definition. . . . In fact neither the Plowden Committee nor anybody else can stop children from being future adults short of killing them, but my point is that when they say "a school is" what they mean is "a school ought to be regarded as", which is not a definition at all but an obvious prescription.'[90]

Index 4 – Confusions concerning means and ends

EXPLANATION

We cite instances here where questions about means are made prior to those about ends – that is to say, where questions about means are raised, discussed and purportedly answered, without any adequate discussion of what ends either are in fact sought, or ought to be sought. Confusions of this kind may indicate a failure to realize that the settling of some issues is dependent on prior, and at least prima facie, settling of others.

EXAMPLE

Burgess

p. 7   So we come to the last unwarranted assumption behind selection: that separate schools are needed for separate abilities. Of course children differ, and have different needs. The question is how these needs should be met. And it is fanciful to suppose that the wild diversity of children can somehow be matched by two (or at most three) types of secondary school. We need in fact the greatest variety of provision, and the argument should be about how to secure it.

p. 17   To sum up, the educational case for comprehensive schools is that

---

[90] R. F. Dearden, 'Philosophy and curriculum innovation', in *Curriculum Development, Themes in Education*, No. 21, Conference Report, University of Exeter (1969), p. 8. R. S. Peters, in his article 'A recognizable philosophy of education: a constructive critique', in *Perspectives on Plowden*, R. S. Peters, ed. (Routledge and Kegan Paul, 1969), pp. 2–3, comments on how paragraph 505 of the Plowden Report conceals 'value judgements in descriptions'. It might be argued that the statement from Plowden discussed above, and others in paragraph 505, could be plausibly interpreted as empirical. In fact, the whole paragraph trades on ambiguities arising from confusions of conceptual, empirical, and normative matters. As such, it might well be cited under Dimension I Index 1 – Ambiguity.

only in this way is it possible to give a genuine secondary education for all children.

We discuss these quotations together. Both appear to assume that the question at issue is about means – that is about how children's needs should be met, or how to secure 'the greatest variety of provision' or 'a genuine secondary education for all children'. The prior question is one about ends – that is about what the children's needs are, what exactly constitutes 'a genuine secondary education' and 'the greatest variety of provision'. It might be thought that the discussion takes it for granted that there is general and genuine (as opposed to pseudo) agreement on ends, but there is no indication in the text that this is the case. In fact it contains no non-vacuous statements about ends.[91] Until there is some reasonably precise and concrete account of what, for example, 'a genuine secondary education' is (which may well be different for different children) there is no way of knowing whether going comprehensive is a way of achieving it, let alone the only way or the best way.

Index 5 – Inconsistency

EXPLANATION

Statements may be said to be inconsistent when they cannot in logic be true at the same time – that is when they are either contradictions or contraries.[92] Inconsistencies can be said to be explicit when the statements that are inconsistent appear in the document, and implicit if at least one

[91] This partly arises from Burgess' use of the word 'need'. For relevant discussions see R. D. Archambault, 'The concept of need and its relation to certain aspects of educational theory', *Harvard Educational Review*, Vol. 27 (1957), pp. 38–62; B. P. Komisar, '"Needs" and the needs-curriculum', in *Language and Concepts in Education*, B. O. Smith and R. H. Ennis, eds (Chicago: Rand McNally, 1961); B. P. Komisar, 'Should we meet the needs of students?', in *Philosophy of Education: Essays and Commentaries*, H. W. Burns and C. J. Brauner, eds (New York: Ronald Press, 1962), pp. 397–402; R. F. Dearden, '"Needs" in education ', *British Journal of Educational Studies*, Vol. 14 (1966), pp. 5–17; P. H. Hirst and R. S. Peters, *The Logic of Education* (Routledge & Kegan Paul, 1970), pp. 32–6. Komisar concludes his 1962 paper by stating that 'The continued wanton use of "need" to pose important educational ideas and issues results in vague, indeterminate, often trivial cliches which sacrifice clarity to obfuscation and generally do treason to the cause of understanding.' He notes in his 1961 paper (p. 41) that in educational writing and discussion 'its vagueness and multiplicity of meaning, far from impairing its usefulness enhances it. For its utterance in a slogan in a suitable setting may further or maintain some educational enterprises. Consider the role of the administrator with its attendant conflicts and dilemmas. The person occupying such a position is frequently called upon to announce policy statements to a public replete with competing and incompatible educational expectations. The energy given in defense of a seemingly partisan policy would detract from other vital administrative functions. Such assertions as "our schools meet needs . . ." may help, in part at least, to avoid these impairments. For a task is performed and a "policy" announced which is least apt to require lengthy debilitating defense.'

[92] For a discussion of inconsistency, contradictions, and contraries see P. F. Strawson, *An Introduction to Logical Theory* (Methuen, 1952), Chapter 1.

of the statements does not appear in the document, but is entailed by a statement or statements that do.

Sometimes statements which appear to be inconsistent turn out not to be so in virtue of some special explanation of their meaning.[93] No such explanation is given in the case of the examples taken from Burgess that we cite here.

EXAMPLE

Burgess

(a) p. 7   Of course children differ, and have different needs.

     p. 13 The Circular recognised that although the needs of children were much the same anywhere . . .

(b) p. 7   We need in fact the greatest variety of provision, and the argument should be about how to secure it.

     p. 11 It is perhaps enough to say briefly here that the positive benefits of comprehensive reorganization are that opportunities remain open for all children, up to the school leaving age . . . and that all children share a common educational experience.

(c) p. 7   And it is fanciful to suppose that the wild diversity of children can somehow be matched by two (or at most three) types of secondary school.

     p. 13 The Circular recognised that although the needs of children were much the same anywhere . . .

Each of the pairs of statements cited here – namely (a), (b) and (c) is inconsistent. (a) Requires no comment. It can be asked of (b) how there is to be great *variety*[94] of provision, and yet all children are to share a common educational experience. It can be said about (c) that if at least one of the criteria for saying that there is a wild diversity of children is that they have different needs, then it is inconsistent to assert both that there is such a diversity and that the needs of the children are much the same anywhere. This latter statement should be considered in the light of Chapter 5 of the Plowden Report entitled 'Educational Priority Areas', and of such notions as 'positive discrimination' (see para. 151, p. 57 of the report).

Further, there are grounds for thinking there is another inconsistency in the statements Burgess makes on page 7. He holds both that the two or three types of secondary school in the tripartite system could not match 'the wild diversity of children', and that 'the greatest variety of provision' is needed. One implication of these views is that the tripartite system was inadequate since the number of types of school was less than the number of types of children. But if the term 'comprehensive' is a unitary

[93] P. F. Strawson, op. cit. (1952), Chapter 1, Part 1.
[94] Our italics.

concept, and thus if comprehensive schools are one type of school, Burgess advocates a reform which is inconsistent with what he previously implied was necessary. This charge of inconsistency might be met, however, by saying that this one type of school is a type in name only, and not in fact, since it admits of great variety of provision. In this case, the notion of types of school is irrelevant to the argument. For it now becomes perfectly possible to say that, though there were only three types of school in the tripartite system, this, taken by itself, does not preclude great variety of provision.[95]

DIMENSION II – USE OF EVIDENCE

Index I – Degrees of assent

EXPLANATION
Under this index we cite cases where:

(*i*) grounds are not offered in support of statements;
(*ii*) grounds are not offered in support of statements, which nevertheless are explicitly claimed to be true;
(*iii*) grounds are adduced in support of statements, but the degree of assent invited is unwarranted.

To offer statements for assent,[96] and at the same time not to offer grounds in support of them, or to offer grounds but to ask for a degree of assent greater than is thereby warranted is to ask for what it would be irrational to give.[97] It is further to invite confusion between (*a*) what there might be grounds for thinking is the case; (*b*) what we might wish to be the case; and (*c*) what we might wish others should believe to be the case.[98]

---

[95] The general inconsistency underlying the inconsistencies on page 7 is that Burgess appears to hold both that in a comprehensive scheme (unlike in a tripartite one) everyone will be treated the same (cf. 'share a common educational experience' and 'the needs of children were much the same anywhere') and that they will be treated differently (cf. 'children have different needs' and 'greatest variety of provision'). For another example that might be cited under this index and for further discussion, see pp. 75 and 101–2.

[96] The phrase 'for assent' is important here. The statements made in the documents are put forward for assent. They are intended to be taken as embodying truths or, at least, as embodying claims which there are reasonable grounds for believing are true. They are not put forward as candidates for discussion, nor as speculations or hypotheses whose truth is a more or less open matter. Cf. the comments in the article by G. Smith and N. Stockman on 'the context of assertion' (pp. 43–49).

[97] Cf. D. J. O'Connor, *An Introduction to the Philosophy of Education*, op. cit. p. 27, 'The use of reason consists in proportioning the degrees of conviction with which we hold our various beliefs to the strength of the evidence that we have to support them. The abuse of reason consists in holding beliefs on insufficient evidence or holding them with a degree of certainty that the evidence does not justify', and p. 28, 'The holding of beliefs on insufficient evidence is superstition.'

[98] Cf. the discussion in R. Crawshay-Williams, *The Comforts of Unreason* (Routledge & Kegan Paul, 1947), pp. 4–10.

It might be argued that, in documents of the sort we are discussing, it is not possible or even desirable, perhaps for reasons of space among others, to give in the text the grounds in support of the views expressed. We do not therefore claim that grounds are not given when references are made to relevant literature. We illustrate (*i*) and (*ii*), here and refer to a later discussion for (*iii*).[99]

EXAMPLES

To illustrate (*i*) we use the following example from Rée.[100]

p. 14 This new, greatly augmented, middle class, wooed by the politicians, by the advertisers, and by the purveyors of entertainment, have suddenly become aware of their own importance; and, as they are ambitious and respectable, they are all expecting at least a Grammar School education for their children. This means that the support for the Grammar Schools is often coming from people who themselves have had no experience of Grammar School education. The working class father and mother who left school at fourteen tend to accept all that a Grammar School can offer their children and be thankful.

Rée offers no evidence to support these statements.
To illustrate (ii) we use the following examples from Burgess.

p. 3 They saw, *rightly*, that there was a lot wrong with the traditional syllabuses and methods.
p. 5 What is more, we are gradually coming to *realise* that although the tests seem to be educational, they are in effect social.

To use the words italicized is to claim explicitly that the views with which they are associated are true. It is inconsistent to say, for example, that people realized that the tests were social and at the same time to deny that they are. Further, the use of such words cannot be justified unless there are grounds which can reasonably be taken to establish the truth of the views associated with them. For their use implies that the views are not merely true but are known to be and, as such, have appropriate evidential backing. No evidence is offered here by Burgess.

For an example of (*iii*) see our discussion under Dimension II, Index 4, Overgeneralization (pp. 70–81). We argue there that the evidence Burgess cites from Sweden, and in addition what he describes as 'all our experience in Britain', cannot support a generalization of the extent that Burgess wishes to make. It can equally well be argued that the evidence

[99] See pp. 79–81.
[100] For a number of comparable and equally unsupported claims see pp. 10–11 of Burgess, op. cit.

cited by Burgess there does not warrant the degree of assent his discussion appears to invite.

Index 2 – Selective use of evidence[101]

EXPLANATION

In very many practical and theoretical[102] issues, particularly where they are complex as many in education are, there will be reasons both for and against adopting any one of a number of competing views.[103] Nagel's example of the reading scheme offers a useful illustration of this in the practical sphere, where consideration about faster learning will generally be held to constitute reasons why a scheme should be adopted, and those about increased misspelling reasons why it should not.[104] Something similar will hold for many theoretical statements, particularly, though not only, for those which fall within academic disciplines such as psychology, sociology, history and philosophy. There may be a number of incompatible views about any one issue in these areas, and of the considerations reasonably held to be relevant to any one view, some will reasonably be held to offer grounds for holding that it is true and others that it is false. What the import of these various and apparently competing considerations is, what views they justify, if any, and what degree of conviction they warrant, may all be difficult to determine.[105] Where not all relevant considerations are given, evidence may be said to be used selectively.[106] We are concerned in particular to identify cases where there are grounds for thinking that only those considerations favourable

[101] A complete justification of our citing passages under various indices, whether in Dimension I or II, has usually been possible up till now, simply by the use of data contained in the documents themselves. But for the next four indices, 2–5, this is not the case, and a complete justification for citing a passage under any of these may well require extensive knowledge of, and reference to, data that are not contained in the documents. The data might come from sociology or psychology or other disciplines. Further, a complete justification might require a long and complex discussion. To deal adequately with the Plowden Report's use of psychological evidence, for example, or with Burgess' use of evidence from Sweden would require a number of papers. The degree of support given in this paper to citings under indices 2–5 will not on the whole amount to more than at best a strong *prima facie* case. Sometimes such a *prima facie* case can be made from statements in the documents themselves. In the case of the Burgess examples used in this index and of the possible example from the Plowden Report, Chapter 16 (see footnote on p. 76), there are indications in the actual texts that evidence has been selectively used.

[102] For the distinction see the discussion in Vol. I, Section 1, pp. 94–121.

[103] See the discussion in Volume I, Section 1, pp. 103–7 and Volume II, pp. 111–15.

[104] See page 21 of this book.

[105] See the discussion in Volume II, p. 163 fn 91, and the references to the articles by Feldman, and by Light and Smith on pp. 157–70.

[106] We are here using 'evidence' in a wider sense than usual – to cover not only considerations relevant to empirical claims but also to normative ones. In the latter case, the considerations are not usually called 'evidence' but rather 'reasons' or 'grounds'.

to a particular view are given, and that those which are unfavourable are omitted.

EXAMPLES
Burgess
pp. 7–8　Will bright children be held back if they are not taught separately from the others? Most of the fears about this come from what people think happens in American high schools, which have always been comprehensive. But the traditions and practices of American education are so different from our own that the faults and virtues of their schools do not come only from their comprehensiveness. On the other hand, far more of the bright children 'get on' and go further in higher education in America than in Britain.

The whole of page 8 is relevant here but for reasons of space we give only two brief quotations from it.

p. 8　But perhaps the most remarkable evidence about this came not from Britain but from Sweden. In view of what I said about American experience, I ought to say at once that the Swedish system was very much like our own, in that it selected children for the equivalent of our grammar schools.
p. 8　The Swedes are also ahead in noting the weaknesses of their new system.

Evidence from the USA that might be taken not to support comprehensive schools in the UK is discounted on the ground that the system in the USA is 'different' from that in the UK. Evidence from Sweden that might be used to support comprehensive schools in the UK, in that it purports to show that 'the more able' (p. 8) do not 'suffer' 'if they are not taught separately from the others' (p. 7), is accepted on the grounds that 'the Swedish system was very much like our own'. But the senses of 'like' and 'different' which are relevant here are those which imply that if two things are like or different, evidence concerning the one is relevant, or irrelevant, respectively, to assertions about the other. The question which needs to be asked is in what respects do cases have to be similar so that evidence from one case can justifiably be used to back assertions about the other? This cannot be answered *a priori*.[107] In the absence of work which could show the relevance or irrelevance of Swedish and American experience, we have no adequate idea of what its bearing is. Burgess accepts evidence from Sweden which he takes to support his case, but not that from the USA, some of which seems to go against it.
　　In addition, the last of these three quotations suggests that Burgess

[107] For a closely related point see K. R. Popper, *The Poverty of Historicism* (Hutchinson, 1961) paperback ed., pp. 93–7.

believes that the Swedish experience could provide grounds against going comprehensive. These grounds are not given, though those from Sweden *for* going comprehensive are. Thus without offering any account as to how this is to be justified Burgess (*i*) selects what he believes to be favourable evidence from Sweden, and rejects what he believes to be unfavourable from the USA; (*ii*) selects from Sweden that evidence only which he believes supports his view and ignores that which does not – even though (*a*) he states that there is some unfavourable evidence ('weakness' (p. 8)); and (*b*) he states that 'the Swedish system was very much like our own. . . .'[108]

The extent to which Burgess has failed to call on all of what he should take the evidence from Sweden to be, is seen by the fact that in his discussion of the evidence from Sweden on page 8, he appears to have isolated for special mention one study from the many studies of the 'fifties and 'sixties carried out in the official 'Experimental Schools', and by such researches as Elmgren, Härnqvist, Bromsjö, Dahllöf, Husén, Marklund, Johannesson, Carlsson, Magnusson, Henricson, Rudberg, Orring, and others. He uses a study which supports his view, but to do this without reference either to the limitations of that study, or to the inclusive nature of the then available evidence, gives a misleading impression of what conclusions it might be held legitimate to draw from a consideration of *all* the studies. Comments by Swedish research workers about the nature of the conclusions that the studies could be held to support are given in the next index (pp. 77–9).

There are further suggestions of selectivity on page 11 of Burgess.

p. 11 So far I have been talking almost entirely in terms of what was wrong with selection and of the arguments for abolishing it.

p. 11 I have mentioned the arguments against selection: the whole of the rest of this book is in a sense the argument for comprehensives.

It has not been shown that there are no arguments for the 11-plus, nor that there are none against comprehensives, though it has been implied that there are some of the latter. No evidence in fact is produced in favour of selection; and none against comprehensive except that heads may not know 'every boy by name' (p. 14) and that 'two tier' arrangements (p. 15) may have disadvantages. What force these two considerations might be held to have is in any case minimized by other remarks close to them. Yet if the issue is to be adequately discussed, both the considerations for and against the 11-plus, and those for and against going comprehensive,

---

[108]The discussion by Burgess on pages 7–8 could, in any case, be cited also under Dimension I Index (5), since it is inconsistent to state that 'the Swedish system was very much like our own' and thus to imply that the evidence in general from there is relevant to practice in the UK and then to imply, by only using part of the evidence, that only some is.

need to be given. The choice between them can be rationally made only by comparing the overall weight of argument for the 11-plus (derived from the reasons *both* for *and* against) with the overall weight of the argument for going comprehensive (derived again from the reasons *both* for *and* against).[109]

[109] Another possible example of this index (and one which readers might wish to look into for themselves) is the Plowden Report, Chapter 16, 'Children learning in school'. Grounds for saying that evidence from psychological research has been used there selectively can be derived from: (*a*) the text itself; and (*b*) B. Foss, 'Other aspects of child psychology', in R. S. Peters, ed., *Perspectives on Plowden* (Routledge & Kegan Paul, 1969), pp. 42–54. Briefly, the report relies on what it takes to be the work of non-behaviourist psychologists (para. 521). It believes that the work of 'behaviourist' psychologists (para. 519) does not, in general, offer much help to teachers. But such work is used where it is thought to support the report's recommendations and is ignored or discounted where it is thought not to. Foss, op. cit., p. 43, suggests that the report underestimates the contribution of 'experimental psychology' which seems to be roughly what the report calls 'behaviourist'.

There are grounds for thinking that the committee did not have an adequate understanding of relevant psychological research. An important paper by D. P. Ausubel, 'Learning by discovery: rationale and mystique', *Bulletin of the National Association of Secondary School Principals*, Vol. 45 (1961), pp. 18–58, which surveys studies on discovery methods, appears to have been unknown to the committee. Foss, op. cit., p. 49, suggests that the report classifies the psychologists it mentions misleadingly. The report (para. 521) appears to overestimate such consensus about the developmental process as there is among those whom it takes to be non-behaviourist psychologists. Its reliance on Piaget's work may be ill-advised since it may be irrelevant to the report's recommendations. Foss, op. cit., p. 49, states that 'Piaget is not basically classed as a learning theorist. Unfortunately he says very little about the learning process. Learning is said to occur through the processes of assimilation and accommodation. Perhaps it does, but the teacher does not get much practical help from this discovery ... Piaget's enormous contribution has not been on the understanding of learning, but in demonstrating how a child's *thinking* differs from that of an intelligent adult, and how the child shows changes in *capacity* for solving problems needing certain concepts.' See also R. F. Dearden, 'What is discovery learning'? *Education 3–13*, Vol. 1, No. 1 (1973), who writes on page 13 that 'The Plowden Report's strong backing for discovery methods is in terms of the Piagetian doctrine that "the child is agent of his own learning". What that doctrine means, I take it, is that each child actively constructs his own mind through a process of interaction with his environment. Certainly the spontaneous "construction of reality" in babies is deeply impressive. But the truth of the Piagetian doctrine cannot be used to justify preferring learning by discovery to learning from instruction, because the doctrine is compatible with *both* ways of learning. The learner just interacts with something different in each case.' See, too, E. V. Sullivan, *Piaget and the School Curriculum* (Ontario Institute for Studies in Education, 1967, Bulletin No. 2), pp. 31–3, who after examining the main areas of Piaget's thought and the use made of it in education concludes, 'It is interesting that so many educators have followed a model of development – prescribing a particular type of learning atmosphere – that has no substantial backing in developmental psychology. ... For education in the 1960s, Piaget is the psychological arm for the proponents of discovery-learning methods. The fact that Piaget's equilibration model is considered deficient by his critics does not hamper those educators who use this model to justify their particular points of view. ... Thus the educator who justifies his particular program by scattered statements made by Piaget is deluding himself into a state of false security.' D. P. Ausubel's comments in the introduction to Sullivan's monograph are also to the point here as are those of Liam Hudson quoted in Volume II, page 165 fn 96.

Index 3 – Inaccurate account of evidence

EXPLANATION

We cite cases here where evidence is given or referred to but where the account given of it is inaccurate. We are not concerned here (as we were in the preceding index) with whether all the relevant evidence is cited but with whether whatever is cited (whole or part), is reported accurately. On this account, therefore, it is a further question whether evidence that is used selectively is also reported inaccurately.

EXAMPLE

One example is Burgess' account of evidence from Sweden about going comprehensive which takes up a large part of page 8 of his book. Burgess can be held to have offered there an inaccurate account of even that part of the evidence he does give. Although he gives no reference, his account appears to refer to the study by Svensson.[110] This study resulted from the situation which existed in Stockholm in 1955, when the city authorities had kept the northern half of the city with traditional parallel school forms, and had set up experimental schools under the 1950 programme in the southern half. There were in fact three sorts of experimental school which between them gave seven different patterns of schooling from 13 to 16. The Teachers High School in Stockholm took this opportunity, with official approval and help, to look at some aspects of this organization – not 'to decide' (Burgess, p. 8). Further, to say that the decision relating to school organization was based on empirical data is again in violation of the historical evidence. The decision to abolish selection between schools was taken, if not in 1950, certainly in 1956 by the Swedish parliament[111] *before* the Svensson study was completed.

Burgess' account is further incompatible with Husén's description of the discussions he had with the Swedish Royal Committee which dealt with the structure and curriculum of the comprehensive school, and which sponsored the Stockholm study. Of these discussions Husén says that 'as the results from the evaluation emerged at the successive grade levels, they were reported to the Committee, with the Minister of Education in the chair and representatives of political parties among members. We met several times with the Committee and discussed at some

---

(Ftn. 109 cont.)

The points made in this footnote, Foss' comment (in Foss, op. cit., p. 42) that the report's recommendations 'could have been arrived at without considering any psychological evidence at all', and comments in paragraph 553 of the report, tend to suggest, in fact, that decisions about what teaching methods to recommend were taken prior to any survey of relevant research, and that then various bits of psychological research were surveyed simply in the hope of finding support for decisions already taken.

[110]N. E. Svensson, 'Ability grouping and scholastic achievement: Report on a five-year follow up study in Stockholm' (Stockholm, 1962).

[111]Swedish Parliamentary Papers, Special Committee SaV. 1950: I, pp. 179–90 and* Parliamentary Debate SV 1956: 102, p. 21.

length the *possible*[112] interpretations of the findings we had submitted. These deliberations often touched upon thorny and highly technical problems.'[113]

Marklund, too, gives an account of the role played by empirical research during the period of school reform which again offers grounds for holding that Burgess' account is not merely inaccurate but perhaps grossly so. Marklund claims that 'the scientific contribution to the experimental work on the 13–16 stage of the compulsory school . . . has seemingly given poor answers. The results are often unclear, and are strongly dependent upon certain presuppositions. . . . The greatest importance of the investigations should be seen in the contributions they make to the dispersion of a number of preconceptions, and how they show that the questions concern values rather than facts. School reform is in the last resort a political question.'[114] In the Swedish context, the OECD Reports make clear that in the interplay between politicians and social scientists, the dialogue was often inconclusive, and policy in the end was based on judgement aided, but not determined, by research.[115] That judgement recognized, as had the researchers themselves, the difficulty of evaluating organizational changes because of the complexity of the processes involved, and the number of variables which require to be considered. Among these were severely circumscribed financial and material resources, and what might be called the human limitations deriving in part from the personalities, skills and attitudes of those involved in the changes – for example, the teachers. Though they in general supported the stated aims of the reorganized schools, a majority of them felt unable to achieve those aims.[116] Pressures from them became so great[117] that in 1970 a committee of inquiry chaired by the Director of the National Board of Education,[118] was set up to examine problems

[112] Our italics.

[113] T. Husén, 'Educational research and the State', in W. D. Wall and T. Husén, *Educational Research and Policy-Making* (National Foundation for Educational Research in England and Wales, 1968), pp. 13–22. (Quote from pp. 14–15).

[114] S. Marklund, *Vår Nya Skola* (Our New School) (Stockholm: 1970), p. 75. Marklund was a member of the Swedish National Board of Education and his studies contributed to the body of empirical work in the 1960s about school reform.

[115] OECD, *Educational Policy and Planning in Sweden* (Paris: 1967), and OECD, *Innovation in Education – Sweden* (Paris: 1971).

[116] *Insyn I Skolan (Insight into the School)*, Lärartidningen/Svensk Skoltidning, 19–20/1971. (Summaries of the inquiry into working conditions in schools carried out by Sveriges Lärarförbund, the Swedish 'NUT'.)

[117] Ibid. For examples of teacher problems as seen by members of Lärarnas Riksförbund, the Swedish 'AMA', see Skolvärlden, 14/1970, p. 25; 15/1970; pp. 3–4, 12; 16/1970, pp. 3–4, 6–7; 19/1970, p. 4. Similar references can be found throughout the 1960s, and were well known before Burgess went to print. See also Volume I, Section 2, pp. 190–204.

[118] Utredning om Skolans Inre Arbets (Inquiry on the Inner Work of Schools): SIA, Skoloverstyrelsen, Stockholm. For the committee's report see, Skolans Arbetsmiljö: Betänkande avgivit av Utredninger om Skolans Inre Arbete – SIA Statens Offentliga Utredningar (SOU) 1974: 53, Stockholm, 1974.

which had arisen. Problems of a similar kind appear to have arisen in this country. One reason given in the James Report for the need for in-service training for teachers was the problems that they met in situations created by comprehensive schools, among other factors.[119]

Our discussion, as a whole, under this index provides grounds for thinking that Burgess' account of the Swedish evidence is inaccurate.[120]

Index 4 – Overgeneralization

EXPLANATION

An argument may be said to be an example of generalization when it is of the following form: some As are Bs; therefore some further As (or indeed all As) are, or are likely to be, Bs.[121] There is overgeneralization where the premise does not support the extent of the generalization in the conclusion.

EXAMPLE

The passage we discuss is from Burgess and runs from the last paragraph on page 7 to all of page 8, except the last three lines. It concerns the evidence from Sweden. The best way of reading the argument here would seem to be as follows. In a study of children of all abilities in Stockholm, it was shown that all groups in the reorganized section did either as well as, or better than, those in the other section (except for a small group of very bright working class boys whose performance was probably affected by the upheaval, and this setback was eliminated in two years). It can be inferred from this that in comprehensive schools in Britain the more able do not, and will not, suffer.

Burgess describes the evidence from Sweden (p. 8) as 'perhaps the most remarkable evidence' that there is concerning the issue under discussion. The evidence that Burgess refers to appears to be that derived from Svensson's study published in 1962,[122] and although it is remarkable as regards the issues that Svensson was examining, Burgess appears to have misused it, as the following remarks suggest.

(i) Svensson's study took a 25 per cent to 30 per cent sample of children in Stockholm who (a) were aged 12 to 15, and (b) were aged 15 to 16 in the 'theoretical' classes of either schools of the traditional grammar-school types, or the various 'experimental schools'. It was concerned with the interrelationships between, on the one hand, the dependent variables of

---

[119] The James Report, *Teacher Education and Training* (HMSO, 1972), p. 8.

[120] It is also worth noting that Burgess fails to mention the teachers' difficulties in Sweden. This failure might itself be cited under Dimension III (proponent and target groups) since, though the point appears both to be true, and relevant to the issue of comprehensive reorganization, mentioning it is not likely to make that policy readily acceptable to those who for the most part are implementing it – namely, the teachers.

[121] For a discussion of generalization see R. H. Ennis, *Logic in Teaching* (New Jersey: Prentice Hall, 1969), Chapter 22.

[122] H. E. Svensson, op. cit. (1962).

social class, scholastic achievement (as measured by standardized tests) and ability (as measured by IQ tests) and, on the other hand, the independent variables of patterns of school organization. One of the latter factors was the presence or absence of classes which had been positively selected, or negatively non-selected, for the more 'theoretical' courses of study. Factors such as discipline, internal school organization, pupil attitudes and adjustment to school, teacher attitudes, and parental attitudes formed no part of the work.

(*ii*) The data and methodology by which Svensson arrived at his conclusions – basically analyses of co-variance – have since been re-examined by Dahllöf using more complex techniques.[123] The data can be shown to give different results.

(*iii*) The circumstances in Stockholm are not necessarily applicable throughout Sweden, a country in which urban–rural differences in educational opportunity and achievement have been known for decades.[124]

(*iv*) A follow-up study in Stockholm is impossible since all schools have been reorganized since 1962. It can therefore be no more than an an assumption that Svensson's results would have been replicated, say in 1970 when Burgess' book was published, even if the same methodology had been employed.

(*v*) Yet, in spite of all this, Burgess appears to generalize (*a*) in time, for the eight years 1962–1970 and beyond; and (*b*) in place, not merely from Stockholm to Britain, but from Stockholm to the rest of Sweden and then to Britain, since whatever the bearing of Svensson's study it is *prima facie* unlikely to be relevant to Britain without being relevant to Sweden as a whole. Burgess appears to imply that one study in one city in Sweden gives firm grounds for believing that since 1962 at the latest, the more able in comprehensive schools have not suffered, whether in Sweden or in Britain, and furthermore that they are unlikely to. For a different view of the implications of the evidence see the following comments of A. Morrison and D. McIntyre. In discussing Svensson's conclusions, they

---

[123] U. Dahllöf, *Skoldifferentiering och Undervisningsförlopp*, Göteberg Studies in Educational Sciences, 2 (Stockholm: Almqvist and Wiksell, 1967). See also a subsequent English version of the above, namely, U. Dahllöf, *Ability Grouping, Content Validity and Curriculum Process Analysis* (New York: Teachers College Press, Columbia University, 1971), and in addition, U. Dahllöf, 'Curriculum process analysis and comparative evaluation of school systems, *Paedagogica Europaea*, Vol. VI (1970–71), pp. 21–36, and V. P. Lundgren, *Frame Factors and the Teaching Process*, Goteberg Studies in Educational Sciences, 8 (Stockholm: Almqvist and Wiksell, 1972).

[124] H. Swedner, G. Ekstrand, 'Skolsegregation i Malmö, 1969'; B–E. Andersson, M. Hallborg G. Ekholm, 'Skolsegration: förekomst och vissa effekter därav' (1970); A. Nygren, 'Social differentiering inom Örebros grundskolor' (1970); B–O. 'Ljung, C. Hansson, S. Jansson, L. Lundman, 'Preliminär rapport gällande effekter av klassers socio-ekonomiska struktur inom Västmanlandsundersökningen' (1970). All these studies are summarized in 'Bebyggelsestrukturen vigtigast vid sociala skillnader' (Structure of the locality is the most important in social differences), *Lärartidningen/Svensk Skoltidning* 15 (1970), pp. 10–12.

write that 'the attainment of the more able pupils was not affected by the age at which they were selected, but less able pupils scored better if they had been to the ... comprehensive schools', and they comment that 'in the very different social and educational conditions of Britain, however, the same may not apply'.[125]

Each of these five points throws doubt on the legitimacy of the generalization that Burgess makes.

Index 5 – Irrelevance

EXPLANATION

Considerations offered in support of the truth or falsity of a claim will be said to be irrelevant when they have no such bearing, that is, when they are not to the point.

EXAMPLE

Burgess

p. 7   And of course the numbers going to grammar schools varied from one part of the country to another. In some places in Wales, 40% of the children were selected for grammar schools, in some Lancashire boroughs only 15% were selected. It seemed awfully far-fetched to believe that the minority capable of benefiting from grammar schools was 40% in one place and 15% in another. In fact the faith that this minority must be about 20% overall stemmed from nothing more scientific than that about 20% had had grammar school education in the past.

The gist of this paragraph appears to be that the belief that only about 20 per cent overall were capable of benefiting from a grammar school education was false, because it arose from the fact that this percentage had attended such schools in the past. Burgess offers nothing else in support of its falsity. Nor does he offer any evidence to support his view of the origin of the belief.

But considerations about how or why beliefs arose are not relevant to determining their truth or falsity. Whether the belief about the 20 per cent arose in the way suggested or in some other way, says nothing at all about whether or not 20 per cent should, or should not, attend grammar schools. It could be perfectly justifiable to agree to Burgess' account of the origin of the belief and still hold that the belief is true (or for that matter false). The argument is an example of the genetic fallacy since in it Burgess fails to distinguish explaining or accounting for the origins of a belief from justifying it.[126]

[125] A. Morrison and D. McIntyre, *Schools and Socialisation* (Penguin Books, 1971), p. 63. Their subsequent discussion about the number of pupils staying on and getting successes in external examinations in comprehensive schools is also relevant.
[126] Cf. D. J. O'Connor, *An Introduction to the Philosophy of Education*, op. cit. p. 68.

Index 6 – Appeals to consensus

EXPLANATION

In cases of appeal to a consensus it will be implied that some class of people, more or less as a whole, know or believe a statement or statements to be true, and therefore that assent to it or them is rational. There are relationships between concepts like truth, knowledge, fact, rational assent and consensus and agreement.[127] Nevertheless, the fact that there is a consensus about some view or other does not make that view correct, nor even assent to it rational.[128] A necessary condition of such assent being rational is that the consensus should be among those who, independently of each other, are in a position to have well grounded evidentially-backed beliefs about matters in the area within which the statement falls – that is, are in a position to understand and assess the evidential argument offered in support of the statement and, further, have done so. Appeals to consensus which are not of this sort, or appeals to a consensus for the existence of which no evidence is offered anyway, offer very little that would show assent to be rational.

EXAMPLES

Rée
p. 17   The advantages of a Grammar School education are coming to be recognized, not only by parents and potential parents from the new middle classes, but also by the users of the Grammar School product, the universities, the Services, industry and commerce.

Rée is here comparing grammar schools with boarding schools, and in particular with comprehensive schools. This can be seen from pages 14–21 of his book.

The passage that we cite from Rée makes various claims. Among them are: (*i*) that, compared with boarding schools and in particular with comprehensive schools, a grammar school education offers advantages; and (*ii*) that parents, potential parents, etc. recognized this. The claim that a grammar school offers such advantages is a normative one, and what is to count as an advantage may be difficult to settle. But if there were agreement about what constitutes an advantage in this context, the empirical task of showing that grammar schools, as a whole, have such advantages is likely to be long and complex; no grounds are offered by Rée to support the claim that grammar schools have them. None is offered to show that parents or potential parents are particularly competent at recognizing them (even if there were known to be some), nor

---

[127] See the comment of E. Nagel (1969) quoted on page 158. See also D. W. Hamlyn's comments on 'agreement' in his book, *The Theory of Knowledge* (Macmillan, 1970), for example, pp. 177–8.
[128] A. G. N. Flew, op. cit. (1971), p. 20.

p. 3 As late as 1961 *an American visitor* could describe these [secondary modern schools] as 'custodial' rather than educational institutions.
p. 6 This new view of ability was accepted *officially* by 1963 ...
p. 7 In one *official* report after another there were surveys showing that there were as many able children outside grammar schools as inside them.

On page 3 the appeal is to what can be described as a disinterested party – one of whose identity and competence (and indeed of whose existence) we are given no information. The views in the quotations from pages 6 and 7 are associated in the one case with an official body (presumably the DES or its predecessor) and in the other with government (among other) reports. The effect of associating all these views with such individuals and bodies is to give them some sort of ratification and so to imply that they are true, or that there are strong grounds for believing they are. In none of these cases is any reference to original sources made. This is particularly unfortunate in the case of the American visitor, not only because of the lack of information about him, but because we do not know what 'these' is supposed to refer to – to many, most, all, some or how many secondary modern schools? If, as the context seems to imply, the claim is a general one referring to at the least 'many, perhaps most' (p. 3) secondary modern schools, his stay in England must have been long and arduous.

Index 8 – Appeals to self-evidence

EXPLANATION
Under this index are cited claims that are implied to be self-evidently true. The implication of an appeal to self-evidence is that the claim in question is true, and moreover that its truth can be (and indeed has been) directly ascertained and apprehended by anyone placed in the relevant circumstances. It is further implied that no evidential argument is needed to establish the truth of the claim and so to justify assent to it.

EXAMPLE
The example under this index is from Burgess. The claim which the italicized vocabulary implies is self-evident does not seem to us to be so. It requires evidential backing if assent to it is to be justified, and no such backing is given.

p. 8 Our old arrangements, like those of Sweden, caused *visible* damage to the children of average and less than average intelligence, with no added advantages to the clever.

It is implied in this quotation that the truth of the claim in it is 'manifest', to use K. R. Popper's word, and that in general its truth is ascertainable by direct observation or some analogous process.[133] Yet not only does the claim raise complex empirical issues, it raises normative ones also about the criteria for identifying cases of 'damage' and 'advantage'.

Index 9 – Appeals to conventional wisdom

EXPLANATION

We cite here cases where a claim is associated with common sense or with a related notion, and where it is thereby implied that assent to the truth of the claim is justified. Appeals to common sense are most directly contrasted with appeals to considerations deriving from specialized intellectual procedures.

We do not wish to assert that claims based on common sense are generally false, nor for that matter that they are generally true. There are, however, limits to what they can offer, in our view, in complex social and institutional situations, and so in matters concerning educational institutions and systems. We may have nothing better by which such claims can be replaced. Even so, the weight that they can justifiably be given may not be very much.

EXAMPLE
Burgess
p. 10   Their dislike was founded on common sense and expressed in common sense terms.

The implication of this passage, taken in the context of page 10 as a whole, seems to be that the dislike of selection by all parents who had experience of it was justified, that what justified it was their realization that it was wrong, and that this realization was justified because it was based on common sense.[134] It does not seem to us that the issue about whether selection is right or wrong is one that common sense can competently decide. Reference to available data, from at least psychology or sociology, will need to be made and some of this may be technical. If common sense could decide the issue, then there would be little need for Burgess' and Rée's books.

If the quotation is interpreted as a purely historical claim about the

---

[133] The notions of self-evidence and related ones, such as intuition, have had a long philosophical history – as reference to any standard history of philosophy will show. P. Winch, in his inaugural lecture, *Moral Integrity* (Basil Blackwell, 1968), p. 8, suggests that the effect of words like 'self-evidence' and 'intuition' is 'to suggest a sort of justification whilst freeing oneself from the burden of actually supplying any'. There are long-standing disputes about which statements, if any, are self-evidently true. This might be one relevant consideration against there being any.

[134] It would be interesting to know what grounds there are for believing that selection was as unpopular as Burgess states, particularly because it appears to contradict Rée's view (quoted on page 72) which is also unsupported.

parents' dislike, then it might be cited under Dimension II Index 5 – Irrelevance. On the historical interpretation, it is not clear what bearing the claim has on whether selection is right or wrong.

Index 10 – Special vocabulary

EXPLANATION
We wish to identify here particular words or phrases which are used either (*i*) in an implicitly commendatory sense about some view, person, object or course of action, or (*ii*) in an implicitly derogatory sense.[135] This vocabulary is related to assent in the following way. To use (*i*) is to imply that whatever it refers to is to be approved of. To use (*ii*) is to imply that it is to be disapproved of. In so far as such vocabulary is used without grounds being given, there is nothing which might show that the attitude of approval or disapproval that it is intended to evoke is justified. In such cases assent or dismissal of a view is asked for which it would not be rational to give.

EXAMPLES
The relevant words and phrases are in italics. It is not implied that they are always used in a commendatory or derogatory sense, even in the same document, but merely that they are in the quotations given below.

We give examples from *Working Paper 27*, from *Burgess*, and from *Black Paper One*.
(*i*) Words used with an implicitly commendatory sense.
Working Paper 27
pp. 78–9   There is much in a lively secondary school that is *new*, *exciting*, and *challenging* to the most handicapped new entrant, and which can be used as the basis for a *new* vocabulary offered in a *new* and interesting way, as if it were a *new* language. The *newer* audio-visual methods of teaching languages can equally well be applied to teaching a *new* reading skill, and we would urge that all teachers, not only teachers of English, should accept responsibility for helping newcomers in this way. The following words are examples of what might be *new* and *exciting*: laboratory, gymnastics, workshop, chemical, deputy, photography, kiln, pattern, chisel – the list is as endless as the teacher's imaginative use of opportunity.

The eulogistic import of 'new', particularly in an almost incantatory role, in *Working Paper 27*, should not be hard to apprehend. It might be argued perhaps that 'new' here means roughly 'to be approved of

[135] For a brief relevant comment see J. Hospers on emotive meaning in *An Introduction to Philosophical Analysis*, op. cit., pp. 51–3.

because (very) recent',[136] and that grounds for approval are at least implied. The inadequacy of these grounds should be noted.
(*ii*) Words used in an implicitly derogatory sense.

Burgess

p. 3   They distrusted the more *arid* aspects of the *old academic* curriculum.

p. 4   And from this[137] arose *the whole apparatus* of selection known as the 11 plus.

Black Paper One

p. 36   In a modern society, education can only thrive in a context of examinations. Those who deny this most probably have ignored the practical realities behind the teaching situation in schools and universities, and succumbed to a prevalent *romantic sentimentalism*.

The dyslogistic import of the italicized words and phrases should not be hard to apprehend.

DIMENSION III – PROPONENT AND TARGET GROUPS

Index – Proponent and target groups

EXPLANATION

We have already drawn attention to Krause's[138] distinction between proponent and target groups. In the case of documents, educational or otherwise, proponent groups consist of those who are responsible for producing the documents (for example, the author or authors and, where appropriate, the institutions and organizations on whose behalf the author is writing or by whom he is commissioned). Target groups consist of those whose support the documents are intended to win, confirm, or strengthen. In many cases it will be possible to identify from the documents themselves those who constitute at least part of the proponent and target groups. In the case of Burgess' book, for example, the cover, among other things, indicates that the proponent group is, at least, the DES. Remarks in the introduction and in Chapter 1, indicate that the target group is, at least, parents, teachers, and administrators.

We make the following two assumptions about proponent and target groups:

(*i*)   A proponent group will wish to appear in a good light in the eyes of its target group, and will almost never wish to appear in a bad one.

---

[136] See the comments in Vol. I, Section 2, page 199, and the quotation from Bernice Martin.
[137] i.e. the situation which existed after the 1944 Education Act, (Eds).
[138] See E. A. Krause, op. cit. (1968), and page 60 of this book.

(*ii*) A proponent group, given its persuasive role, will wish to keep the goodwill (or at the very least not to incur the ill-will) of its target group. For this group will contain both those who might become a proponent sub-group,[139] and those who might make the implementation of a policy difficult or even impossible.[140]

We cite cases where there are prima facie grounds for saying that considerations deriving from these two assumptions, rather than from a concern to justify the policy in question, have had a bearing on what was excluded from the document, or on what was included, and on how this was expressed. We give examples of where (*a*) the proponent group, or possible proponent sub-groups or other allied groups, are put in a good light, and where (*b*) there is at least a prima facie case for saying that the proponent group was concerned not to offend its target group and felt constraints on what it could say to it. There may be grounds for believing that what is said in all or some of the quotations given here is true. There also may not be. But the truth of statements does not alone justify their inclusion in documents. Relevance to the policy issue is also required. The statements cited in this index may be true, and yet have no bearing on justifying the policy in question. They may, even so, have a part in a proponent group's task of making the policy acceptable to a target group.

EXAMPLES

We cite first, from Burgess, cases where the proponent group and a possible proponent sub-group are put in a good light. The view in the quotation is not accompanied by any evidence which could support it.

p. 14 The Department and the local authorities are getting very good at this: school building is one of the greatest triumphs of the welfare state.

(The word 'this' refers to designing school buildings from the school's educational principles.)

Our next quotation from Burgess concerns the inspectorate who, at least in its official role, is·seen as part of the proponent group.

p. 3 The spread of new ideas through the inspectorate was sure but slow. The discussion about what Burgess describes as 'the old academic curri-

---

[139] Consider (*a*) the role of some teachers' unions in secondary-school reorganization, or in raising the school leaving age, and (*b*) the role of teachers, among others, as contributors to the Schools Council's newsletter *Dialogue*. It is worth noting that the membership of proponent and target groups is not fixed. One reason for this is that an aim of proponent groups is likely to be to cannibalize, as it were, members of its target group, and turn them into a proponent sub-group. Further in the case of the Plowden Report, though The Plowden Committee were the original members of the proponent group, the DES and governments have become part of it, in so far as they have accepted, advocated, and attempted to implement its recommendations.

[140] In education, teachers and parents, for example.

culum' (of which the preceding quotation is part) might be taken to censure at least implicitly the inspectorate and so to put it in a bad light. For the question arises – why did not the inspectorate (since there was neither the Schools Council nor the Nuffield Foundation) take a hand in devising new courses? The question is answered by attributing to the inspectorate what might be described as 'rational caution'. It is held to have been a steadying influence on proposed innovations, and to have subjected them to a thorough, if slow, scrutiny.[141]

To cope with the question this way is to avoid putting the inspectorate in a bad light. Why praise is not more forthcoming may be because Burgess believes that at least part of the target group (some teachers perhaps) has an ambivalent attitude towards the inspectorate.

We now look at a case where a proponent group is concerned to win or keep the goodwill of a target group. We list some comments from Burgess about parents.

Introduction, last page
      ... I believe that the present reform of secondary education owes a great deal to parents. Comprehensive schools are their schools, and I hope this book will make clear what they have done.

p. 10 (a) Most parents would not have been able (reasonably enough) to say why the educational assumptions behind selection were wrong, but they did know how selection affected their children.

p. 10 (b) All parents knew from simple observation that children develop at different rates ...

p. 10 (c) The upshot of all this was that by the middle 1950s parents as a whole had decided that selection was wrong. Without this public opinion selection would probably have survived.

p. 11 Parents may not know very much about detail and although they are quite capable of seeing when the results of a policy are dreadful, they may not know what policy would improve things.

The goodwill of parents is asked for in various ways.
    (i) Knowledge is attributed to parents about the consequences of selection and of having a tripartite scheme, and their views about these matters are said to be, in part, responsible for the abolition of selection, and for reorganization on comprehensive lines, though this actual policy originated elsewhere (p. 11).

---

[141] Cf. the Plowden Report on the inspectorate, paragraph 509. 'In the earlier part of the period, too, H.M. Inspectors, who for the previous thirty years had been examiners, were probably restraining influences on innovation, though as time went on they tended increasingly to be agents of experiment and change.' The period referred to is 1898–1944. See also the discussion on the inspectorate in 'Some issues arising from the readings', in Vol. II of this book (pp. 172–3 fn 126).

(*ii*) Where parents are said not to know, their lack of knowledge is said to be a reasonable one (p. 10 (*a*)). This is also implied on page 11, where parents are held to be ignorant only of details and of what policies are required to improve matters. Parents' lack of knowledge in these cases might be said to be reasonable on the grounds that they may not be specialists in educational affairs. The last sentence of the quotation from page 11 is one which appears to rule out parents from participation in decisions about what the new policy should be though comprehensive schools are said to be 'their schools'.[142] Further, where lack of knowledge is attributed to parents, it is either not attributed to all parents (cf. p. 10 (*a*) 'most parents') whereas knowledge is (cf. p. 10 (*b*) 'all parents'); or it is attributed to them only as a possibility (cf. p. 11 'may not know').

(*iii*) In order to justify the change to comprehensive schools, Burgess appears to believe that he needs to show that selection and the tripartite system as a whole were very bad. But to admit both that they were very bad, and that parents had not noticed it would be to imply one or other of the following: that the tripartite system was not really so bad; that parents failed to see what was before their very eyes, as it were, in matters which affected their children; that, though the tripartite system was very bad, the DES, the schools, and LEAs had deceived parents by keeping things covered up.

None of these would be likely to make parents well disposed towards the proponent group.[143]

Conclusions

The concluding section of the paper contains four parts entitled respectively, The Dimensions, Indices, and Ideology; Use and Limitations of the Dimensions and Indices; Origins of Ideological Documents; Origins of Ideological Documents, and Justifying their Use. The central argument of the paper as a whole consists of the introduction to it, the critical

---

[142] T. Burgess, op. cit., Introduction, last page.

[143] Burgess is concerned not to offend (in addition to parents) teachers, particularly those in secondary-modern schools. From remarks on pages 3, 7 and 9 of his book, it can be seen that he generally assigns credit for whatever was good in those schools to teachers and places blame for whatever was bad elsewhere. The credit and blame might be justifiably divided in this way. They also might not. Burgess cites no evidence to support his view. Rée's concern not to offend the inspectorate can be seen from his remarks on pages 61–2 of his book. See, too, page 8 of his book where at least part of his target group is described as 'well-informed, thinking people'. For the Plowden Report's concern not to offend headmasters see paragraph 500 of the report.

apparatus, and the first part of the conclusions. The last three parts of the conclusions raise a number of issues related to the central argument.

THE DIMENSIONS, INDICES AND IDEOLOGY

This part of the conclusions is divided into three sub-sections: Some Current Notions of Ideology; Current Notions of Ideology and the Dimensions and Indices; The Dimensions and Indices and the Standards of Rational Argument. These three sub-sections are intended, taken together, to constitute an argument to the effect that the dimensions and indices might reasonably be held to offer a way of identifying ideological material.

Some current notions of ideology

An adequate justification of why the indices might reasonably, and use-fully, be taken as indicators of material that is ideological would require a long and detailed discussion, and would involve two sorts of consideration. The first would be to show that the conception of the ideological proposed in this paper is consonant with some of the literature on ideology,[144] and the second that it might be useful in the study of the origins, causes, and effects of ideologies, and in what Edel calls 'the critique of ideological judgement'.[145]

Very little is said here about the second sort of consideration, partly because the value of such a conception for research, particularly empirical research, is unlikely to be known before it is tried. Even so, there seem to be some gains in adopting an account of what is ideological which does not depend on what in fact is believed, and is linked to specific concrete discussions.[146] One advantage of such a link is that it should become more difficult for anyone engaged in studying ideologies to attribute to a group views which reflect what he expects the ideology of the group to be, rather than those which on investigation they might be discovered to hold. In particular, it might avoid what can be called 'general ideologies' described by such phrases as 'the grammar school ideology', 'the comprehensive school ideology' etc., which, though apparently no more than social scientists' abstractions, are often held to embody what the supporters of grammar schools, and comprehensive schools believe.[147]

[144] It could only be consonant with some of the literature since the literature is contradictory.

[145] See A. Edel, op. cit. (1968), pp. 82–6.

[146] See the introduction to this paper for a brief discussion of this point.

[147] The attribution of a general ideology to a group (say to supporters of comprehensive schools) may tend to disguise the extent of *dis*agreement within the group. Individuals may support the same policy for a number of different reasons, and on the basis of different empirical beliefs.

As for considerations of the first sort, we believe a detailed case can be made out to show that our stipulation of what is ideological is not arbitrary or unreasonable. But all that can be done here is to make out a brief case by indicating the lines along which a justification of our conception of what is ideological might proceed. We do this by making some general points about ideology and then relating the dimensions and indices to them.

1. IDEOLOGY AND CONFLICT

Ideologies are likely to arise in areas of uncertainty or conflict about practical issues, that is to say, about what should be done. Brown, for example, suggests that mass-media ideologies are most likely to be developed in 'areas where there is potential or actual conflict with members of other interest groups'.[148] King suggests that political leaders are likely to 'demand an ideology or regret the absence of one, and *possibly* with reason in either case' in an unsettled political order where 'there are few publicly recognised guidelines that can be followed'.[149] He notes *àpropos* of nationalist ideologies, that 'the fact of diversity, which is to say, the popular and psychological perception of barriers between peoples within the state, often increases the felt need for an ideological identity'.[150] Geertz makes a number of points which might be held to support King's first contention, and goes on to say that it is 'a loss of orientation that most directly gives rise to ideological activity, an inability, for lack of usable models, to comprehend the universe of civic rights and responsibilities in which one finds oneself located'.[151] All of the points we have noted in this paragraph are reflected either in the strain theory, or the interest theory of ideology, which, according to Geertz, are 'currently two main approaches to the study of the social determinants of ideology'.[152]

2. IDEOLOGY AND ACTION

An inference that can be drawn from (1) is that ideologies are likely to have a role in minimizing uncertainty and conflict about what should be done, and in generating concerted action towards some goal or other. The goal may be to effect change or to preserve the status quo. Krause draws attention to the link between ideology and concerted action. He writes that one strong tradition in the current literature is that ideologies

---

[148] R. Brown, 'Some aspects of mass media ideologies', *Sociological Review Monograph*, No. 13 (January 1969), p. 160. Cf. E. Sagarin (1968), pp. 85–6 op. cit.

[149] P. King, 'An ideological fallacy', in P. King and B. C. Parekh, eds, *Politics and Experience* (Cambridge University Press, 1968), p. 343. See also page 357 where it is stated that in some cases 'ideological formulae, ubiquitous as they are, do not so much represent a unity, as a tenuous and final effort to constitute a unity.'

[150] P. King, op. cit., 1968, pp. 380–1.

[151] C. Geertz, 'Ideology as a cultural system', in D. E. Apter, ed., *Ideology and Discontent*, (New York: Free Press, 1964), p. 64.   (A.D. Aptor)

[152] C. Geertz, op. cit. (1964), p. 52.

are 'people energizing, political program statements'.[153] Some remarks
of King suggest that ideologies might be used 'to marshall a group to
attain a particular aim',[154] and that their acceptance 'creates an identity,
and is intended to promote action'.[155] Lunsford suggests both that ideologies are likely to be demanded where orientations are vague, and
(following Selznick) that ideologies might be seen as '"socially integrating myths" that help to hold the loosely coordinated organization together
and give its members "a sense of mission".'[156] Geertz suggests that ideologies might in part be 'matrices for the creation of a collective con-
science'.[157]

3. IDEOLOGY AND CONSENSUS
The preceding points relate ideology to action. Equally they suggest that
one important role of ideology is to create a consensus about what should
be done. The number of those among whom consensus is sought will vary.
Ideologies may have wide-ranging or restricted target groups. If, for the
sake of argument, Christianity is taken to be an ideology, then the consensus it seeks (that is its target group) is world-wide. But an ideology might
be intended to unify, and prepare for action against a threat from outside,
a *particular* group within which there was actual or potential conflict. An
ideology of this kind might be said to be for internal consumption only.
Another ideology might be used to explain and justify the actions of a
group to those outside it who might be able to affect its actions, favour-
ably or unfavourably.[158] An ideology of this sort might be said to be
intended for external consumption. Another ideology might be intended
to do both these things.

Further, the consensus sought is likely to be not only on the recommendations for action, but also on other value judgements, and on
empirical and historical statements and so on, by which the recommendations are supported. For differences about these might well give rise
to differences about recommendations. Ideologies are likely to contain,
therefore, definitions of the situations in which action has to take place,
and consensus will be sought for those definitions.

4. IDEOLOGY AND THE USE OF EVIDENCE
It might be said that the points made in (1)–(3) are not distinctive of ideologies (though they might be closely associated with them) but might be
held of non-ideological justifications which, like ideologies, are likely

[153] E. A. Krause, 'Functions of a bureaucratic ideology: "citizen participation"', *Social Problems*, Vol. 16, No. 2 (1968), p. 130.
[154] P. King, op. cit. (1968), p. 353; cf. p. 343.
[155] Ibid., p. 390.
[156] T. F. Lunsford, op. cit. (1968), p. 11.
[157] C. Geertz, op. cit. (1963), p. 64.
[158] Mass-media ideologies (R. Brown, op. cit., 1969) and those of sexual deviants (E. Sagarin, op. cit., 1968) might in many cases be of this sort.

to appear more often in time of explicit conflict when the need to seek consensus, and to promote concerted action, is more readily acknowledged.

There is, however, a feature of ideologies that might be used particularly to distinguish them from other sorts of justification, and that is the way in which they seek to achieve consensus and promote action. They seek to do this in ways that are not intellectually respectable and, because of this, ideologies can be said to be epistemologically unsound in that much of what they assert is inadequately grounded. This is reflected in the literature. Marx for example linked ideologies with distortion.[159] Mannheim notes that 'ideology' is used as a dyslogistic term, and writes that 'if the theoretical implications of this contempt are examined, it will be found that the depreciative attitude involved is, at bottom, of an epistemological and ontological nature. What is depreciated is the validity of the adversary's thought because it is regarded as unrealistic.'[160] Geertz notes this tradition in his article.[161] Krause suggests that one major type of definition of 'ideology' is in terms of 'lies to protect the interest of groups in power' and he associates this use with Marx.[162] MacRae suggests that one customary sense of ideology is 'both the distortion of thought by interest – public or private, consciously or unconsciously known – and the study of such distortion'.[163]

What these comments suggest is that ideologies are likely to contain empirical and other statements which are made, not because there are appropriate or relevant grounds for them, but rather because they are believed to support an independently adopted normative position. Thus Roucek writes, 'Ideological thinking is one form of "wishful thinking" – employed particularly in the field of social action. The ideologist, hoping to bring about a "better" world, is interested not in a scientific knowledge of the "truth" but in his political or philosophical "ideal". His ideology does not include social facts in their complex and kaleidoscopic relations, but constructs them according to this ideal in a well-prepared picture. Ideologies are therefore a synthesis of facts and assumptions arranged to support an ideal which is not always in accord with social facts'.[164] Sagarin makes a similar claim about the ideologies constructed by sexual deviants, and about those constructed by some social scientists who

---

[159] J. Plamenatz, *Ideology* (Pall Mall Press, 1970), pp. 23–4.

[160] K. Mannheim, *Ideology and Utopia* (Routledge & Kegan Paul, 1936), p. 64.

[161] C. Geertz, op. cit. (1964), pp. 49–52.

[162] E. A. Krause, op. cit. (1968), pp. 130–1.

[163] D. G. MacRae, *Ideology and Society* (Heinemann, 1961), p. 64.

[164] J. S. Roucek, 'A history of the concept of ideology', *Journal of the History of Ideas*, Vol. 5 (1944), p. 480. See also page 483 where Roucek quotes a remark of Engels that 'a clear ideology is the deduction of a reality not from reality itself, but from imagination'. For some remarks relevant to Roucek's point about 'truth' and 'ideal' see P. King, op. cit. (1968), p. 353.

[165] - MARX- G. "A DAY AT THE RACES" (MGM)

study such deviants.[165] Sagarin writes of the latter that, having arrived at a conclusion about how deviants should be treated in society, 'they proceed to arrange reality in such a manner as to support the conclusion, and in so doing they do violence to evidence, truth, self-consistency and impartial objectivity.'[166] White even offers a definition of 'ideology' as 'a selective interpretation of the state of affairs in society made by those who share some particular conception of what it ought to be.'[167]

5. IDEOLOGY AND IGNORANCE

Further, there are suggestions in the literature that ideologies are likely to arise in areas where knowledge is in short supply. The lack of orient-ation, which it is claimed, is associated with the rise of ideologies, might have its origins in the fact that the situation in which action has to be taken is not fully, and is perhaps very inadequately, understood.[168] The causes of particular states of affairs may be unknown, the details of these states themselves may also be unknown, as well as the outcomes of proposed courses of action in them. Ideologies may fill the gap, as it were. Brown, for example, referring to the mass media, states that 'because it is difficult or impossible to demonstrate the actual effects and consequences (par-ticularly of a single programme or article) the affirmation of ideology replaces scientific measurements.'[169] Geertz suggests that ideologies attempt to render 'otherwise incomprehensible social situations meaning-ful, to so construe them as to make it possible to act purposefully within them',[170] and he talks of them as 'maps of problematic social reality'. Though he goes on to contrast science and ideology, he suggests they are alike in that they are both 'concerned with the definition of a problematic situation and are responses to a felt lack of needed information.'[171] A consequence of this is that ideologies are likely to contain empirical and other claims that lack adequate evidential support. This lack of support is not likely to be made explicit, since where the jejune knowledge base of a policy is apparent and where it is admitted that outcomes are unknown, it might be harder to achieve consensus among the target group.[172]

---

[165]E. Sagarin, op. cit. (1968), p. 86.

[166]E. Sagarin, op. cit. 1968, p. 92. Cf. A. Edel, 'Reflection on the concept of ideology', *Praxis*, Vol. 4, (1967), pp. 571–2.

[167]W. White, *Beyond Conformity* (Glencoe: Free Press, 1961), p. 6.

[168]C. Geertz, op. cit. (1964), p. 64. See D. Emmet's discussion of 'bounded rationality' Volume I, Section 1, pp. 53–4.

[169]R. Brown, op. cit. (1969), p. 162. This offers a clue to a possible function of educa-tional ideologies.

[170]C. Geertz, op. cit. (1964), p. 64.

[171]C. Geertz, op. cit. (1964), pp. 64 and 71. These definitions, to which Geertz refers, though themselves problematic in many cases, might nevertheless (as Brown, op. cit. (1969), p. 166, suggests) 'assume a considerable degree of objective reality and come to define situations, not only for their originators, but for society at large as well.'

[172]As we pointed out (Vol. I, p. 105) uncertainty about outcomes does not entail uncertainty (or disagreement) about what to do. See the discussion of the Gross study in Vol. I, Section 2, pp. 196–202.

6. IDEOLOGY AND SCIENCE

Reflected in (4) above is the contrast between ideology and science, which appears in the literature. The contrast is seen in Marx.[173] Plamenatz notes, 'Ideology in narrower senses can, of course, be distinguished from thought that is not ideological. For example, it is often distinguished from what is called 'scientific' thought . . .'[174] Edel suggests that there are at least two concepts of ideology and that one of them 'is embedded in the slogan "Science vs. ideology".'[175] Geertz discusses the contrast and says that 'though science and ideology are different enterprises, they are not unrelated ones. Ideologies do make empirical claims about the condition and direction of society, which it is the business of science (and, where scientific knowledge is lacking, common sense) to assess.'[176] He suggests there are differences in the 'symbolic strategy for encompassing situations that they respectively represent. Science names the structure of situations in such a way that the attitude contained toward them is one of disinterestedness. Its style is restrained, spare, resolutely analytic: by shunning the semantic devices that most effectively formulate moral sentiment, it seeks to maximize intellectual clarity. But ideology names the structure of situations in such a way that the attitude contained toward them is one of commitment. Its style is ornate, vivid, deliberately suggestive: by objectifying moral sentiment through the same devices that science shuns, it seeks to motivate action.'[177] Eastman comments similarly on differences in style between ideologies and theories (among which he includes scientific theories).[178] These and other authors draw attention to the intensity with which ideologies are typically held, and contrast this with the way scientific theories (ideally) should be held.[179]

The general distinction between science and ideology gives rise to a number of important issues. One of these is whether, and if so in what sense, scientific truth is socially determined, whether scientific and other truth is relative, and whether science is one more ideology among others.[180] These complex epistemological and sociological issues are

---

[173] Cf. H. M. Drucker, 'Marx's concept of ideology', *Philosophy*, Vol. 47 (1972), p. 157.

[174] J. Plamenatz, op. cit. (1970), p. 29.

[175] A. Edel, op. cit. (1968), p. 74.

[176] C. Geertz, op. cit. (1964), p. 72. Cf. T. Parsons, 'An approach to the sociology of knowledge', *Transactions of the Fourth World Congress of Sociology*, Volume IV (International Sociological Association, 1959), pp. 25–49.

[177] C. Geertz, op. cit., p. 71. Whether Geertz's comment on style in ideologies is unqualifiedly true is doubtful. A. MacIntyre in *The Listener* (29 July 1971), pp. 150–1 argues that the 'turgid and vapid' style of H. Wilson's *The Labour Government 1966–1970: a Personal Record* has an ideological function in that, taken with one or two other features of the writing, it makes the book so boring that 'it tends to disable any reflection on the memoirs as a whole . . .' What stylistic features might be expected to do is to make ideological discussion less open to criticism.

[178] G. Eastman, op. cit. (1967).

[179] Ibid., p. 108; J. S. Roucek, op. cit. (1944), p. 480.

[180] Cf. A. Edel, *Ethical Judgement: the Use of Science in Ethics* (Free Press of Glencoe,

not discussed here. We are rather concerned to make a number of brief points about the distinction between science and ideology.

The distinction seems to presuppose that science is a unitary concept that might unambiguously provide a point of contrast with ideology. But it is not clear whether this is so. Black for example states that he believes 'the term "science" has no definite and unambiguous application';[181] Gallie says that 'there is a marked variety in our uses of the term [science] in different kinds of context',[182] and talks of 'the application rules of the term or concept "science"'[183] as being untidy or sprawling. Even so one central feature of scientific enterprises is suggested by Nagel's comment that science is generated by 'the desire for explanations which are at once systematic and controllable by factual evidence'[184] – that is with the creation of theories that are testable against experience. Popper in fact claims 'that the criterion of the scientific status of a theory is its falsifiability, or refutability, or testability.'[185] A necessary condition of the evidential control implied by the remarks of Nagel and Popper is that scientific theories are stated as clearly, precisely, and unambiguously as possible. This is Geertz's point about science seeking to maximize intellectual clarity.[186] For unless this is done, it becomes impossible to assess adequately, if at all, the bearing on the theory of any set of findings which might be relevant to it.

But if one of the functions of ideologies is to minimize conflict, and to persuade target groups to agree on policies and action (and this at the expense of evidential control as our discussion in (4) suggests), then intellectual clarity is not likely to have high priority, and at least some of the claims made in ideologies are unlikely to be clearly, precisely, and unambiguously expressed. For if, as is likely, the proponent group takes the target group to consist, at least in part, of individuals who hold different views, empirical and evaluative, about the issues under discussion, then the proponent group's statement of its policies is likely to be sufficiently loose not only to give members of the target group some room to interpret it in a way that is consonant with their already existing beliefs, but also to allow them to appear to be in agreement with others who have

(Ftn. 180 cont.)

1958), p. 282 onwards; P. King, op. cit. (1968): J. Plamenatz, op. cit. (1970), Chapter 3. More generally see W. W. Bartley, *The Retreat to Commitment* (Chatto & Windus, 1964); I. Scheffler, *Science and Subjectivity* (New York: Bobbs-Merrill, 1967); R. Trigg, *Reason and Commitment* (Cambridge University Press, 1973).

[181] M. Black, 'The definition of scientific method', in R. C. Stauffer, ed., *Science and Civilisation* (Madison, Wisconsin: University of Wisconsin Press, 1949), p. 69.

[182] W. B. Gallie, 'What makes a subject scientific?', *British Journal for the Philosophy of Science*, Vol. 8 (1957–8), p. 132.

[183] Ibid.

[184] E. Nagel, *The Structure of Science* (Routledge & Kegan Paul, 1961), p. 4.

[185] K. R. Popper, 'Science: conjectures and refutations', reprinted in K. R. Popper, *Conjectures and Refutations* (Routledge & Kegan Paul, 3rd edn, 1969), paperback, p. 37.

[186] C. Geertz, op. cit. (1964), p. 71.

accepted it. In general, where claims are vacuous, vague, imprecise, ambiguous and generally unclear, conflicts are likely to be minimized and go unnoticed because the empirical and evaluative claims can be interpreted in a number of ways. Thus the possibility of any individual finding the claims acceptable is greater than if they were precisely stated.

There is another reason why ideologies are not likely to be over-concerned with intellectual clarity. Like scientific theories, they are corrigible*(in principle at least) in the light of later experience – and this is particularly likely where evidence is misused or claims are made that are inadequately supported. If claims are expressed clearly, falsification of them is made easier.[187] But the easier falsification is, the less effective an ideology is likely to be in creating a consensus. Further, where claims are expressed unclearly, such evidential feedback as there is can be coped with more easily. It can be interpreted to a greater degree as supporting the claims made in the ideology, and where this is impossible, it can be more easily discounted.[188]

We might say from our discussion here (and from the points in (4) and (5) too) that ideologies are not likely to give the same importance to intellectual clarity and evidential control that should ideally mark scientific and other intellectual work.

Current notions of ideology and the dimensions and indices

We relate here the dimensions and indices to the points made in the preceding discussion.[189]

DIMENSION I

Index 1 – Ambiguity. Ambiguities do not make for intellectual clarity, and where this is missing, it becomes more difficult to show that a statement has been falsified. In particular, where ambiguities are implicit and unnoticed, apparently falsifying evidence can be countered by moving from one sense to another. Further, evidence favourable to a

---

[187] Cf. Volume I, Section 2, page 200 on this.

[188] For other defence mechanisms which limit effective evidential feedback see C. P. Ormell, 'Ideology and the reform of school mathematics', Philosophy of Education Society of Great Britain, *Proceedings of the Annual Conference*, Vol. 3, (January 1969), p. 41. The closed nature of ideologies is mentioned by J. S. Roucek, op. cit. (1944), p. 480, and G. Eastman, op. cit. (1967), p. 108. The points discussed in (6) and to a slightly lesser extent those discussed in (4) and (5) can account, to a large degree, for what P. King, op. cit. (1968), p. 391, implies is the 'a priori, analytical, arbitrary' nature of ideological recommendations. Roucek, op. cit. (1944), p. 480, described ideologists as having 'the a priori theological temperament'. It needs to be noticed that theories and other claims, even where clearly expressed, can be made immune to feedback if those who are in a position to test them are not prepared to test them. This is, in part, what G. Eastman, op. cit. (1967), means when he talks of theories being ideologized.

[189] For a detailed discussion of the dimensions and indices see pp. 61–91.

can be corrected.

statement that is interpreted in one sense, may unknowingly and illegitimately be used to support it when interpreted in another. Ambiguities, that is, may be traded upon.[190] Statements that are ambiguous become apparently easier for proponent groups to justify and so to make more acceptable. Further, the difficulty in showing that such a statement has been falsified may make its rejection by a target group less likely.

In addition, where policies are stated ambiguously and where this goes unnoticed, the risk of conflict might be lessened, because the policy statement can be interpreted in a number of ways.[191] Individual members of a target group might more easily be led to believe that the policy is in accordance with their existing beliefs, and that they agree with other members of the group. Much the same will hold for Index 2, Vacuity.

Index 2 – Vacuity. Vacuous statements are difficult to falsify since there is almost no limit to the substantive interpretations they can be given. Conflict about what is the case, or about what ought to be done is likely to be minimized, in that individuals who give substantively different interpretations to a vacuous statement may in fact believe they agree. The advantage of vacuous statements to a proponent group is that it can propose a policy with least risk of causing conflict between it and its target group, and between members of the target group itself.

Index 3 – Confusions between conceptual, empirical, and normative issues. Proponent groups may attempt to reduce normative issues to empirical ones in the hope of minimizing explicit conflict about them.[192] Another possible advantage, for proponent groups, of such reductions, particularly to areas of empirical inquiry such as psychology or sociology, is that the view of proponent groups can be associated with authorities in these fields, whose views might carry weight with the target group.

The reduction of normative or empirical statements to analytic ones makes, apparently, falsification impossible in that analytic statements are necessarily true. The advantage of such a reduction for a proponent group is not merely that the claim thus reduced appears to be unfalsifiable but that it can be shown, apparently, to be true.[193]

---

[190] For a discussion of fallacies of ambiguity see I. M. Copi, op. cit. (1961), pp. 73–82.

[191] See Vol. I, page 199, fn 101 for some comments on this.

[192] Cf. G. Bergmann, op. cit. (1951), p. 210, where he states that he will call 'a value judgement disguised as, or mistaken for, a statement of fact' an 'ideological statement'. See too, K. Nielsen; 'On talk about God', *Journal of Philosophy*, Vol. 55 (1958) p. 889.

[193] D. M. Taylor, *The Explanation of Meaning* (Cambridge University Press, 1970), pp. 24–8, has a discussion relevant to the points we make about unfalsifiability in the discussion of Dimension I. He writes (p. 28), 'Scientific theories or hypotheses which are unfalsifiable, or untestable, are all unsatisfactory, not just because they are unfalsifiable, but because their unfalsifiability reflects their insulation from the world. The causes of unfalsifiability considered above, inconsistency, vagueness, tautology all have this in common.' Taylor's remarks are usefully read in the light of P. King's (op. cit. (1968), pp. 390–2) comments on the non-contextual nature of ideological claims.

Index 4 – Confusions concerning means and ends. To make questions of means prior to those of ends is another way of minimizing explicit conflict about values. What is likely to be an intractable value question is turned into a technical question of one sort or another. As a class, these are usually held to be easier to settle. Where statements of aims are made they are often vacuous, and explicit value conflict is again avoided.[194]

Index 5 – Inconsistency. Strictly speaking a person who makes inconsistent statements imparts no information at all.[195] Nevertheless inconsistencies that are unnoticed may have a function.[196] If a proponent group makes inconsistent claims and the inconsistency goes unnoticed, then (*a*) if the claims are contradictions, any member of the target group must agree with one of them; and (*b*) if they are contraries, though it is possible to agree with neither, a choice of views on the matter under discussion is offered.

In the example of inconsistency cited in the critical apparatus, Burgess says both that children's needs are the same and that they are different.[197] Any individual must believe one of these. Each is used as an argument for comprehensive schools. Because children's needs are the same they need 'a common educational experience' which they cannot get under the tripartite scheme. Because children's needs are different, they need 'the greatest variety of provision' which the 'two (or at most three) types of secondary school' in the tripartite scheme cannot provide. The first of these arguments for comprehensive schools is likely (it might be tentatively said) to appeal to those members of the target group who believe comprehensive schools will promote equality of educational opportunity (where some flat-rate notion of equality is to be understood), and remove social privilege. The second sort of argument is likely to appeal to members of the target group who might be conventionally described as 'child-centred', and who stress the uniqueness of each individual child.

There is a similar inconsistency in the Plowden Report, to which R. S. Peters had drawn attention.[198] Paragraph 505 of that report advocates that in schools children should not live as future adults, whereas paragraphs 494 and 496 advocate a programme which implies that they should. The support of the non-child-centred members of the target group is asked for in paragraphs 494 and 496, and that of the child-centred in paragraph 505.

Both Burgess and the Plowden Report try to have it both ways, to put

[194] See also the preceding comments on Dimension I, Indices 2 and 3.
[195] P. F. Strawson, op. cit. (1952), p. 2.
[196] For an interesting discussion on some social functions of inconsistency, see R. Gotesky, 'The uses of inconsistency', *Philosophy and Phenomenological Research*, Vol. 28 (1967–8), pp. 471–500.
[197] See page 70.
[198] See R. S. Peters, ed., *Perspectives on Plowden* (Routledge & Kegan Paul, 1969), p. 2.

it colloquially, and to offer something to please everyone.[199] By their use of inconsistencies they invite the support of the largest possible number of members of their target groups.

DIMENSION II

The discussion on page 96 suggests that ideologies are likely to arise when knowledge is in short supply, that they are likely to offer definitions of situations, that evidence is likely to be selectively used, and that they are not likely to have a high degree of evidential control. In general, therefore, ideologies are likely to be epistemologically unsound, in that the claims they make are not likely to be adequately supported.[200] The indices in Dimension II draw attention to a number of different ways in which the support might be less than adequate.

One reason for requiring appropriate backing to claims can be seen if Burgess' and Rée's books are each read together, since a good many of Rée's claims are inconsistent with those of Burgess. For example, Rée says, 'the fact that selection is made solely on intellectual calibre and potential seems justified' [sic].[201] The tenor of Chapter I of Burgess' book is that this is not so. Burgess states that 'we are gradually coming to realise that although the tests seem to be educational, they are in effect social.'[202] These two claims, as far as the somewhat imprecise vocabulary allows one to judge, seem to be inconsistent. Neither author offers any evidence to support his claim and, as a consequence, it is not possible to decide which of them (if either) is to be believed and, if so, how firm one's belief might reasonably be.[203]

Not much requires to be said about the individual indices here, since the important points are given in the critical apparatus.[204] Indices 1 to 5

[199] An example, at the level of secondary education, is seen in A. Rowe, 'The dead end kids', *The Guardian*, 15 February 1972, p. 15. Rowe states that pupils' 'working class culture should be accepted to be as valid as anyone else's, which it in fact is. Not inferior, simply different.' He goes on to say that 'Their culture doesn't need changing in its fundamentals: the aim should be to sensitise it and substantially expand and enrich it.' But 'sensitise', 'expand', and 'enrich' are in this context implicitly all value terms or, if they are not, they must for Rowe to make his point, imply a value term such as 'improve'. But does a culture which is 'valid' need improving? If it does and if all cultures are equally valid, why is it working-class culture alone, and not that of the middle class, for example, that schools need to improve? The inconsistency that Rowe is trying to cope with is that working-class culture is both perfectly alright and needs improving. In the context of ideology, it is interesting to note that the normative issues raised by 'sensitising' working-class culture are left entirely implicit. See also Vol. I, Section 2, pages 149–88.

[200] For a discussion of general relevance to this dimension see M. Black, *Critical Thinking*, (New Jersey: Prentice Hall, 1946), Chapter 13.

[201] H. A. Rée, op. cit. (1956), p. 40.

[202] T. Burgess, op. cit. (1970), p. 5.

[203] I. Scheffler, *Science and Subjectivity* (New York: Bobbs-Merrill, 1967), pp. 1–4 points out that reason is 'a moral as well as an intellectual notion' (p. 4) and that the demand for evidentially controlled assertion is not only an intellectual one but also a moral one.

[204] See pp. 71–88.

draw attention to cases where evidence is entirely missing, used selectively, or given inaccurately, where it is made to yield a stronger conclusion that it should, or is not to the point. Index 6 is a way of getting assent by arguing that since there is widespread agreement on some matters, dissent is unreasonable and unjustified. Index 7 allows the proponent group to associate views with individuals or institutions which might carry weight with the target group and, where the referencing is inadequate, to preclude the target group from checking the credentials of the authority and whether the attribution of the views to the authority is justified. Index 8 allows the proponent group to state that a claim is so manifestly true that dissent is unreasonable. Index 9 allows it to claim that all that is required to recognize the truth of a claim is the presence of common sense, and thus that dissent is unreasonable and to be put down to the absence of common sense. The role of the special vocabulary, cited in Index 10, in getting claims accepted and rejected can be seen from our comments in the index, and the examples given there.

DIMENSION III

The sole index under this dimension arises from Krause's[205] distinction between proponent and target groups, together with a suggestion of Brown's that ideological utterances are likely to be tailored for specific audiences.[206] It can be admitted that certain sorts of tailoring are permissible or desirable. The examples cited in the index, however, are unlikely to be of this sort. They appear to have no role in justifying the central normative and other claims made in the document but they are likely, even so, to have (and may have been intended to have) a role in getting the claims accepted by the target group. This index provides one means (among others) of identifying ways by which a consensus is sought by irrelevant considerations. A conversion to a view achieved by the strategy cited in this index is not one that can be justified.

The Dimensions and indices, and standards of rational argument

We have tried to show that the indices given in the critical apparatus relate to some of the things said about ideology in the literature. To that extent our stipulation for 'ideological' cannot be said to be arbitrary.

What, very generally, the indices can be used to identify are discussions where attempts are made to achieve a consensus, and to minimize conflicts about certain normative and other related claims, in ways that do not depend on rational considerations. The distinction, therefore, between seeking to persuade people to believe things by rational argument and seeking to persuade them to believe things by non-rational discussion

---

[205] E. A. Krause, op. cit. (1968).
[206] R. Brown, op. cit. (1969), pp. 160–1.

is central to our account of 'ideological'.[207] To make this distinction we use the criteria for rationality of thought and conduct proposed by Feigl.[208] These criteria, quoted below, can be seen to be related to our indices which thereby become indicators of discussions that are less than fully rational. Feigl writes:

'Rationality' connotes a variety of virtues of thought and conduct. The following list may not be complete, but it will be sufficiently suggestive:

1. *Clarity of Thought.* This implies the meaningful use of language, the ability to distinguish sense from nonsense and thus avoid gratuitous perplexities over unanswerable questions. It also implies a sufficient degree of specification of definition of meanings so that communication may be as unambiguous and concepts be as precise as the task on hand requires.

2. *Consistency and Conclusiveness of Reasoning.* This is 'logicality' in the narrower sense of absence of self-contradictions and of analytically necessary implications between the premises and the conclusions of valid deductive arguments. Conformity with the principles of formal logic ensures fulfilment of this requirement.

3. *Factual Adequacy and Reliability of Knowledge Claims.* These are the virtues of thought usually summarized under the caption 'truth'. Truth may be semantically defined as correspondence of statements and facts. But this rather formal definition is insufficient if a characterization of the confirmation of truth is to be given. Wherever a complete confrontation of statement and corresponding fact is impossible, principles of inductive probability for the partial and/or indirect verification of generalizations, hypotheses, or theories have to be respected. Generally the degree of confirmation (or of the reliability) of factual statemments is to be maximized in accordance with the rules of inductive logic. Wherever the evidence is too weak, belief should be withheld until further evidence turns up to decide the issue on hand.

4. *Objectivity of Knowledge Claims.* This comprises intersubjectivity and impartiality in cognitive issues. Objectivity in this sense involves not only absence of personal or cultural bias but also the requirement that knowledge claims be testable by any person sufficiently equipped with intelligence and the instrumental devices for performing the test of the knowledge-claim in question.

5. *Rationality of Purposive Behavior.* Rationality in this sense may be explicated as the main feature of behavior which achieves its purposes by a proper choice of means. Behavior which defeats its own purposes is generally con-

[207] Cf. W. D. Hudson, *Modern Moral Philosophy* (Macmillan, 1970), p. 76, who says it is 'one thing to present considerations which "determine the intellect" in the sense of persuading people to believe something and quite another to present considerations which show the belief in question to be rational.' For a relevant discussion of persuasion see J. N. Garver, 'The rationality of persuasion', *Mind*, Vol. LXIX (1960), pp. 163–74. See also G. R. Morrow, 'Plato's concept of persuasion', *Philosophical Review*, Vol. 62 (1953), pp. 234–50.
[208] H. Feigl, op. cit. (1955), pp. 335–6. For a more detailed discussion, see H. Feigl, 'De principiis non est disputandum', in J. Hospers ed., *Readings in Introductory Philosophical Analysis* (Routledge and Kegan Paul, 1969) pp. 111–135.

sidered 'irrational'. This criterion of rationality is closely related to a similar but more specialized concept in economics. Generally speaking, we have here a conception of rationality which amounts to a minimum–maximum ('minimax') principle according to which a maximum of positive value is to be produced by means which involve a minimum of negative value.

6. *Moral Rationality.* This comprises: (*a*) Adherence to principles of justice, equity, or impartiality. If there is no morally relevant or sufficient reason to allow greater privileges to one person than another, they are to be *equal* before the moral law. This exclusion of special privilege rules out the sort of arbitrary arrogation of rights on the part of individuals who are unwilling to accept the correlative obligations. (*b*) The abstention from coercion and violence in the settlement of conflicts of interest. 'Appeal to reason' in the sense of all the connotations of 'rationality' thus far enumerated (from 1 through 6a) is deemed as the only morally acceptable method for the adjudication of disputes.[209]

The dimensions and the indices grouped under them relate to Feigl's criteria in the following way. Feigl's first criterion is concerned with clarity of thought, and the second with consistency and validity. Dimension I is concerned with these. His third criterion is concerned with factual adequacy, and the reliability of knowledge claims; the fourth with their objectivity; the fifth with a specific sense of rationality where the overall worth of a course of action is determined by a 'principle according to which a maximum of positive value is to be produced by means which involve a minimum of negative value.' This last criterion has relevance to issues of selectivity – though not only so. Dimension II is concerned with issues that fall under these third, fourth, and fifth criteria. For Feigl's sixth criterion which concerns considerations (*a*) of equity, and (*b*) of abstention from violence and coercion, we have not, as yet, found it necessary to provide an index. Citation under the index in Dimension III is an indication of a less than fully rational discussion for the following reason. If statements are included in documents which do not bear on the justification of the central claims in it, but, even so, have a role in getting the claims accepted by the target group, then to that extent, assent to the claims is invited which it would not be rational to give, since it does not depend on relevant considerations.[210] Dimension III can be said to relate to Feigl's third criterion.

[209] For an interesting discussion which raises a number of important questions about this view of rationality see D. C. Morton and D. R. Watson, 'Compensatory education and contemporary liberalism in the United States: a sociological view', *International Review of Education*, Vol. XVII, No. 3 (1971), pp. 289–306. Some of these issues are examined in A. Hartnett and M. Naish, eds., *Knowledge, Ideology and Educational Practice*, op. cit. (in preparation). See also R. Trigg, op. cit., and B. Wilson, ed., *Rationality* (Oxford: Blackwell, 1970).

[210] Dimension III, Index 1 differs from Dimension II, Index 5 in that though both depend on gaining assent by the production of irrelevant considerations, Dimension III, Index 1 depends on softening up the target group – that is on making it well disposed, or at least not ill-disposed, towards the proponent group, and so more ready to accept the claims it makes.

USE AND LIMITATIONS OF THE DIMENSIONS AND INDICES

Reliability: an aspect

One way in which the limitations of the indices might be seen is by comparing the results achieved by a number of people using them, independently, on the same material. Ideally, the results ought to be the same, but there are a number of reasons why this might not be so.[211] There are at least four sources of discrepancies. They are: (*i*) the definitions of the indices; (*ii*) difficulties in interpreting the material contained in the document; (*iii*) the nature of the theoretical work used in the document; (*iv*) the abilities of the analyst (the user of the indices).

(*i*) Some discrepancies might arise because the indices are not precisely enough defined, and therefore allow different analysts scope in the way they interpret them. These discrepancies can be reduced but not entirely eliminated, because even the best definition cannot preclude there being borderline cases about which there might be justified differences of opinion.

(*ii*) Though the indices might be clearly defined, there might be different views about how the material is to be interpreted. One or other of these views might be seen to be ill-founded by additional work on the document (for example, by paying closer attention to contexts). But this might not be true in all cases. There might be justifiable differences, for example, about whether an apparent contradiction is really a contradiction, or whether material has been included in a document simply to make the target group well-disposed to the views advocated without having a bearing on their justification.[212]

(*iii*) The citations under some of the indices in Dimension II will involve understanding data from theoretical disciplines, such as psychology or sociology, and there might be justifiable differences of opinion as to the import of the relevant theoretical work, and so as to whether the account of it given in the document is in fact selective, or inaccurate, or used to support generalizations that are beyond its power.[213]

(*iv*) A fourth source of discrepancies is constituted by the intellectual capacities and limitations of the analysts. To use the indices to their fullest extent requires a reasonable amount of conceptual, logical, and theoretical sophistication. Analysts must be able to distinguish empirical issues from evaluative ones, to detect ambiguities and contradictions, to

---

[211] See G. W. Budd, R. V. Thorp and L. Donahew, *Content Analysis of Communications* (New York: Macmillan, 1967), for a useful discussion of some issues that are relevant here. In this paper, the discussion is presented in nontechnical language and is based on our own experience in constructing and applying the indices, and on a pilot study carried out by Miss Lois Benyon in her unpublished Master of Education dissertation, *An Analysis of Some of the Literature Relating to the Education of Children under Social Handicap* (University of Liverpool, 1973).

[212] See pp. 69–71 and pp. 86–91.

[213] See pp. 71–88.

identify irrelevant considerations, to determine where theoretical work has been misused. In so far as analysts vary in their ability to carry out these tasks, there are likely to be discrepancies in the results they obtain. One likely way of reducing such discrepancies is to use a number of analysts on the same document and to assign to each of them an index or those indices which are most suited to their abilities.[214] People who are philosophically trained to some extent might be set to look for ambiguities and contradictions; others who have some grasp of sociology or of psychology might work on some of the earlier indices in Dimension II; the ability to identify unsupported claims, or to identify citations under Dimension III, requires less specialized knowledge.

What these four points amount to is that in practice discrepancies in results are likely to occur and that even the results independently achieved by two fully competent analysts on the same material are likely to be similar rather than identical.

It can be seen from our remarks here, and from the critical apparatus itself, that to analyse fully by means of the dimensions and indices other than short documents is likely to be a lengthy task requiring various sorts of expertise. Nevertheless, the apparatus might well have a useful role in less time-consuming, less demanding, and less rigorous analyses. It might act as a sensitizing device to show ways in which discussions in educational documents might be less than rational, and in which agreement is sought other than by rational argument. It might also act as a sampling device which gives a rough and ready estimate of the quality of the arguments contained in documents, and which might indicate whether they are worth further investigation, and what sort of questions might be asked about them.

Quantification

We have suggested that if a document is cited under the indices, it can to that extent be said to be ideological. One purpose of the indices was to provide a way of identifying individual discussions as ideological rather than to offer an account of the term 'ideological' which would enable us to assess whether one discussion was more ideological than another. But it might be hoped that from an approach such as ours a means of making such assessments might be devised, by constructing a scale which would measure the extent to which discussions in different documents were ideological. We briefly raise a number of considerations about this.

We can and do make rough and ready judgements about whether one

---

[214] Individuals or groups, in so far as more than one index is assigned to them, can *either* (*i*) go through the document looking for examples of each index in turn, *or* (*ii*) hold all the indices in mind and scan the document for all of them simultaneously. (*i*) is likely to lead to greater reliability, because (*ii*) makes much greater cognitive demands on the analysts and so may make errors more likely.

discussion is more, or less, ideological than another just as we can and do say that one set of beliefs is more, or less, rational than another, without at the same time relying on any quantified notion of 'more' or of 'less'. But one document cannot usefully be said to be more ideological (as defined by the critical apparatus) than another, simply by reference to the number of times it is cited under the indices, since a discussion in a document which is cited more frequently, but is longer, might overall contain a much more rationally argued case than one that is cited less but is shorter. The raw numerical scores of the citations, except perhaps in occasional and rare cases, such as where one document is cited and another not at all, is largely useless as a measure of how ideological one document is compared with another. What is required is some measure of the *density* of the citations. Densities are expressed in terms of ratios, but if one term of the ratio either is, or is derived from, the number of citations, what is the other term to be? What, that is to say, is the basis of comparison between documents to be? It cannot, as our remarks above indicate, be the number of words. Further, the conciseness with which a case is argued may vary from document to document, and this makes length (in terms of number of words) an even less adequate base for comparison. It might be suggested that the ratio should be in terms of the number of citations relative to the amount of information each document contains. But information (in the everyday sense of the term) is not quantifiable, even though we can and do talk of one book or article containing more, or less, information than another. If 'information' is given some stipulated meaning, so that it can be expressed in terms of a number of units of one sort or another, it ceases to be information as it is ordinarily understood. This is not necessarily a defect. But there might be a number of possible stipulations and so of different ways of deciding how many units of information a discussion contains. One such way might be to use the notion of 'a communication unit'.[215] But only by stipulatively defining them can each communication unit be said to contain the same amount of information. There is a further point. Are citations under each index to count the same? Might not citations under one index be said to have more ideological import than those under another? Might not citations, for example, under Dimension I, Index 2 – Vacuity, be said to have more ideological import than those under Dimension II, Index 5 – Irrelevance? If citations are not to count the same, which ones are to count more and how is this to be described numerically?

It follows that though a meaning for 'ideological' can be stipulated in such a way that the extent to which different documents are ideological can be quantified and compared, a number of such stipulations are possible. Whether anything useful either for the theoretical study of

---

[215]See W. D. Loban, *The Language of Elementary School Children* (Illinois: National Council of Teachers of English, 1936).

ideology, or in terms of practical consequences, can be derived from defining 'ideological' in one or other of these ways is an open question.

Extending the indices

There are a number of ways in which the indices might be extended, and we suggest three. The first is concerned with metaphor; the other two are not concerned with the language of the document, but with its presentation.

METAPHOR

In the light of Cheverst's comment that 'it is precisely in the employment of metaphors that a rich cargo of assumptions can be smuggled into seemingly descriptive discourse',[216] it might be useful to have an index or indices for metaphor. Cheverst's point has close connexions with the fact/value confusions in Dimension I, Index 3. He goes on to say that metaphors often have a 'direction' which may be either 'favourable or unfavourable towards the aspects of education that they describe'.[217] This point is related to Dimension II, Index 10. He suggests that a metaphor's intensity needs to be noted and whether it has 'a part to play in the argument', or whether it is 'rhetorical, seeking to persuade rather than convince'. One educational metaphor which might be said to have an ideological role is that of 'growth', some assumptions of which R. F. Dearden has examined.[218]

TYPOGRAPHY

Under an index such as this could be cited typographical devices, in so far as they could be said to contribute to one or other of the functions of ideologies.

Inverted commas. In the chapter by Burgess[219] from which we cite a number of examples in the indices, inverted commas can on occasions be said to have an ideological role. Though they are used to indicate quotations, they appear to be used also to indicate to target groups that a word belongs to a technical or semi-specialized vocabulary, and in consequence that no stigma accrues from not knowing it, and even that kudos accrues from knowing it. Examples from Burgess are (p. 5) 'intelligence quotient', and (p. 9) 'streaming'. These examples can be related to Dimension III.

Capital letters. In the book by Rée[220] from which we cite a number of

[216] W. J. Cheverst, 'The role of metaphor in educational thought: an essay in content analysis', *Journal of Curriculum Studies*, Vol. 4 (1972), p. 71. See also C. Geertz, op. cit. (1964), pp. 57–60 for a discussion of metaphor and ideology.

[217] W. J. Cheverst, op. cit. (1972), p. 75.

[218] R. F. Dearden, op. cit. (1968), Chapter 3; see also I. Scheffler, op. cit. (1960), Chapter 3.

[219] T. Burgess, op. cit., Chapter 1 (HMSO, 1970).

[220] H. A. Rée, op. cit. (Harrap 1956).

examples in the indices, capital letters are used as follows: Grammar
School, Primary School, Preparatory School, Secondary Modern School,
Independent School, Public School, Comprehensive School, State
System, Elementary School, Primary Heads, Record Cards, Prefects'
Room, Cadet Corps, Services, Intelligence Tests, Common Room,
Governors' Meeting, Women Students, Schoolgirls. It is not clear what
the function of capital letters is in all of these cases, but in some it appears
to be analogous with 'God', 'Christian', and so on. By his use of capitals,
Rée appears to offer to Primary Schools, Grammar Schools, Prefects'
Room, Governors' Meetings, Women Students and so on, a sort of secular
sanctification. In so doing, he indicates to his readers what he values. The
comprehensiveness of his evaluations (so indicated) may play a role in
gaining the good will of the target group. This use of capital letters,
therefore, can be related to Dimension III.

Other features of typography worth looking at are the use of italics,
and exclamation marks. The former are often used as a way of putting
pressure on readers;[221] the latter are often used with the force of 'But we
know better now'. An example is this comment of Burgess, 'Ironically,
one authority, Westmorland, wanted to go comprehensive after the war
but was prevented by the then Labour Government!'[222]

PHOTOGRAPHS AND ILLUSTRATIONS
Illustrations may embody implicit educational claims, normative and
empirical. In the photographs in the Plowden report, for example,
teachers rarely appear (this might have been predicted from the title –
Children and their Primary Schools).[223] When they do appear, they are
sitting on the same level as the children. In plate 4 the teacher and some
of the pupils are sitting on a tree trunk; in plate 7, both are sitting on the
floor; in plate 5, both are sitting at the same (pupil's) desk. All of this
has implications for practice as does the conjunction of plates 2 and 3.
This pair of illustrations is particularly interesting. They share the following caption – 'Children at work 1937 and 1966'. Unfortunately, in the
1937 school the children are not at work, but are posing for the photo-
graph. The conjunction of these two plates has intended implications for
both teaching methods, and the design of buildings. Further, though

---

[221] Cf. L. R. Perry's review of *Interest and Discipline in Education*, by P. S. Wilson, in
British Journal of Educational Studies, Vol. XX, No. 3 (October 1973), pp. 350–1. Perry
writes of Wilson's book, 'There are many instances, e.g. page 40, page 62 and page 69,
where a point of view is being strongly pushed. One telling sign of the degree of pressure
to which the reader is subjected is the enormous number of italicised words in the text
of the book.'

[222] Burgess, op. cit. (1970), p. 12.

[223] The use of the possessive adjective here has an ideological role. Cf. Burgess, op. cit.
(1970), Introduction, last page, where it is stated that 'comprehensive schools are their
schools' – namely, parents' schools. Vocabulary associated with ownership often has an
ideological role, though the rights claimed by its use vary with contexts.

in the illustrations there are long shots of where the schools are sited, and some are stated to be below minimum standard (cf. plate 23) the interiors of the contemporary primary schools shown in other plates appear to be well lit, pleasant, etc. In the light of the age, overcrowding, and admitted inadequacy, of much educational building this is surprising.[224]

THE ORIGINS OF IDEOLOGICAL DOCUMENTS

To call a document 'ideological' is on our account, to make an adverse criticism of the quality of the argument contained in it. However no inference can be drawn *from this alone* about the extent to which those who produced the document are liable to censure for the quality of the argument it contains. It would be over-simple to believe that all ideological documents are deliberately produced, as a result of their authors' Machiavellian tendencies, in order to further their own interests or the interests of some favoured group. Some ideological documents might be produced in this way, others not at all, some only partially. Issues about authors' and proponent groups' motives, and their liability to censure, cannot be answered until some empirically based explanations can be given about how the document originated, and how it came to have the content it has. What the identification of a document as ideological might do, is to suggest what kind of explanation is appropriate.[225] All we offer here are a number of speculative comments about the origin of ideological documents in education.

Our discussion in Volume I, and some of that in Volume II, suggests: (*i*) education is an area where there are serious and complex value disputes; (*ii*) education is an area where some of the disputes may in practice, and in principle, be insoluble;[226] (*iii*) education is an area where relevant theoretical knowledge, particularly about the feasibility of goals and outcomes of decisions, is in short supply; (*iv*) the understanding of the nature and limitations of relevant theoretical work in education requires a fair amount of intellectual expertise; (*v*) expectations about what can be achieved by changes in educational practice and policy are high.

There are at least two further points about education that are relevant here: (*vi*) educational issues are in many cases also political issues, and educational policies and practices need to be publicly explained, defended and advocated; (*vii*) traditionally, teachers, heads, and local education authorities, have been said to have a reasonable amount of autonomy.

---

[224]Similar points to those we make about the photographs in the Plowden Report can be made about the photographs in Burgess' book. On school buildings see Volume I, Section 2, pp. 174–77.

[225] See the reading by Smith and Stockman, pp. 39–55, and our comments on it, pp. 5–10.

[226] For a discussion of insolubility and the related question of what might be meant by saying that a dispute is settled, see Vol. I, Section 1, pp. 100–3.

A number of tentative inferences might be drawn from these points.

(*i*) Because some educational issues are political issues, the public at large will need to believe that policies are justified. This is likely to be true in particular for the parents of children of school age.

(*ii*) Because teachers, heads, and local education authorities are said to have, and may see themselves as having or having a right to, a reasonable degree of autonomy, and because policy decisions are implemented by them, their co-operation needs to appear to be won rather than forced.

(*iii*) There are likely to be disputes among members of target groups about normative issues of educational practice and policy. It may be impossible to get agreement about solutions to these disputes,[227] and the existence or even possibility of such a dissensus is likely to give rise to educational documents which attempt to explain, defend, and justify the policies or practices.[228] Those who are responsible for running the educational system may well feel that the more open dissensus there is, the more difficult the system is to run.

(*iv*) Both proponent groups (for example, political parties) and target groups may have an inadequate understanding of the issues, because of their complexity and the nature of the intellectual expertise required. They may, for example, have an incomplete grasp of the limitations of the social sciences, or of the nature of moral justification. They may even not be open to rational argument on certain issues because of emotional or other psychological factors. Not all members of target groups, therefore, are likely to be persuaded by rational arguments, nor are all proponent groups likely to be able to offer them.

(*v*) Policies and practices may be advocated which do not take full account of relevant theoretical work, just because it requires a specialized understanding. Further, even if it were understood, policies at the political level in particular are likely to some extent to be adopted because of their efficacy in winning elections, and not simply, if at all, because they are justified in terms of the interests of those to whom they apply.[229] In this case theoretical work is likely to be scanned *after* the decision is taken, in an attempt to supply backing for the policy.[230]

(*vi*) A proponent group may believe that a policy or practice will become more acceptable to a target group, the more it can persuade the

---

[227] See the discussion in Vol. I, Section 1, pp. 100–3, for some sources of disagreement.

[228] See the discussion about ideology, conflict and consensus on pages 93–4.

[229] Cf. A. Downs, *Economic Theory and Democracy* (New York: Harper & Row, 1957), p. 28, and E. Waugh, *The Ordeal of Gilbert Pinfold* (Chapman & Hall, 1957), p. 44. We ignore here the difficulty in identifying these interests. See the reading by Dumont and Wax, Vol. I, pp. 158–73. It is important to notice that the ability to gain support is *a* reason for adopting a policy, but that, even so, policies might gain widespread support, and at the same time be immoral.

[230] Cf. I. L. Horowitz, 'Social science mandarins: policy making as a political formula', *Policy Sciences*, Vol. I, 1960, pp. 339–60, and Vol. II, pages 164–70.

group that it is *certain* (not merely possible or even probable) that the policy or practice will be beneficial. A policy proposed as a tentative solution to a problem might well not gain much support. To make explicit that only very tentative judgements can be made about outcomes, and so about whether a policy or practice will in fact be beneficial, is likely to make agreement harder to get, and the system harder to run.[231] These difficulties are only likely to increase if additional issues about the criteria for what is to count as beneficial are in turn made explicit.

(*vii*) Finally, the educational system as a whole may feel that it needs to persuade those outside it that its activities are successful. It may need, that is, to provide what might be called 'current images of success', and this in situations where not only are there competing accounts of what constitutes success, and of what outcomes are likely to be, but even where the prevailing state of affairs is at best only partially known and understood. As we pointed out in Volume I, Section 2, not only are the outcomes of policies hard to predict, but the *actual* outcomes of policy decisions in education are hard to investigate and identify.[232] The need for such images of success may be felt at all levels of the system. Politicians may need to explain and justify the current educational system to the public at large; teachers may need to explain and justify what they do to parents, and so on. At the political level, a government may feel the need for such images even where the prevailing situation was brought about by policies of which it disapproved. A Conservative government, for example, might be prepared to present a favourable image of the reorganized part of the secondary education sector, if it felt that it might incur some discredit (even if undeserved), were the results of the reorganization to be thought unsatisfactory, or if it believed that it could sidestep a demand for more money to be spent on that sector – a demand which, in the light of what that government believed to be a justified order of financial priorities, it was unwilling to meet.[233]

We now attempt to draw together some of these points, and relate them to the three dimensions of the critical apparatus. Our discussion sug-

---

[231] On this account, ideological documents and discussions may well act as a series of systems' lubricants.

[232] Cf. Vol. I, Section 2, pages 190–204. See also the comment of R. Brown, about ideology and scientific measurement, quoted on page 96.

[233] A Conservative government *might* also support any reorganization in the secondary sector which had taken place before it came to power, because it believed that such a form of organization lowers costs through the economies of scale. Political parties may also advocate changes in education which appear to provide additional economic resources for education, but which in fact may not do so. It might, for example, be speculatively suggested that the Labour Party's proposed intention to close down private schools is a way of apparently improving the resources available to the state system of education, without having to actually spend more money on state schools. The abolition of privilege will benefit all: exactly how is less than clear. The same arguments could (and have) been applied to private medicine and the National Health Service.

gests that any group or person advocating policies and practices in
education is seeking agreement in an area where there are likely to be
widespread and perhaps insoluble moral disputes; where there are few,
if any, reliable predictions about outcomes; and where a full understanding of many of the issues (for example, the empirical ones arising from
psychological and sociological studies) requires a fairly sophisticated
intellectual expertise.

Further, any such group or person may see its
target group as including not only individuals who lack the requisite
intellectual expertise, and have different values, but also those who are
to some extent not open to persuasion by rational argument. These points
may hold for members of a proponent group too. But to the extent that
they all (publicly at least) agree to the policy, there is likely to be that
much less dispute about values. If these points are accepted, then it might
well be argued that a proponent group may adopt and advocate a policy
which in the light of the available theoretical knowledge is hard to justify.
It might even adopt a policy for political advantage[234] rather than on the
grounds that it serves the morally justifiable interests of one group or
other. A policy so chosen may again be hard to justify, and in so far as
a rational case cannot be made out for a policy, agreement to it cannot
be obtained by rational argument. Further, even if a proponent group has
an adequate grasp of the practical and theoretical issues involved, and has
adopted a policy for which a rational justification is forthcoming, it might
believe that a full and rational presentation of its case might not win the
support required. Members of the target group might not understand the
discussion, and the very explicitness of the value positions adopted (and
with it the overt rejection of others), and the acknowledged tentativeness
of the predictions about outcomes, might not only fail to bring agreement but might increase dissensus.

What these points amount to is that policies might be advocated which,
given current knowledge, cannot be justified; that policies might be
knowingly chosen for reasons which might only have a limited role in
their justification and that, as a consequence, no rational case can again
be made out for the policies; and finally, that even where a proponent
group advocates a policy which can be justified, and knows how to give
such a justification, it might feel that it is better, and justifiable, to gain
support in another way. At least some educational documents, therefore,
are unlikely to present a fully rational case in support of policies or
practices. Value issues may be left implicit, either because a proponent
group draws no very sharp distinction between them and issues of other

---

[234]The very difficulty in investigating actual outcomes of educational policies makes
it easier for failures of policy to go undiscovered, and for successes to be claimed.
Proponent groups in education, therefore, might feel less cautious in proposing changes in
educational policy and practice than other proponent groups might in their respective
areas (for example, medicine).

sorts, or because it believes that to make them explicit is to risk losing the agreement required and sought. Discussions may be general, imprecise, vacuous, contain contradictions, and be capable of a number of interpretations, in the hope of securing as extensive agreement as possible. These points are reflected in the indices in Dimension I, in particular.

Moreover, because relevant theoretical work is not fully understood, because there is less than is ideally required, and because to make explicit the uncertainty about outcomes may be to risk losing at least some of the agreement sought, claims may be made that are unsupported, or supported by evidence that is misused in some way, or other sources of support may be appealed to (for example, consensus or self-evidence). Relevant literature may not be cited, perhaps because a proponent group might feel that it makes the document less acceptable to a target group, or less presentable, or perhaps because the literature is not known, or because it might undermine or make less certain some of the claims made in the document. These points are reflected in Dimension II, in particular.

Where attempts are made to get agreement about policies and practices in areas of wide dissensus, and particularly where a proponent group is responsible for a decision, the implementation of which depends on the goodwill of the target group, it becomes particularly important that a target group is well disposed towards its proponent group. In some cases, therefore, documents are likely to contain statements whose function is to make the target group so disposed (and to foster good relations generally), and which have little or no bearing on the justification of the policy. Such statements may often act as signs to the target group that the proponent group at least publicly values and respects it, its opinions, and work. They may make the target group more disposed both to accept other claims contained in the document, and to carry out the policies and practices advocated. These points are reflected in Dimension III.

THE ORIGINS OF IDEOLOGICAL DOCUMENTS, AND JUSTIFYING THEIR USE

We have suggested that answers to questions about the origins of ideological documents (as identified by the critical apparatus) depend upon empirical investigation.[235] It can also be seen that their origins are likely to be explained in one or other of at least three ways. Ideological documents might: (*i*) be unknowingly produced and used; (*ii*) be deliberately and knowingly produced and used, and their producers and users admit that their use is not morally justified; (*iii*) be deliberately and knowingly produced and used, and their producers and users believe, and be prepared to argue, that their use is morally justified.

What we wish to comment on here is how the producers and users of ideological documents under (*iii*) might justify their use. (The question

[235] See page 111.

does not arise under (*i*) and (*ii*) since it is inappropriate to ask anyone to justify what he did unknowingly, or what he did when he believed he ought not to have done it.) This issue of justification is important for a number of reasons. One is that it might be argued that in areas, such as education, where it is difficult to get agreement on policies and practices, the use of ideological documents is, on occasions, justified. It might be argued that in certain circumstances the consequences of presenting a non-ideological case for a policy or practice might be so adverse (for example, divisive), and might make concerted effort impossible or so hard to get that it is better to implement the policy by using, to some extent, ideological documents than to attempt to implement the policy without them or to abandon it altogether.

It does not appear that the deliberate use of such documents can be shown, by *a priori* argument, to be never justfied. An argument of the form outlined above might, on occasions, justify their use. But because the use of such documents involves a departure from the standards of rational argument, and depends upon misrepresentation and deception, in that the intention is to persuade people that a case is rationally argued when it is not, the deliberate use of ideological documents can be held to be presumptively wrong. This means that the onus of proof is on the ideologue, and where the presumption cannot be defeated by considerations adduced by him, then their use is categorically wrong.[236] If the deliberate use of ideological documents in support of a policy or practice is to be justified, a non-ideological, that is rationally argued, case for the policy or practice must have been made out, and one consideration included in such a case must be that ideological documents will be used in implementing the policy. This means that the deliberate use of ideological documents must be justified by a non-ideological argument. Further, the deliberate use of ideological documents may involve denying people access to material and data relevant to the issue under discussion. For if access is granted, the ideological nature of the documents might more readily be revealed, and their effectiveness be reduced. Moreover, the ideological nature of the documents will need to be concealed even when the policy or practice has been successfully implemented, because the more that documents are revealed as deliberately (or indeed as accidentally) ideological, the greater the risk might be that documents from a given source will not be believed. A document that is deliberately ideological will need to remain unrecognized as such, and this may involve a denial of access to information. If, however, such a document is revealed as ideo-

---

[236] For a similar claim about indoctrination see A. G. N. Flew, 'Against indoctrination', in A. J. Ayer, ed., *The Humanist Outlook* (Pemberton & Barne & Rockliff, 1968).

logical, it will need to be passed off as accidentally so, and this in its turn may involve a similar denial. The lack of public accountability,[237] and of informed public discussion, that the deliberate use of ideological documents is likely to require, has great dangers and implications which need not be pointed out here.

What this brief discussion suggests is, not that the deliberate use of ideological documents is never justified, but that its justification is not likely to be simple.[238]

12 Sociology of education and the Education of teachers   D. R. McNAMARA
(*British Journal of Educational Studies*, Vol. 20, No. 2, June 1972, pp. 137–47)

The particular concern of this paper is with the place of the sociology of education in the professional training of teachers. In recent years the sociology of education has been established in education courses as one of the foundation disciplines of education.[239] However, we often hear of headteachers, in charge of probationers who have had 'four hours of the teaching of reading and forty hours of the sociology of education' in their college courses, complaining about the value of sociology in training programmes and questioning its relevance for classroom practice. The purpose here is to review the development of the sociology of education in this country, to consider its content and also to ask what is its value in the training of teachers. Finally a tentative proposal for a sociology of education which would be of value for the classroom teacher is outlined.

In order to understand the development of the sociology of education in colleges of education it is helpful to locate the growth of the subject within the wider context of the growth of sociology in this country during the last decade. In 1962 there were five University chairs in sociology in this country, now nearly every University has its professor of sociology and some have two or three. It is now possible to take sociology as a main subject in 50 colleges of education and at 29 of these it is possible

[237]It can be seen that if there were to be an occasion on which the deliberate use of ideological material was justified, the proponent group could not *publicly* justify it, since this would be self-defeating.

[238]Also implicit here are important issues for teacher education which are discussed in A. Hartnett and M. Naish eds., *Knowledge, Ideology and Educational Practice*, op. cit. (in preparation). There is likely to be an incompatibility between deliberately using ideological documents, and having an *educated* teaching profession.

[239]For an outline of the development of the education course in Colleges of Education see W. Taylor, *Society and the Education of Teachers*, London 1969, 117–124.

to go on and offer the subject for the B. Ed. degree.[240] Coupled with this burgeoning development of sociology there has been a vast increase in the number of sociologists interested in the educational system. A survey conducted by the British Sociological Association in 1968 reported that one quarter of the respondents gave sociology of education as a main interest.[241] Many of the increasing number of sociologists trained in university departments of sociology go on to teach their subject at various levels within the educational system. These people are likely to be of the opinion that they are professionals working in a field which has now been clearly delineated and become academically respectable. And in so far as many of these people take up posts in colleges of education or university departments of education the influence of the sociologist with an academic perspective is likely to be felt on courses in sociology for intending teachers. Therefore it is interesting to note that accompanying the rapid growth rate of the subject there has been a movement by many of the more respected commentators in the field to advocate a shift in emphasis in the subject from the study of educational sociology to the study of the sociology of education.[242] It has been argued[243] that the term 'educational sociology' should refer to the discipline as practised in the early years of its development when the emphasis was on the practical problems facing the teacher; the approach was pragmatic and polemical. 'Findings' based upon rudimentary research techniques were used to support particular educational philosophies. The main practitioners in the field were educationalists rather than sociologists who were abreast of the main developments in the discipline. Swift[244] illustrates the distinction between 'educational sociology' and the 'sociology of education' by referring to the distinction between technology and pure science. Where the research emphasis is of no practical importance but is concerned with improving our understanding of how society works, and when the educational system provides an experimental or observational situation for the sociologist we may refer to the 'sociology of education'. 'Educational sociology', on

[240] *Handbook of Colleges and Departments of Education*, London 1970. For a detailed account of the development of sociology in colleges of education see *Sociology in the Education of Teachers*, the Association of Teachers in Colleges and Departments of Education (Sociology Section), 1969.

[241] M. P. Carter, Report on a survey of social researchers in Britain, *Sociological Review*, XVI, No. 1, 1968, 5–40.

[242] The discussion over the distinction between 'sociology of education' and 'educational sociology' is comparatively recent in this country. However, in the USA the debate goes back to the 1920s. See W. B. Brookover, 'Sociology of Education: A Definition,' *American Sociological Review*, XIV, 1949, 407–15. A particularly good discussion is: D. A. Hansen, 'The Uncomfortable Relation of Sociology and Education', in D. A. Hansen and J. E. Gerstl (eds.) *On Education: Sociological Perspectives*, New York, 1967.

[243] O. Banks, *The Sociology of Education*, London 1968, 7–9.

[244] D. F. Swift, *The Sociology of Education: Introductory Analytical Perspectives*, London 1969, 2–6.

the other hand, is the applied branch of the subject where the concern is with solving practical problems which are likely to arise for the educationalist. Possibly the baldest definition of what is the sociology of education is that by Pavalko:[245] 'Basically, sociologists regard education as a distinctly social phenomenon or "institution" which, like other social phenomena, is amenable to objective scientific analysis'. He considers that it is the prime concern of the sociologist to build up a verified body of knowledge about education. Only secondarily are sociologists concerned about applying their findings and conclusions to the concerns of educational practitioners.[246] However, the statement on the subject which has probably had most influence in colleges of education is one by Taylor[247] in that seminal work edited by Tibble *The Study of Education*. He argues that the perspectives of the sociologist and educationalist are different. The sociologist is interested in education because it is one of the central activities of industrialized societies; he studies educational institutions in order to improve his understanding of the structure and institutions of industrial societies and the way in which the young are inducted into full membership of them. The educationalist, on the other hand, is interested in the contribution that specialist studies make to the practical activity of educating; if he wishes to make use of sociological evidence he usually has a useful purpose in mind. And herein Taylor sees a danger; namely that when sociological insights are brought to bear in the training of teachers they have usually been to support an educational philosophy, or an educationalist's point of view. The emphasis has been hortatory rather than empirical, inspirational rather than objective, and synoptic rather than analytic. Educational sociology has been given a normative orientation, being particularly concerned with solving problems, with fulfilling a social welfare role and with an emphasis on what seems to be sociologically significant. The result is disjointed courses dealing with the burning issues of the day and a concern with problems that teachers may be able to solve. He advocates, therefore, that the emphasis should be placed upon the sociological perspective rather than on the educational one in courses in the sociology of education.

In sum the argument is that sociology is a science and that when its theories and methods are brought to bear on the educational system the 'sociology of education' will provide objective knowledge and understanding about education which will be of value to the teacher in training.

The argument which will be put forward against this position should not be seen as in any way denigrating the study of the sociology of education

[245] R. M. Pavalko (ed.), *Sociology of Education: A Book of Readings*, Utasca, Illinois 1968, 4.
[246] Ibid., 3–5.
[247] W. Taylor, 'The Sociology of Education', in J. W. Tibble (ed.), *The Study of Education*, London 1966, 179–213.

in university sociology departments or on advanced courses in education. Remember we are here concerned with the initial three-year training of teachers. Neither is the imputation to be made that student teachers are not intellectually capable of coping with the demands of a rigorous course in the sociology of education.

The argument will proceed in four stages: First, it will be argued that what used to be termed 'educational sociology' is of no value in college courses; it can be misleading and often contains within it an implicit ideology not apparent to the students. Second, that it is an open question whether or not sociology of education is a science. It is suggested that the quality of its discourse resembles that of literary or philosophical criticism and that while sociological evidence may provide valuable insights into the educational system it must argue its claim for a place in education courses with literary writings about education, social history and so on. Third, that despite the interest expressed by sociologists in education there is possibly not enough research evidence which is distinctly sociological to justify courses in the subject. Fourth, that we must accept as 'given' that the student teacher's frame of reference is more likely to be 'professional' than 'academic' and that it is necessary to develop a sociology of education which will be of value to him in the classroom.

To return to the first point. It is agreed that problem orientated, hortatory, educational sociology is to be avoided. The point may be made by giving an example.

A considerable number of educationalists would agree with Miss M. S. Valentine in her presidential address to the A.T.C.D.E.,[248] when she said, 'the harsh facts of life within Educational Priority Areas come as a shock to many young people, but their understanding is deepened by the study of the Sociology of Education'. It is arguable that this is not necessarily the case. Much of the discussion about the child living in E.P.A.s is couched in the language of the 'culturally deprived'. Now sociologically the term culture may be defined as 'an interdependent system of institutionalized patterns of living which lend a considerable measure of regularity and orderliness to man's social behaviour and the material and non-material products (goods, ideas, values etc.) of these institutional patterns.'[249] That is, from the sociological perspective, everyone who lives within a social context possesses culture; clearly for a sociologist the term 'cultural deprivation' is a misnomer – man cannot be deprived of his culture. The point that it is important to note is that all too easily discussion in this

[248] *Education for Teaching*, Spring 1970, 2–11.
[249] This definition is from R. A. Kurtz and W. Wolfensberger, 'Cultural deprivation lower class and mental retardation: certain terminological and conceptual confusions', *Social Science and Medicine*, III, 1969, 229–237.

area slips from using the term 'culture' in a sociological sense to using it in an evaluative sense. That is in terms of the distinction between 'High Culture' and 'Low Culture'. And as we are all aware, typically it is the children from the lower socio-economic classes who are seen as culturally deprived – cultural deprivation becomes the monopoly of the lower classes, the poor. For example Riesman in his book *The Culturally Deprived Child*[250] states 'the terms culturally deprived, educationally deprived, deprived, underprivileged, disadvantaged, lower class, low socio-economic group are used interchangeably throughout this book.'

Bernstein[251] has pointed out some of the implications of labelling a child 'culturally deprived'. The parents come to be seen as inadequate, teachers will have lower expectations of their children. All that informs the child and gives meaning and purpose to him outside the school ceases to be valid or accorded significance and opportunity for enhancement within the school. The child is expected to drop his social identity and his way of life at the school gate. For, by definition, the child's culture is inadequate. And, more importantly, the concept detracts from the deficiencies of the school itself and focuses upon deficiencies within the community, the family, the child itself.

It may be argued that the conceptual models and research in this field have been guided by and have implicit within them an ideology which is similar to the ethnocentric liberal ideology implicit in the research on the deprived American Negro child which denies cultural differences and thus acts against the best interests of the people it wishes to understand and eventually help.[252]

The point to make, then, is that often what passes for a sociological explanation of a problem contains within it its own ideology and that a certain sociological acumen is necessary before the student is in a position to evaluate problem orientated research. This is not to say that sociologists should not be involved in helping solve educationalists' problems,[253] but rather that before one is able to evaluate critically the significance of the sociologists' perspective on a problem one needs a considerable sociological training oneself. This cannot be provided in the time available in education courses.

To take up now the second line in the argument; namely the question as to whether or not sociology of education is a science. Here it will be

[250]New York, 1962, 1.

[251]B. Bernstein, 'Education Cannot Compensate for Society', *New Society*, 26 February 1970, 344–347.

[252]S. S. Baratz and J. C. Baratz, 'Early Childhood Intervention: the Social Science Base of Institutional Racism', *Harvard Educational Review*, XL, 1970, 29–50.

[253]See for example, N. Gross and J. A. Fishman, 'The Management of Educational Establishments', in Paul F. Lazarsfeld *et al.* (eds.), *The Uses of Sociology*, London 1967, 304–358.

argued that this is not the case, and it is important to remember that this is a point of contention among sociologists.[254]

Consider first general sociological theory. Nisbet[255] has argued that the great classical themes of sociology are characterized by: first, a moral aspiration; the great ideas of sociology have been generated by individuals with a moral commitment, and second, the frames of thought and ideas of sociologists are the result of artistic imagination,[256] vision and intuition. Horton[257] in a similar vein has argued that the classical definitions of anomie and alienation (to take two key sociological ideas) rest on opposed utopian descriptions of essentially the same social discontent. He goes on to argue that the evolving history of these concepts has not led to the emergence of value free concepts but the transformation of values. He suggests that these ideological changes might be explained sociologically in terms of the changing class position of the sociologist and the organization of sociology. We must also agree with Nisbet and other sociologists[258] who have pointed out that we can only understand the fundamental ideas of sociology if we realise that sociology is an attempt by industrial man to understand industrial man. The matrix of sociological thought was the industrial revolution. Further, Runciman[259] has questioned the whole notion of whether there are general theories of social science which can be applied to substantive areas of human behaviour. He suggests that to talk of social science only becomes relevant when a particular area of human behaviour is isolated and a theory or model put forward to explain it. So far, then, the argument is that general sociological theory is not 'objective' or scientific and that in any case it is a mistake to apply general theory to a particular area of behaviour. Substantive theory must be generated for each particular area of human behaviour.

However, it may be argued against the above position that objectivity is a predicate of method rather than of theory and that it is by the use of rigorous research and experimental techniques that one ensures objectivity. But as Berlin[260] has pointed out there exist two classes of problems

[254]There is an extensive literature on this subject. Authorities who advocate that sociology is a science include: G. A. Lunderg et al., *Sociology* (3rd Edn.), New York 1963; R. S. Rudner, *Philosophy of Social Science*, Prentice Hall, 1966; and H. L. Zetterberg, *On Theory and Verification in Sociology* (3rd Edn.), Bedminster Press, 1965. For the argument that the Sociology of Education is a science see Pavalko op. cit., and Swift op. cit.

[255]R. A. Nisbet, *The Sociological Tradition*, London 1966, Part 1.

[256]For the argument that the language of sociology has a poetic form see: *M. R. Atein*, 'The Poetic Metaphors of Sociology' in M. Stein and A. Vidieh (eds.), *Sociology on Trial*, Prentice Hall Inc., 1963.

[257]J. Horton, 'The Dehumanization of Anomie and Alienation: A Problem in the Ideology of Sociology', *British Journal of Sociology*, XV, 283–300.

[258]For example E. Gellner, *Thought and Change*, 1965.

[259]W. G. Runciman, *Social Science and Political Theory* (2nd edn.), Cambridge, 1969, Ch. 1.

[260]I. Berlin, 'Does Political Theory Still Exist?', in Peter Laslett and W. G. Runciman (eds.), *Philosophy, Politics and Society* (2nd series), Oxford, 1967, 1–33.

to which men have succeeded in obtaining clear answers. The first have been so formulated so that they can (at least in principle, if not always in practice) be answered by observation or by inference from observed data. These determine the domains of natural science and every day common sense. These are empirical questions and he argues that all generalizations and hypotheses and models with which the most sophisticated sciences work can be established and discredited ultimately only by the data and inspection and introspection. The second type of question to which we can hope to obtain clear answers he calls formal. That is given certain propositions called axioms, together with rules for deducing other propositions from them we may proceed by mere calculation. Characteristics of both types of question are that even if we do not know the answer to a given question we know what kinds of methods are appropriate in looking for the answer and this means, in effect, that it is only where the concepts are firm, clear and generally accepted and the methods of reasoning and arriving at conclusions etc. are agreed between men is it possible to construct a formal or empirical science. Whenever this is not the case, where the concepts are vague or too much in dispute, where methods of argument and the minimum qualifications that constitute an expert are not generally agreed, where we find frequent recriminations about what can or cannot claim to be a law, an established hypothesis or an undisputed truth, then we are at the best in the realm of quasi science. The candidates for inclusion in this group include (for Berlin) psychology, sociology, linguistic analysis and literary criticism.

We may emphasize Berlin's point by taking a particular example. In 1958 Gross[261] wrote a paper in which he attempted 'to delineate for the educational practitioner some specific contributions of sociological analysis to the field of education'. The first of these was the relevance of the sociology of formal organizations to the organizational setting of the school.[262] Now the argument is that it may well be the case that organizational analysis provides valuable 'insights' into the functioning of schools but it is not the case that it provides a scientific analysis of the school. The following quotations from a comprehensive review of the contribution of organizational analysis to the study of educational institutions[263] makes Berlin's point without further comment:[264]

[261]N. Gross, Some Contributions of Sociology to the Field of Education, in *Harvard Educational Review*, XXIX, 1959, 275–87.

[262]For good overviews of the work in this field see C. G. Bidwell, 'The School as a Formal Organisation' in J. G. March (ed.) *Handbook of Organisations*, Rand McNally, 1965, 972–1022; R. C. Corwin, 'Education and the Sociology of Complex Organisations' in D. A. Hansen and J. G. Gerstl, *op. cit.*; and E. Hoyle, 'Organisational Analysis in the Field of Education', *Educational Research*, VII, No. 2, Feb. 1965, 97–114.

[263]W. B. Davies, *On the Contribution of Organizational Analysis to the Study of Educational Institutions*. Paper read to the British Sociological Association Annual Conference, 1970.

[264]As does the critique by M. Albrow, 'The Study of Organizations—Objectivity or Bias?', in Julius Gould (ed.), *Penguin Social Sciences Survey 1968*, 146–167.

'The divisions reflect, to a very large extent, the historical divisions within sociology – the unreconciled differences between conflict, social action and system approaches, between rational change and natural growth, power and consensus, and so on.'
'there is an ecumenical stir in the air',
'Clearly all research reflects the values and commitments of those who conduct and finance it',
'Indeed, sociological studies of educational organizations exhibit their own fashions.'

It is suggested therefore that if the sociology of education cannot claim to be a science it does not have a necessary claim to be included in the education syllabuses of colleges of education. It is an open question as to whether the insights of the sociologist are more valuable than those of the literary critic, linguistic philosopher or social historian. And it may well be the case that if the terminology which sociologists use to analyse schools as organizations seems somewhat remote and irrelevant to the classroom situation then other disciplines which may also be able to provide insights into how institutions operate, for example social history and literature, may have a valid claim for inclusion in the education course at this point.

Before closing this section one should note that the distinction between a 'pure' and 'applied' science which provides one of the criteria for the sociologist's distinction between 'sociology of education' and 'educational sociology' is not quite so clear cut as some sociologists[265] would like to think.[266] The distinction is a particularly British phenomenon[267]

Moving on to the third strand in the argument the question is: Is there enough research evidence which is distinctly sociological to justify courses in the sociology of education for teachers? And here we are particularly concerned with British research. While there is a considerable American research literature it is questionable whether it is generalizable to the North American Continent let alone to Britain where the relationships between school and society and the organizational structures of schools are different from those in USA.[268]

The authors[269] of a review of the recent literature in this country stated that 'We have made no more than a half-hearted attempt to be sociological – the application of anything but a very tolerant set of criteria for defining sociology would have excluded almost everything' (from their biblio-

---

[265] Swift, *op. cit.* is a notable exception.
[266] See for example S. D. Beck, *The Simplicity of Science*, Pelican Books, 1960, Ch. I.
[267] P. B. Medawar, 'Two Conceptions of Science' in P. B. Medawar, *The Art of the Soluble*, Pelican Books, 1969, 125–143. (See too, L. Stevenson, 'Applied Philosophy', *Metaphilosophy*, **1**, 1970, pp. 258–67, eds.).
[268] See N. Gross, *op. cit.*
[269] D. F. Swift and H. D. Acland, *The Sociology of Education in Britain, 1960–68*, a paper presented to the European Seminar on Sociology of Education, Noordwijk/Zee, Netherlands, 1968.

graphy). It is suggested following this comment that except for a few notable exceptions[270] there is little empirical research reported in this country which is distinctly sociological and which has a necessary claim to be included in sociology courses. Neither does one need to be a sociologist to understand this research – although a sociological background is necessary to evaluate this research when it claims to be sociology. However, often the research does not claim to be sociological – this is a claim made by lecturers who need empirical work to include in their courses. It is suggested that much of the research literature included in sociology of education courses could be included in general education courses and this may, in fact, demonstrate the relevance of the material to the student.[271]

One may note in passing that the considerable body of data pertaining to the relationship between social class and educational achievement is not in itself sociological. It is data which provides a description of the social structure of our society. Of course it is possible to provide a sociological explanation of this phenomenon. However, it is equally possible to provide a psychological explanation. And it may, in fact, be more worth-while to combine both psychological and sociological explanation when trying to understand the relationships between social class and educational achievement.[272]

To proceed to the final strand of the argument. To look for a moment at the process of teacher training 'sociologically' it is necessary to realize that from the time when he enters college the student has made at least some commitment to the teaching profession and that he is being socialized into an occupational role.[273] It may well be the case that the college authorities also expect him to fulfil the role of 'academic student', but for the student his frame of reference is likely to be the classroom rather than the groves of academe. We would suggest that it is possible to develop a

---

[270] For example: C. Lacey, 'Some Sociological Concomitants of Academic Streaming in a Grammar School', *B.J.S.* XVII 245–262 (1966); B. Sugarman, 'Involvement in Youth Culture, Academic Achievement and Conformity in School: an Empirical Study of London Schoolboys', *B.J.S.*, XVIII, 151–64 (1967); M. Shipman, 'Education and College culture', *B.J.S.*, XVIII, 425–34 (1967).

[271] Works which would come into his category would include J. W. B. Douglas, *The Home and the School*, London, 1964, and S. Wiseman, *Education and Environment*, University of Manchester Press, 1964.

[272] For a useful discussion on this point see: D. F. Swift, 'Educational Psychology, Sociology and the Environment: a Controversy at Cross-purposes', *British Journal of Sociology*, XVI, 334–50 (1965).

[273] There is a considerable amount of American literature in this field. Selection is invidious but see: J. W. Carper and H. S. Becker, 'Adjustments to Conflicting Expectations in the Development of Identification with an Occupation', *Social Forces*, XXXVI, 51–6 (1957–8); E. C. Hughes, 'Stress and Strain in Professional Education', *Harvard Education Review*, 319–329 (1959); W. L. Wallace, 'Institutional and Life Cycle Socialization of College Freshmen', *American Journal of Sociology*, LXX, 303–318 (1964).

sociology of education which recognizes this fact and which is at the same time academically respectable. One may illustrate this point by looking, with Jackson,[274] at the life of the teacher in the classroom. He argues following interviews with highly respected members of the profession that teachers' talk is characterized by conceptual simplicity, four aspects of which are: (1) an uncomplicated view of causality; (2) an intuitive, rather than rational approach to classroom events; (3) an opinionated, as opposed to an open-minded, stance when confronted with alternative teaching practices; and (4) narrowness in the working definitions assigned to abstract terms. He is not trying to sneer at teachers, he goes on to argue that this may be necessary if the teacher is to cope successfully with the exigencies of classroom life. To quote:

'The personal qualities enabling teachers to withstand the demands of classroom life have never been adequately described but among these qualities is surely the ability to tolerate the enormous amount of ambiguity, unpredictability and occasional chaos created each hour by 25 or 30 not-so-willing learners. What is here called the conceptual simplicity evident in teachers' language may be related to that ability. If teachers sought a more thorough understanding of their world, insisted on greater rationality in their actions, were completely open-minded in their consideration of pedagogical choices, and profound in their views of the human condition, they might well receive greater applause from intellectuals, but it is doubtful that they would perform with greater efficiency in the classroom. On the contrary, it is quite possible that such paragons of virtue, if they could be found to exist, would actually have a deuce of a time coping in any sustained way with a class of third graders or a play-yard full of nursery school tots.'[275]

The point that we can make from this picture of life in classrooms is that the teacher and by implication the student concerned with his own behaviour in classrooms after he has finished training and during school practice is not likely to take into account the findings of sociologists about education while he is actually working in the classroom. Not particularly because he does not want to but because the pressures of work and the practical demands of the situation in which he finds himself make it particularly difficult to stand back and look objectively at what he is doing. It may be as Jackson suggests that good teachers are those who are completely involved in the work which they are doing.

However, rather than conclude the jeremiad at this point we would like to go on to suggest that it may be well be possible to develop a rigorous sociology of education which may be of practical benefit to the student or teacher and which may be of relevance to the classroom situation. The basis for this rather 'optimistic' statement is the work of two

[274] P. W. Jackson, *Life in Classrooms*, New York, 1968.
[275] *Ibid.*, 149.

sociologists who have argued that the major task confronting sociology today is the development of *grounded theory*.[276] They are concerned that for too long sociologists have been interested in the process of how they should go about verifying their theories and in developing rather general theories which they then impose upon some social situation. They argue that what sociologists should do is systematically obtain data in particular social situations and then develop theories which actually fit the empirical situation they have been studying. As they say 'The basic theme in our book is the discovery of theory from data systematically obtained from social research.'[277] Their argument is fully outlined in the following quotation:

> 'Theory in sociology is a strategy for handling data in research, providing modes of conceptualization for describing and explaining. The theory should provide clear enough categories and hypotheses so that crucial ones can be verified in present and future research; they must be clear enough to be readily operationalized in quantitative studies when these are appropriate. The theory must also be readily understandable *to sociologists of any viewpoint, to students and to significant laymen.*[278] Theory that can meet these requirements must fit the situation being researched and work when put into use. By 'fit' we mean that the categories must be readily (not forcibly) applicable to and indicated by the data under study; by 'work' we mean that they must be meaningfully relevant to and be able to explain the behaviour under study.
>
> 'To generate theory that fills this large order, we suggest as the best approach an initial, systematic discovery of the theory from the data of social research. Then one can be relatively sure that the theory will fit and work. And since the categories are discovered by examination of the data, laymen involved in the area to which the theory applies will usually be able to understand it, while sociologists who work in other areas will recognize and understand theory linked with the data of a given area.'[279]

They suggest that this procedure[280] will avoid the opportunist use of theory for example when a sociological study has a tacked on explanation from a logically deduced theory. And it avoids the procedure of selecting examples chosen for their confirming power.

Thus it is arguable that at least potentially it is possible to develop a sociology of education which is based upon observation and research in school situations and which is concerned with deriving explanations of the behaviour of individuals in schools from the data collected in schools

---

[276] B. G. Glaser and A. L. Strauss, *The Discovery of Grounded Theory: Strategies for Qualitative Research*, London, 1968.

[277] *Ibid.*, 2.

[278] My italics.

[279] *Op. cit.*, 3–4.

[280] For a particularly illuminating use of this procedure in hospital situations see: B. G. Glaser and A. L. Strauss, *Time for Dying*, Aldine Publishing Co., 1968.

rather than applying theoretical perspectives elsewhere which look as though they may be illuminating.[281]

The suggestion is, therefore, that if sociologists become concerned with what actually goes on in schools[282] it may be possible to generate a sociology which is particularly beneficial to the student in training and to the serving teacher because it will be a sociology which will be both rigorous and seen to have a practical application in the classroom.

13 University scholarship and the education of teachers
ISRAEL SCHEFFLER
(The Record, Vol. 70, 1968–69, pp. 1–12)

What are the ingredients of a teacher's education? The question is old and controversial, surely not to be settled in a single discourse. Yet certain of its philosophical aspects may perhaps profitably be explored in brief compass, and it is such aspects that I wish here to treat, especially as they relate to the general role of university scholarship in the preparation of teachers.

This latter theme has, I believe, been relatively underplayed in contemporary treatments of the question. Recent educational reforms have largely addressed themselves to the proper structuring of subject-matter and its articulation in the teaching process. Discussion of the teacher's education has tended accordingly to concern itself, not with the general strengthening of his powers through scholarly studies, but rather with improving his grasp of the particular subject to be taught and providing him with practical experience in its classroom presentation.

In earlier days, there was also, to be sure, much confident talk of a putative science of education. The first annual convention of American normal-school principals in 1859, for example, passed a resolution proclaiming that 'education is a science.' Richard Edwards, later president of Illinois Normal University, protested in vain on that occasion that sciences are built not by proclamation but by research.[283] Yet even he was convinced that research would yield such a science, of fundamental importance in the training of teachers. In 1865, he declared:

---

[281] The application of the concept of 'Total Institutions' developed by Goffman is a useful example. E. Goffman, 'The Characteristics of Total Institutions' in *Symposium on Preventive and Social Psychiatry*, Walter Reed Army Institute of Research, Washington, D. C., 1957.

[282] The recent interest by a group of sociologists in the curriculum of the school is of significance. See for example: I. Davies, 'The Management of Knowledge: A Critique of the Use of Typologies in Educational Sociology', *Sociology*, IV (1), 1–22 (1970). M. F. D. Young, *Curricula and the Social Organization of Knowledge*, paper read at the British Sociological Association Annual Conference, 1970.

[283] See Merle L. Borrowman, *Teacher Education in America: A Documentary History*. New York: Teachers College Press, 1965.

It is not, I trust, necessary, at this late day, to assure you that there is here as noble a science as ever engaged the thought of man. There are immutable principles here, that ought to be studied and comprehended by every young person entering upon the work of teaching. There is, in the nature of things, a foundation for a profession of teachers.[284]

The development of a distinctive science of education has not, however, come about, and with increasing rejection of the idea of such a science in recent years,[285] there has been a growing tendency to exalt either specific subject-matter competence or classroom practice into a position of primacy in the preparation of teachers, with moderates striving, as ever, for an even balance between the two.

My own view is that the whole framework of this latter discussion has been too constricted, and that the preparation of teachers in a university setting, in particular, offers the special opportunity to develop a broader conception. Beyond a teacher's knowledge of his subject and his practice in the art of teaching under supervision, he needs to be helped, I am convinced, to relate his work in suitable manner to the family of scholarly and research disciplines represented by the university at large.[286]

No science of education. Nor does such a conviction imply a return to the fruitless quest for a distinctive science of education, as a foundation for the teaching profession. There is indeed, I believe, little to support the faith that such a distinctive science will one day to developed. The belief that the profession requires such a science as its foundation is, however, misguided. For if there be no distinctive science or special discipline of education, there are surely multiple modes of analyzing educational problems in a scientific spirit and a disciplined manner.[287] The teacher's preparation should lead him to relate his own tasks to such modes, and teacher education should thus be an integral undertaking of the whole university.

The underlying point was well put by the American philosopher Josiah Royce, in 1891. Arguing against the conception of education as a science, Royce insisted nevertheless that 'the undertakings of pedagogy' are 'capable of scientific and general discussion.'[288] Indeed, there is, he wrote, 'no science of education. But what there is, is the world of science furnishing material for the educator to study,' offering 'aid from the scientific spirit and counsel from scientific inductions.'[289] It is, I suggest, the family

[284] Richard Edwards, 'Normal Schools in the United States,' 1865. Reprinted in Borrowman, *op. cit.*

[285] See John Walton and James L. Kuethe, eds., *The Discipline of Education.* Madison, Wis.: University of Wisconsin Press, 1963.

[286] See *The Graduate Study of Education: Report of the Harvard Committee.* Cambridge: Harvard University Press, 1966.

[287] See I. Scheffler 'Is Education a Discipline?' in Walton and Kuethe, *op. cit.*

[288] Josiah Royce, 'Is There a Science of Education?' Reprinted in Borrowman, *op. cit.*

[289] *Ibid.*

of university studies, representing the world of science and the material of general discussion, that needs to be brought to bear on the teacher's work. I am, of course, not arguing for some particular administrative arrangement. Alternative arrangements are compatible with the general idea of initiating the teacher into disciplined perspectives, scholarly and humanistic, from which his professional work may be viewed.

Towards disciplined perspectives. To set forth such a general idea is in itself, however, hardly to persuade. Indeed, doubts are encountered almost immediately upon reflection. What is the point of a scholarly emphasis in the education of teachers?, asks the sceptic in each of us. Can an initiation into disciplined analyses of education really be thought necessary for effective teaching? What is the use of theoretical sophistication that is not translatable into subject-matter competence or strengthened practical skills? Have we not all known teachers of power and resourcefulness, innocent of educational history and philosophy, ignorant of psychology and the social sciences, and yet capable of transmitting their subjects effectively to the minds of their students? Is not the emphasis on scholarly disciplines then merely an eccentricity natural to scholars or, worse still, a fraudulent attempt to give education the aura of professionalism? So speaks the sceptic, and he deserves a serious answer, for he raises questions fundamental to any philosophy of teaching. Let me, then, sketch the sort of reply I am myself inclined to give to his challenge.

In general, though I hold the sceptic's doubts to be searching and important, I believe they flow from faulty reasoning. Consider his stress on what is necessary for effective teaching, indeed his appeal to such presumed necessity as a criterion for evaluating the education of teachers. By this criterion, he implies, we must admit the importance of subject matter competence and practical training. For, surely, without a knowledge of the subject to be taught, and without practical classroom procedures mastered through experience, a man cannot teach effectively; justification is thus conceded to these ingredients in the preparation of teachers. However, continues the sceptic, application of the same necessity criterion serves to exclude the ingredient of scholarly sophistications, since effective teaching may perfectly well proceed without an initiation into critical and disciplined approaches to the educational process. Such approaches, he concludes, therefore have no justification in the preparation of teachers.

The limits of necessity. From the reasonable premise that whatever is necessary for effective teaching is thereby justified as an element of training, the sceptic has invalidly concluded that *only* what is thus necessary can be justified. He has, in effect, exalted necessity into a unique position and ruled out all other principles of justification. Such exclusion is, however, quite vulnerable on general grounds. For by parallel reasoning one might argue, for example, that shock absorbers and automatic trans-missions ought to be done away with since they are not essential to effec-tive transportation, that carpets and paintings have no legitimate place in the home because they do not contribute to effective shelter, that literature and the fine arts are unjustified as civilized pursuits because they are unnecessary to sustain life.

Surely, the sceptic's attitude is too reductive. Justification is not, as he supposes, simply a matter of minimal necessity. It is, rather, a matter of desirability, and a thing may be desirable not because it is something we could not do without, but because it transforms and enhances the quality of what we do and how we live. If a justification is needed for the teacher's scholarly and theoretical sophistication regarding his work, it is not that, lacking it he cannot manage to teach, but that having it, the quality of his effort and role is likely to be enhanced. It is a maximal rather than a minimal interpretation of the teacher's work that is thus relevant to a philosophical assessment of his education.

In what, however, does such an enhancement of quality as has been mentioned consist? What are its concrete manifestations? How, specific-ally, does it show itself if, while inessential to mastery of the subject to be taught, it is also, by hypothesis, not transmuted into practical skill or improved maxims of classroom procedure? Does not theory, in general, refine the operations of craft through developing its technology? Is not a theoretical study of education therefore exposed as utterly irrelevant to the practice of teaching if it fails to foster new devices and specialized procedures for the conduct of schooling? Here is a further, and a persua-sive challenge of the sceptic.

Arguments from technology.   It should first be noted, however, that an important concession underlies this new challenge. The earlier complaint against a theoretical ingredient in the teacher's education was that it was not required for effective teaching. Now it seems to be allowed that such an ingredient might be independently justified, after all, as advancing the technology of education. Though the individual teacher does not require theoretical sophistication in order to perform his own work effectively, such sophistication may, it is now suggested, facilitate the invention of new methods and techniques, with a resultant improvement in the general state of the art. The sceptic therefore implicitly grants a place to theory provided it promises to yield technological improvements in educational practice. Against all other theory he is adamant.

One difficulty in this new position of the sceptic is that there is no sure way of telling in advance if, when, or how a bit of theoretical sophistica-tion will transform practice. If he interprets his new doctrine so liberally as to admit all basic theory that might conceivably yield practical change, he virtually abandons his opposition altogether. On the other hand, if he is to maintain effective opposition to specified bodies of theoretical content on the ground that they do not presently seem to him technologically promising, he cannot provide a principled basis for his judgement that will be generally acceptable to others, and he runs the real risk, moreover, of excluding technologically fruitful material. In sum, if the sceptic's present criterion is to avoid being simply vacuous, it must run the risk of being applied in a manner that is arbitrary and short-sighted, even from a technological point of view.

There is, however, a more fundamental reply that needs to be made to the present challenge of the sceptic. For he may argue that, although there is no generally acceptable, principled basis for estimating technological promise in advance, there is at least a rough intuitive ranking of theories that can be made, with respect to their relative promise. And he may add that, while some risk is admittedly involved in excluding theories beyond a certain designated point in the ranking, such a risk is inevitable in all estimation, and is well worth taking, here as elsewhere, in order to facilitate the making of practical decisions.

The more fundamental reply hinges then, not on the problem of applying the sceptic's present criterion, but rather on its basic concept of technological promise. For he construes the import of theory in education as consisting wholly in its power to transform the technology of teaching through providing new maxims of procedure. Educational improvement is seen as consisting altogether in a refinement of the teacher's operations in the pursuit of his craft. It is this implicit assimilation of educational improvement to technological development that I believe to be inappropriate, for the reduction of the teacher's role to the set of operations performed by him is, in fact, impossible.

Teacher vs. technician. It has, indeed, become increasingly fashionable in recent years to construe the teacher's work as that of 'a minor technician within an industrial process, the overall goals ... [of which are to be] ... set in advance in terms of national needs, the curricular materials prepacked by the disciplinary experts, the methods developed by educational engineers – and the teacher's job ... just to supervise the last operational stage, the methodical insertion of ordered facts into the student's mind.'[290] The trouble with this picture is that it is radically wrong, both normatively and descriptively. The teacher, in a free society at least, is not just a technician, but also one of the shapers of the educational process. Moreover, he influences students not only through his activity, but by his identity.

In the paradigmatic case of industrial design and manufacture, the technician operates upon inert materials, he does things to these materials under the guidance of rules improvable through investigation and experi-

---

[290] I. Scheffler, 'Concepts of Education: Some Philosophical Reflections on the Current Scene' in Edward Landy and Paul A. Perry, editors, *Guidance in American Education: Backgrounds and Prospects*, Cambridge: Harvard University Press, 1963.

ment. These materials are shaped by what he thus does; they are not responsive to what he is. They react to what is done to them by the technician but they do not enter into communication with him. They do not, in the process of their own shaping into output, question his judgements and beliefs, his perspectives and purposes. They present him with no new centers of personal experience, by relating to which his own meanings may be engaged and transformed.

Teaching is, in every crucial respect, vastly different. Although the teacher's procedures are also subject to improvement through scientific research and experiment, the student is not mere inert material to be worked on by rule. He enters into communication with the teacher and, through the teacher, with the heritage of culture common to both. Such communication broadens and refines the student's initial outlook, and thereby increases his understanding.

But the process is not one-sided, for in the student's efforts to understand, he questions and explores, doubts and evaluates. And he thus responds not only to the explicit material of the lesson but to its larger ramifications, not only to what the teacher does, but also to what he intends and represents. He is, in short, alive not simply to the content of classroom activities but to the manner in which they are carried out, the standards and convictions they reflect, and the larger rationale that underlies them. The teacher is, moreover, committed to honoring the student's quest for understanding by providing him with honest answers, that is to say, answers he himself finds genuinely compelling. The teacher is thus called upon to reveal and hence to risk, his own judgements and loyalties in the process of teaching others. In embracing this risk, the teacher is himself forced to a heightened self-awareness, and a more reflective attitude toward his own presuppositions; his own outlook is thereby broadened and refined.

For the teacher to conceive his role after the analogy of industrial production is thus, I believe, a distorting fallacy of far-reaching consequence. His role is not reducible to the operations he performs; it draws heavily upon his capacities for insight into his own principles and allegiances. And it demands an ability to reflect critically on these principles in the face of the searching curiosity of the young.

Quickening critical powers.   His preparation for teaching is thus strengthened not simply through an increased mastery of procedures, but through a development of his resources for carrying on a significant conversation with the young, that is to say, through a widening of his intellectual perspectives, a quickening of his imaginative and critical powers, and a deepening of insight into his purposes as a teacher and the nature of the setting in which these purposes are pursued. Do not scholarly and theoretical studies of educational problems find sufficient justification in the rich opportunities they offer for such a strengthening of the teacher's resources?

But perhaps, it will be thought, the sceptic rejects any such appeal to 'cognitive' rather than 'operational' notions, in the process of justification. Being a sceptic, he is after all professionally hard-headed; he does not look with favour upon concepts of insight, reflection, and intellectual perspective, nor does he relish elusive references to a strengthening of the teacher's resources. He recognizes the importance of mastery of the subject to be taught, and the significance of reliable classroom procedures. But any appeal to a notion of latent intellectual power he finds obscure and therefore unacceptable.

To this line of thought there are, it seems to me, two replies. The sceptic's general aversion to non-operational concepts is, in the first place, not decisive in countering the specific arguments previously offered. If these arguments are sound, they cast doubt on the operational bias motivating the very aversion in question. To insist that the arguments must be wrong simply because they clash with the aversion would be to beg the question.

In the second place, the sceptic must himself acknowledge a principle of justification that ranges beyond what can be reflected in operational maxims of the classroom. For, let us remind him, he has spoken glibly of the necessity of knowledge of a subject for effective teaching. And what, we may ask him, is a subject? Is history, for example, a subject? Surely, effective teaching of a given history lesson or course does not require a general knowledge of history, as such. Nor does effeçtive teaching of a particular topic in mathematics require a knowledge of mathematics, taken as a whole. Nor, finally, does effective teaching of a particular English poem or literary period require a comprehensive mastery of English literature. The boundaries of the subject in every case reach far beyond the scope of the teacher's actual classroom work. If knowledge of the subject is nevertheless justified in the sceptic's eyes, he has implicitly, and despite his vaunted hard-headedness, granted the importance of a non-operational ingredient in the teacher's preparation.

Now it may, perhaps, be objected that this latter reply to the sceptic takes for granted the standard everyday concept of a subject. Subject matter rubrics, it will rightly be said, are crude practical devices of grouping that are variable at will. Mathematics need not be construed so expansively as to embrace all mathematical topics, nor should history be interpreted as covering the whole sweep of human events, when we are concerned with the particular problem of specifying the education of teachers. In dealing with this problem we are, in every case, that is, presupposing a narrower conception of the relevant subject to be mastered by the teacher.

This conclusion, though correct, is not, however, sufficient to save the sceptic from implicit appeal to a non-operational component in the teacher's education. For the sceptic, no matter how narrowly he conceives the subject-matter preparation of the teacher, does not, in practice, construe any subject so narrowly as to collapse it into the single course nor, certainly, into the single lesson being taught for the day. Whatever he means by insisting on the necessity of knowledge of the subject, the subject represents, for him too, a wider circle of materials and instrumentalities surrounding the content to be taught, access to which strengthens the teacher's powers and, in so doing, heightens the possibilities of his art. Though it does not translate itself uniformly into technological improvement, it is acknowledged, even by the sceptic, to be justified as an ingredient of the teacher's education.

Subjects reconceived. And once such a notion is admitted, can we put bounds to it? Can we say: This much surrounding matter represents an important teaching resource, but beyond this nothing significant is to be found? How difficult such a position would be! Indeed, to recognize that the ordinary notion of a subject is artificial should lead us rather to break its pervasive hold over our educational conceptions. Subjects should be taken to represent, not hard bounds of necessity which confine the teacher's training, but centers of intellectual capacity and interest, radiating outward without assignable limit. Anything that widens the context of the teacher's performance, whether it extends his mastery of related subject matter or, rather, his grasp of the social and philosophical dimensions of his work, has a potential contribution to make to his training. It is in the latter respects particularly that scholarly and theoretical studies of education find their proper rationale.

Thus far, in replying to the sceptic, I have addressed myself mainly to the notion of justification, the import of theory, and the nature of subjects. A last, but no means unimportant, aspect of the sceptic's doctrine that remains to be discussed is his emphasis on effective teaching. For, as we have seen, he considers the effective practice of teaching to constitute a basic focus of relevance in evaluating the teacher's preparation. One question that should, however, be raised concerns the clarity of the general idea. Is teaching effectiveness so clear a notion that it can perform properly in the fundamental evaluative role thus assigned to it?

No matter how we initially understand it, I think we must agree, upon reflection, that evaluating the effectiveness of teaching is not a simple thing. Any serious attempt to assess such effectiveness raises not only difficult practical questions of inquiry and measurement but also fundamental issues concerning reasonable criteria of judgement. What qualities of classroom performance should enter into a judgement of effectiveness, and what influences on the students?

Turning first to classroom performance, it is important to stress the subtlety and delicacy of the teacher's interchange with the student. A crude demand for effectiveness easily translates itself into a disastrous emphasis on externals simply because they are easier to get hold of than the central phenomena of insight and the growth of understanding. In an important essay of 1904,[291] John Dewey distinguished between the inner and outer attention of children, the inner attention involving the 'first-hand and personal play of mental powers' and the external 'manifested in certain conventional postures and physical attitudes rather than in the movement of thought.' Children, he noted, 'acquire great dexterity in exhibiting in conventional and expected ways the *form* of attention to school work.' The 'supreme mark and criterion of a teacher,' according to Dewey, is the ability to bypass externals and to 'keep track of [the child's] mental play, to recognize the signs of its presence or absence, to know how it is initiated and maintained, how to test it by results attained, and to test *apparent* results by it.' The teacher 'plunged prematurely into the pressing and practical problem of keeping order in the schoolroom,' Dewey warned, is almost of necessity going 'to make supreme the matter of external attention.' Without the reflective and free opportunity to develop his theoretical conceptions and his psychological insight, he is likely to 'acquire his technique in relation to the outward rather than the inner mode of attention.' Effective classroom performance surely needs to be judged in relation to the subtle engagement of this inner mode, difficult as it may be to do so.

Influence on students. Let us look now at the question of influence on the students, as a component of teaching effectiveness. What sorts of influence are relevant? Is their knowledge of material alone to be considered, or shall we also take into account their problem solving capacity, their attitudes, their propensity for inquiry, the hidden alteration of their perceptions and sensibility which may become manifest, if at all, only long after they have left the classroom? Even the hard knowledge of material is not, despite the confidence of the test-makers, a simple thing to gauge or analyse. William James' comments of nearly eighty years ago are still fresh and instructive on this topic. 'We are all too apt,' he says,

> to measure the gains of our pupils by their proficiency in directly reproduc-ing in a recitation or an examination such matters as they may have learned, and inarticulate power in them is something of which we always under-estimate the value. The boy who tells us, 'I know the answer, but I can't say what it is,' we treat as practically identical with him who knows absolutely nothing about the answer at all. But this is a great mistake. It is but a small part of our experience in life that we are ever able articulately to recall. And yet the whole of it has had its influence in shaping our character and defining our tendencies to judge and act. Although the ready memory is a great blessing to its possessor, the vaguer memory of a subject, of having once had to do with it, of its neighborhood, and of where we may go to recover it again, constitutes in most men and women the chief fruit of their education. This is true even in

[291] John Dewey, 'The Relation of Theory to Practice in Education,' in National Society for the Study of Education, *The Relation of Theory to Practice in Education of Teachers*, Third Year book, Part I. Bloomington: Public School Publishing Co., 1904.

professional education. The doctor, the lawyer, are seldom able to decide upon a case off-hand. They differ from other men only through the fact that they know how to get at the materials for decision in five minutes or half an hour: whereas the layman is unable to get at the materials at all . . .

Be patient, then, and sympathetic with the type of mind that cuts a poor figure in examinations. It may, in the long examination which life sets us, come out in the end in better shape than the glib and ready reproducer, its passions being deeper, its purposes more worthy, its combining power less commonplace, and its total mental output consequently more important.[292]

To take James' words seriously is to realize how complex and subtle is the notion of effectiveness in teaching, how far from providing a firm educational criterion marking an end, rather than an opening, of inquiry and reflection.

The main point to which I would here call attention is, however, a different one. It concerns not the clarity of the notion of teaching effectiveness, but rather the implied emphasis on the teaching performance, in contrast with the role of the teacher.

Understanding the teaching role. How indeed is this role itself to be understood? Is the teacher to be thought of as an intellectual technician, whose teaching performance may be more or less effective by whatever criteria of value and of influence may be chosen, but who has no voice in setting these criteria? Or is he, on the contrary, to be thought of as a man with a calling or vocation committing him to the values of truth, reason, and the enlargement of human powers, dedicated to raising his voice for them, and to shaping the conditions of his work so that these values may flourish? His effectiveness as a teacher, in the light of the latter conception, is quite different from the restricted notion of his effectiveness in classroom performance.

The sceptic's emphasis on effectiveness in teaching is, I should argue, too narrow, for it leads him to conceive teacher training as geared primarily to the refinement of performance, and to underestimate the significance of the teacher's larger role. A society aspiring to be genuinely free cannot afford such a restricted view. It must appreciate, indeed insist on, the fundamental relevance of enlightenment and critical thought in all matters bearing on the nurture of its cultural life. It needs, in particular, to view its teachers not simply as performers professionally equipped to realize effectively any goals that may be set for them. Rather, it should view them as free men and women with a special dedication to the values of the intellect and the enhancement of the critical powers of the young.

In such a role, teachers cannot restrict their attention to the classroom alone, leaving the larger setting and purposes of schooling to be deter-

---

[292] William James, *Talks to Teachers on Psychology: and to Students on Some of Life's Ideals*. New York: W. W. Norton Company, 1958.

mined by others. They must take active responsibility for the goals to which they are committed, and for the social setting in which these goals may prosper. If they are not to be mere agents of others, of the state, of the military, of the media, of the experts and the bureaucrats, they need to determine their own agency through a critical and continual evaluation of the purposes, the consequences, and the social context of their calling.

If we accordingly conceive of the education of teachers not simply as the training of individual classroom performers, but as the development of a class of intellectuals vital to a free society, we can see more clearly the role of educational scholarship and theoretical analysis in the process. For, though the latter do not directly enhance craftsmanship, they raise continually the sorts of questions that concern the larger goals, setting, and meaning of educational practice. It is these questions that students need continually to have before them as they develop into mature teachers, if they are indeed to help shape the purposes and conditions of education. To link the preparation of teachers with such questions is the special opportunity of the university.

The family of studies and disciplines represented by the university is not, let us be clear on this, a happy family. It harbors quarrels and nasty feuds as well as sweetness and light. But the contribution it offers to teacher education presupposes neither an unattainable coherence of perspectives nor an artificial consensus on details. It consists rather in an enlargement of the intellectual context with which a teacher views his work. Such an enlargement centers the work within a web of new relationships, altering its familiar outlines and inviting novel perceptions of its import. In so doing, it continually suggests alternatives to encrusted assumptions, generating insistently larger questions of meaning, setting, and purpose. In its shared commitment to critical thought and responsible inquiry, moreover, the family of scholarly studies spurs the teacher's effort to attain a more rational insight into his task. It is the quest for such insight, within ever growing contexts of meaning, that frees the teacher and fits him to teach free men.

Some issues arising from the readings

Preliminary comments

Here we raise first a number of issues about philosophy and sociology and go on to say that philosophy and sociology do not seem to contain much that can count as securely established knowledge. Next, we suggest that at least some work from theoretical disciplines appears in education in inaccurate and misleading forms. We draw attention to the way that institutional factors may affect the production of theoretical work relevant to education. Finally, we raise some issues about the justification of philosophy and sociology in the education of teachers.

The disciplines of philosophy and sociology: some general comments

1. The nature of philosophy and sociology

The issues raised here all concern the accounts that are (and might be) given of philosophy and sociology, particularly by philosophers of education and sociologists of education.[1] We begin with philosophy and

[1] Our discussion centres on philosophy but a similar case might well be made out for sociology, *mutatis mutandis*. We deliberately refrain from giving accounts of philosophy, sociology, philosophy of education, or sociology of education. Some of the reasons for this should become apparent from our discussion. For a collection of articles concerned with the nature of philosophy of education and for a brief bibliography see C. J. Lucas, ed., *What is Philosophy of Education?* (Collier-Macmillan, 1969). For bibliographies in philosophy of education see, H. S. Broudy, M. J. Parsons, I. A. Snook and R. D. Szoke, eds, *Philosophy of Education: an Organisation of Topics and Selected Sources* (University of Illinois Press, 1967); C. M. Smith and H. S. Broudy, eds, *Philosophy of Education: an Organisation of Topics and Selected Sources*, Supplement 1969 (Urbana Illinois: University of Illinois Press, 1969); J. P. Powell, *Philosophy of Education: a Select Bibliography* (Manchester University Press, 2nd edn, 1970). On the sociology of education see A. Hartnett, ed., *The Sociology of Education: an Introductory Guide to the Literature* (1975), op. cit.

sociology unqualified because it has been argued that 'philosophy' and 'sociology' do not change their meanings by being prefixed to 'of education' any more than by being prefixed to 'of religion'.[2] The accounts individuals give of philosophy of education and sociology of education are, therefore, likely to depend on what they take philosophy and sociology unqualified to be.

Anyone reading some of the recent literature in philosophy of education might be forgiven for believing that the question of what philosophy is can be answered reasonably easily; that contemporary philosophers (in the English-speaking world, at any rate) are fairly clear about the nature of their subject; and that there is one fairly uniform account of it to which, with minor disagreements and reservations, they would nearly all subscribe. We read in a discussion by Peters, that there has been a 'revolution in philosophy'; that as a result of it philosophers have become 'increasingly aware of what is distinctive of philosophical enquiries and more cautious about making pronouncements on matters which are not strictly philosophical in character'; that philosophical questions are 'second order'.[3] Often added to this is the claim that philosophy is analysis – logical, linguistic, or conceptual. A number of things can be said about these claims. In so far as they can be held to imply that questions about the nature of philosophy are relatively unproblematic or that there is current agreement about its nature, there are grounds for thinking they are misleading. Some comments of Ayer suggest this. He says, in a reprinted lecture, 'Yet not only am I not at all confident of my ability to give a satisfactory answer to the question [i.e. What is philosophy?] which you have put to me, but it is very probable that the answers which you obtain from my colleagues will differ quite markedly from my own; it might even be that they are radically divergent.'[4] He goes on to say that

---

[2] Cf. R. F. Dearden, 'The philosophy of education', in J. W. Tibble, ed., *An Introduction to the Study of Education* (Routledge & Kegan Paul, 1971), p. 88, who argues that 'the philosophy of education just is general philosophy when it takes the theory and practice of education as a more narrowing criterion of relevance.' See also R. G. Woods, 'Philosophy of education', in R. G. Woods, ed., *Education and its Disciplines* (University of London Press, 1972) and R. A. Becher, 'A lack of discipline, *Philosophy*, **49**, 1974, pp. 205–11.

[3] R. S. Peters, 'The philosophy of education', in J. W. Tibble, ed., *The Study of Education* (Routledge & Kegan Paul, 1966), p. 59.

[4] A. J. Ayer, 'Philosophy as elucidating concepts', in J. Bobick, ed., *The Nature of Philosophical Inquiry* (Indiana: Notre Dame Press, 1970), p. 101. Ayer also states in A. J. Ayer, ed., *Logical Positivism* (New York: Free Press, 1959), p. 9, that 'It is especially characteristic of philosophers that they tend to disagree not merely about the solution of certain problems but about the very nature of their subject and the methods by which it is to be pursued.' B. Mitchell, in *The Philosophy of Religion* (Oxford University Press, 1971), p. 1, in his introduction as editor states 'It is among the fascinations of philosophy that the nature of philosophy itself is as much a controversial issue as any other that philosophers discuss.' F. Waismann in his article 'How I see philosophy', in H. D. Lewis, ed., *Contemporary British Philosophy* (Allen & Unwin, 1956), p. 445, writes 'What phil-

though there are disputes among specialists in other disciplines about the nature of their subjects, these take place 'against a background of accepted doctrine or, at the very least, a stock of accredited facts. This is not so in philosophy', and that 'the failure of philosophers to come to agreement about the purposes of their activity and the methods by which it should be pursued, has become more marked in recent years and has led, understandably, to a certain crisis of confidence.'[5]

In any case, an account of philosophy that relies upon notions such as 'second order' or 'analysis' is likely to be problematic. Firstly, issues arise about the distinction between first-order and second-order questions. Briefly, what is meant by calling an inquiry 'second order' as opposed to 'first order' is that, given areas of inquiry or discourse such as science, history, or morality, a second-order inquiry is not one which makes, or tries to establish the truth of, statements within these areas. This is the job of the scientist, historian, etc. Rather from a non-participatory and spectatorial viewpoint, it investigates the nature of the thinking that goes on in these areas. Thus A. R. White says that 'What sorts of things are valuable is a first-order question, while inquiries – whether psychological, sociological, or logical – into our thinking about values are second-order.'[6] The second-order inquiries of philosophy are usually held to be of a logical sort. But whether this sharp distinction suggested by White can be maintained is not clear. Mays comments that analytical philosophers assumed that 'formal (structural) questions and substantive questions (i.e. those of content) are separable' and suggests that the assumption might not be justified.[7] Gellner also appears to hold a similar position. He says that 'conceptual investigations are seldom or never separable from either substantive ones or from evaluation. The model on which the contrary assumption was based is false . . . In fact, "analyses" almost always plainly do have evaluative implications.'[8]

(Ftn. 4 cont.)
osophy is? I don't know nor have I a set formula to offer.' Fairly wide differences about the nature of philosophy can be detected in the discussions in B. Magee, ed., *Modern British Philosophy* (Secker & Warburg, 1971). See also the comments of E. Nagel at the very beginning of the article on page 13.

[5] A. J. Ayer, op. cit., (1970), p. 102.

[6] A. R. White, *The Philosophy of Mind* (New York: Random House, 1967), p. 5. Nagel would appear to see philosophy as a second-order discipline. See p. 15.

[7] W. Mays, 'Linguistic analysis and the philosophy of education', *Educational Theory*, Vol. 20 (Summer 1970), p. 273.

[8] E. A. Gellner, *Words and Things* (Penguin Books, 1968), p. 294. For a relevant discussion of this and related issues in the context of moral philosophy, see A. Gewirth, 'Meta-ethics and normative ethics', *Mind*, Vol. LXIX (1960), pp. 187–205, and R. C. Solomon, 'Normative and meta-ethics,' *Philosophy and Phenomenological Research*, Vol. XXXI (1970–71), pp. 97–107. It might be argued, in the light of the comments of Mays and Gellner, that one of the assumptions made by some contemporary philosophers when they give an account of the subject is itself a matter of philosophical dispute.

Secondly, the claim that philosophy is analysis or even conceptual analysis is likely to be ambiguous, and even where unambiguous, programmatic. Ayer lists eight different sorts of activity which might be described as 'philosophical analysis', and of these at least five might be described as 'conceptual analysis'.[9]

In the light of these comments it would be over-ambitious of us to attempt to give an account of what philosophy is, and thus of what philosophy of education is.[10] In our view any such account is probably better understood, not as a factual account of what the discipline is, but rather as a persuasive or programmatic definition of it.[11] Hospers suggests that philosophy has often been persuasively defined. He points out that 'Among the many words and phrases that have been infected by persuasive definition, the one of most interest to us is "philosophy" itself. Different people who all claim to be engaging in the philosophic enterprise have seized upon the aspects of the subject that have interested them most, or those that they consider the most important, and defined

[9] A. J. Ayer, op. cit. (1970), pp. 112–17. He states on page 112 that 'there is no general agreement among those who subscribe to it as to what philosophical analysis consists in.' See also his comment in A. J. Ayer, ed. op. cit. (1959), p. 1, where he says that the scope of what he regards 'as analytical philosophy is wide. It allows for serious disagreement, not only over technical niceties, but on major points of doctrine, including the method and purpose of analysis itself.' S. Körner in his book, *Fundamental Questions in Philosophy* (Allen Lane, The Penguin Press, 1969), p. 26, claims that comparatively few analytical philosophers 'have turned their analytical acumen on the concept of analysis itself. In view of the vast claims made for analysis, especially the claim that there is no other legitimate method in philosophy, some analysis of "analysis" seems desirable.' Körner goes on to make a useful distinction between what he calls 'exhibition-analysis' and 'replacement-analysis'. See also the distinctions between 'therapeutic analysis', 'descriptive analysis', and 'critical analysis' in R. H. Weingartner, 'The meaning of "of" in "Philosophy of ..."', *Journal of Value Inquiry*, Vol. 2 (1968), pp. 79–94.

[10] There may, of course, be some accounts of philosophy of education which depend very little, if at all, on accounts of philosophy as an academic discipline.

[11] For persuasive and programmatic definitions see C. L. Stevenson, 'Persuasive definitions', *Mind*, Vol. XLVII (1938), pp. 331–49; R. Robinson, *Definition* (Oxford University Press, 1950), pp. 165–70; I. Scheffler, *The Language of Education* (Springfield Illinois: Charles C. Thomas, 1960), Chapter 1; J. Hospers, *An Introduction to Philosophical Analysis*, (Routledge & Kegan Paul, 2nd edn, 1967), pp. 53–6. R. F. Dearden, in 'The philosophy of education', in J. W. Tibble, ed., *An Introduction to the Study of Education* (Routledge & Kegan Paul, 1971), p. 83 makes a point similar to ours. He writes, 'It might be thought that an obvious next step, now that the ground has been cleared a little, would be simply to supply the correct definition of philosophy as it is understood by professional philosophers. But there would be difficulties in doing that, and even objections to trying to do it, as much for philosophy as for any other discipline. Most likely such a definition would be the conscious or unconscious expression of a particular orthodoxy, surreptitiously legislating the correctness of its own approach.' A. G. N. Flew, in his introduction to A. G. N. Flew, ed., *Logic and Language*, Second Series (Blackwell, 1953), pp. 7–8, makes a number of important and related points. He notes on page 7 that 'the whole idea that there is or should be some real essence of philosophy which has been or could be expressed in a final, comprehensive, "true definition" is radically misguided.'

"philosophy" in terms of these only, thereby relegating the remainder of the group (including many professors of philosophy at universities and colleges) to the position of non-philosophers. (The group left in the cold by this definition would of course construct a persuasive definition of their own so as to exclude the first group.)'[12]

Nevertheless, given that there are very important distinctions between disciplines, the extent to which any definition can be plausibly argued to be a definition of 'philosophy' will be limited.[13] There are likely to be a number of criteria which mark out an area outside of which accounts of philosophy cannot fall. Danto, for example, argues that no acceptable account of philosophy can be given such that it precludes the question 'What is philosophy?' from being a philosophical question.[14] He holds that by the use of this criterion philosophy can be demarcated from the sciences. Waismann, though on different grounds, holds that 'philosophy, as it is practised today, is very unlike science.'[15] Gellner states that 'philosophy, quite patently and also self-confessedly, is not a kind of thought which stands or falls with factual evidence',[16] and thus would appear to agree with the conclusions of Danto and Waismann, and with that of Hirst who implies that philosophy must be distinguished from sociology and psychology – at least in so far as they are empirical areas of inquiry.[17] Whether or not another negative criterion is that philosophical disputes are not normative we will discuss later.[18]

What we might expect to see therefore, are a number of competing accounts of philosophy which, if they are to have at least *prima facie* plausibility, must fall within an area demarcated, perhaps only roughly, by a number of negative criteria.

We now turn briefly to sociology, where similar factors appear to apply.

Firstly, it is likely that there is considerable variety within sociology courses in higher education. This may apply both within societies and, to an even greater extent, between different societies.[19] Barnes suggests

---

[12] J. Hospers, op. cit. (1967), pp. 54–5. For what he calls the 'partisan' nature of accounts of philosophy, see K. Nielsen, *Reason and Practice* (New York: Harper & Row, 1971), Chapter 1.

[13] Cf. the comments of P. H. Hirst, in 'Educational theory', in J. W. Tibble, ed., *The Study of Education*, (1966) op. cit., p. 33.

[14] A. C. Danto, *What Philosophy Is – a Guide to the Elements* (Penguin Books, 1971), p. 18.

[15] F. Waismann, op. cit., p. 445.

[16] E. Gellner, *Words and Things*, op. cit., p. 255.

[17] P. H. Hirst, 'Educational theory', in J. W. Tibble, ed., (1966) op. cit., p. 33.

[18] See pp. 147–51.

[19] For a comment on national divisions in philosophy see A. J. Ayer, in A. J. Ayer, ed., op. cit. p. 9. See also the discussion between B. Magee and A. Montefiore, in *The Listener*, (4 March 1971), pp. 267–71 and reprinted in B. Magee, ed., op. cit. For sociology see M. Coulson and D. S. Riddell, *Approaching Sociology* (Routledge & Kegan Paul, 1970), pp. 3–4.

that 'the range of variation within Britain as to what goes on in a university under the rubric of sociology is enormous.'[20] Coulson and Riddell note the variations between sociology in Britain and Yugoslavia; within the French and British traditions in Canada; and argue that 'within a country, to a considerable extent the approach which a student finds he is being taught varies according to the particular views of his teacher or his department.'[21]

Secondly, this variety of approach exists at the level of sociological theory, research, and methodology. There is a very considerable literature in this area.[22] The general issue is made explicit by Merton, commenting on a paper by Bendix. He writes, 'Although no one has yet provided systematic evidence bearing on the matter, we provisionally accept as roughly true Professor Bendix's impression that there is less consensus in sociology than in some other contemporary sciences ... The crucial implication is that this social condition of dissensus confronts individual sociologists with great uncertainty about their role as scientists; uncertainty about what to choose to do, how to do it, how to find out whether they have done it effectively and what it all adds up to when they are temporarily done with it. Substantial dissensus means that sociologists are more insecure in their work-roles than other contemporary scientists about the kinds of judgements and choices that scientists in every field must incessantly make.'[23] This statement, if valid, will have implications for the form and content of introductory textbooks in sociology. Coulson and Riddell compare an American and a Yugoslav

[20] J. Barnes, *The Listener* (5 August 1971), p. 174.

[21] M. Coulson and D. S. Riddell, op. cit., p. 1. Given the variety of qualifications and background of those who teach 'sociology of education' in colleges of education, there is likely to be a great range of activities covered by the label 'doing sociology'. See W. Taylor, *Society and the Education of Teachers* (Faber, 1969), pp. 211–18.

[22] See, as examples, R. W. Friedrichs, *A Sociology of Sociology*, op. cit.; E. Tiryakian, ed., *The Phenomenon of Sociology*, op. cit.; J. C. McKinney and E. A. Tiryakian, *Theoretical Sociology Perspectives and Developments* (New York: Appleton-Century-Crofts, 1970); A. W. Gouldner, *The Coming Crisis of Western Sociology* (Heinemann Educational Books, 1971); I. L. Horowitz, ed., *Sociological Self-Images* (Pergamon Press, 1970); M. Popovich, 'What the American sociologists think about their science and its problems', *American Sociologist* (May 1966); J. L. McCartney, 'On being scientific: changing styles of presentation of sociological research', *American Sociologist*, Vol. 5, No. 1, February 1970; Fuad Baali and Michael C. Moore, 'The extended deliberation: definitions of sociology 1951–1970', *Sociology and Social Research*, Vol. 56, No. 4 (July 1972), pp. 433–9. For some of the literature in the sociology of education see Sections 1 and 2 (by Brian Davies) in A. Hartnett ed., op. cit., (1975).

[23] R. Merton, pp. 189–90 in Tiryakian, op. cit. Note B. Bernstein's remarks in his introduction to *Class, Codes and Control* (Routledge & Kegan Paul, 1971), pp. 19–20. He writes 'Theories are rarely refuted: they are explored and replaced by more simple, more explicit, more delicate, more general, indeed, more exciting ideas. It is probably wrong to use the word "theory". The most we seem able to do is to construct weak interpretative frames. Perhaps in the end the sole criterion is: do these encourage a shift in perspective so that we can see received frames differently or even a little beyond them?'

textbook and point out considerable differences.[24] They also make the important point that disagreements and conflicts within sociology may not be made explicit in introductory textbooks.[25]

2. Philosophy and philosophy of education

Our discussion so far suggests, among other things, that there is no one very determinate answer to the question 'What is philosophy?' What are the implications of this for philosophy of education?[26] In so far as definitions or accounts of philosophy of education are held to depend upon those of philosophy, then any account of philosophy of education will be one account among others and is likely to be persuasive or programmatic. Yet there is a danger that this might not be realized. When Peters, for example, explains what he believes to have been the somewhat premature publication of *Ethics and Education*, he says, 'The point is to provide a few signposts for others and to map the contours of the field for others to explore in a more leisurely and detailed manner. The important thing in the philosophy of education is that something should be there to indicate what it is and to provide a determinate structure on which students can train their critical faculties.'[27]

Now admittedly Peters is concerned in *Ethics and Education* with 'the applications of ethics and social philosophy to problems of education' and not with philosophy of education as a whole.[28] Even so the implication of the phrases 'to indicate what it is' and 'to map the contours of the field' is that there is something called 'philosophy of education' which, like a suspect at an identity parade at the back of the local police station, is merely waiting to be picked out by an alleged eyewitness.[29]

[24] Coulson and Riddell, op. cit., pp. 3–4.

[25] Ibid., p. 3, where they cite Bottomore, and p. 6 where they cite Cotgrove. K. R. Minogue, *The Concept of a University* (Weidenfeld and Nicolson, 1973), p. 135, suggests that most textbooks tend 'to encourage a simple and unphilosophical reception of the current categorisation of a subject.' The point about the reception may be true even where more than one categorization is current.

[26] We restrict our discussion here and in the next section to philosophy of education but similar points can almost certainly be made about sociology of education.

[27] R. S. Peters, *Ethics and Education* (Allen & Unwin, 1966), p. 8.

[28] Ibid., p. 19.

[29] A more apt comparison is with a beauty contest. It would probably be unjust to say that Peters is unaware of the programmatic nature of accounts of philosophy of education. But some of his discussions tend to be less than explicit about it. Take for example the following passages from R. S. Peters, in J. W. Tibble, ed., op. cit., (1966), p. 62. 'Before passing to a more positive account of what the philosophy of education ought to be, it will be as well, therefore, to give a brief description of what passes for it at the moment in most Colleges and Departments of Education.

Current conceptions of philosophy of education. There are, roughly speaking, three conceptions of philosophy of education which permeate such institutions, in addition to the conception of philosophy of education which will be later developed in this article.'

Peters' claim is misleadingly put, since far from encapsulating even in part some sort of Platonic essence of philosophy of education, *Ethics and Education* is better seen as one view of part of the subject.[30] One consequence of putting the matter as Peters and others do, is that those who read such discussions, perhaps as part of their introduction to philosophy or philosophy of education, might take them as giving the only possible and universally accepted account of what the subject is, and even of what is taken to be reasonably well established in it, rather as a student might take an introductory textbook in physics.[31] Another consequence might be that instead of the subject developing different perspectives and approaches, it develops within an implicit framework derived from Peters.

But disputes about what philosophy of education is might arise not only from disputes about what philosophy is, but from disputes about the relationship of philosophy to education, expressed by the phrase 'of education'. Remarks of Peters suggest that one source of the difference between, for example, D. J. O'Connor's view of philosophy of education and his is this relationship, irrespective of whatever views they hold about philosophy.[32] Further, B. Williams, who notes that a number of

---

(Ftn. 29 cont.)

On p. 84, having outlined his conception of philosophy of education, Peters writes, 'It is one thing to sketch in outline what the philosophy of education is; it is quite another to decide how it should be taught in colleges and departments of education.'

The ambivalence of these passages can be seen by noting how the force of 'ought' – a word which apparently makes it explicit that a value position is being defended – is minimized by the implication of 'passes for' to the effect that three possible rival candidates are not philosophy of education at all. This implication is, however, partly contradicted by the later admission that there are at least four conceptions of philosophy of education and this is contradicted in turn by the claim that in giving his new conception of philosophy of education Peters is outlining 'what the philosophy of education *is*' – Our italics. Notice, too, the force of the word 'permeate'.

[30] It might be argued that one important topic missing from *Ethics and Education* is that of practical reasoning as, for example, discussed by: F. E. Oppenheim, 'Rational choice', *Journal of Philosophy*, Vol. L (1953), pp. 341–50; K. Baier, *The Moral Point of View* (New York: Cornell University Press, 1958), Chapter 2; N. Rescher, 'Practical reasoning and values', *Philosophical Quarterly*, Vol. 16 (1966), pp. 121–36; J. Wheatley, 'Reasons for acting', *Dialogue: Canadian Philosophical Review*, Vol. VII (1969), pp. 553–67; S. Körner, *Fundamental Questions in Philosophy* (Allen Lane, Penguin Press, 1969), Chapter 7. See also G. Reddiford, 'Philosophy of education and the logic of educational theory', *Education for Teaching*, No. 72 (February 1967), pp. 59–67.

[31] T. S. Kuhn, 'The function of dogma in scientific research', in *Scientific Change*, ed. A. C. Crombie (Heinemann Educational Books, 1963), pp. 350–2, has comments on the use of textbooks in science. It seems to us that, both because of the variety of approaches to philosophy and sociology and because of the lack of accredited facts in these areas, textbooks in philosophy and sociology ought not to play a role in any way similar to the role Kuhn implies that science textbooks play. See also T. S. Kuhn, *The Structure of Scientific Revolutions*, (1970) op. cit., Chapter XI.

[32] R. S. Peters, in J. W. Tibble, ed., (1966) op. cit., pp. 66–9. I. Scheffler, in his review of O'Connor's book *An Introduction to the Philosophy of Education*, suggests that O'Connor himself appears to have two quite different conceptions of philosophy of education. See I. Scheffler, *Reason and Teaching* (Routledge & Kegan Paul, 1973), pp. 162–3.

things might be called philosophy of education, gives three different, though not incompatible, characterizations of philosophy of education which are distinguished not by different definitions of philosophy but rather by their relationship to education.[33]

Definitions of philosophy of education might therefore reflect differences about the nature of philosophy, about its relation to education or both. The variety of definition, however, may be merely a symptom of a more fundamental difference. In some cases disputes about the nature of philosophy of education are likely to be normative in rather a different way from, say, disputes about the nature of philosophy of history or of philosophy of religion or of philosophy of science. Some disputes about philosophy of education are likely to be, at least in part, disputes about what of a philosophical nature should be taught to student teachers, qualified teachers on advanced courses, and to others concerned with education. Definitions of philosophy of education might, therefore, be unlike definitions of philosophy of history or of religion or of science, all of which may well not embody any views about what of a philosophical nature should be taught to historians, clergymen, or scientists, prospective or otherwise. Peters' discussion in the Tibble volume can be seen in fact as an attempt to justify the inclusion of philosophy of education, as conceived by him, in the curricula of colleges of education or of departments of education, in preference to the other conceptions he outlines in the article.[34] One difficulty of making anything other than an incomplete and context-free justification is, as we point out later, that the outcomes of teaching philosophy of education (however defined) seem largely unknown.[35]

3. Philosophy and values: an example of variety within a discipline

One way in which the variety within philosophy, and within philosophy of education can be seen is by asking whether philosophy is value free, where what is understood by the question is whether philosophical arguments can be themselves established normative judgements.[36]

---

[33] B. Williams, 'Philosophy and imagination', *The Times Educational Supplement* (28 April 1972), p. 19. See also B. Williams, 'Philosophy', in M. Yudkin, ed., *General Education* (Allen Lane, Penguin Press, 1969), pp. 138–64. Williams has an interesting discussion of what he calls 'pure' and 'impure' philosophy. He also notes on page 158, 'We have to beware of the formula: if you are primarily studying x, then the best philosophy to study with it is the philosophy of x. It does not follow; and, as we have already seen, "the philosophy of x" may itself mean different things.'

[34] R. S. Peters, in J. W. Tibble, ed., (1966) op. cit. This article is usefully read with P. R. Burke and V. A. Howard, 'On turning the philosophy of education outside-in', *British Journal of Educational Studies*, Vol. XVII (1969), pp. 5–15.

[35] See pp. 175–7.

[36] The question about whether disciplines are value free can be given a number of senses. Some of these are indicated by R. W. Friedrich's comments about research in the social sciences. He writes in 'Choice and commitment in social research', in *The Impact of Socio-*

It can be admitted that answers to specific practical problems cannot be given by philosophy alone, if, as we suggested in Volume I, empirical data are necessary. However, it might be held that normative judgements of a general kind can be established by philosophical argument alone. But even this view appears to be ruled out by some of those who regard philosophy as second order, as our quotation from A. R. White shows (page 141). In support of White we may cite Mackie who states that 'there is no sound way of laying down our initial or fundamental value-judgements or prescriptions *a priori* or on general philosophical grounds, and this holds for our basic educational evaluations as for all others.'[37]

Such a view underlies the claim that philosophers as philosophers cannot make value judgements or that philosophers of education as philosophers of education cannot make value judgements. When the latter do make them, they do so apparently as educational theorists.

But is Mackie's view true? It can be made true, as it were, by a conceptual fiat affecting 'value judgement' and 'philosophical'. But nothing substantive is gained by this manoeuvre. What has to be done is to show that there is no defensible account of philosophy which entails that a philosophical statement can be normative. It is certainly not enough to say that philosophy is second order and so non-normative, since, even if being second order did entail being non-normative, such a view of philosophy might simply be one view of the subject in competition with others. There are, for example, philosophers who think that moral philosophy should and therefore can be concerned with first-order normative issues. C. H. Whiteley writes, 'It is time to reverse the process by which the discussion of ethical problems is being extruded from the domain of philosophy and replaced by a study of the grammar of ethical words ... Moral questions can be rationally discussed, and moral philosophers are

---

(Ftn. 36 cont.)

logy, ed. Jack Douglas (New York, Appleton-Century-Crofts, 1970), p. 89. 'We simply are unable to move through the research task without unavoidably, both in principle and in practice, making choices and taking actions which contravene an ethos of "neutrality". The decisions we make regarding problem selection, the appropriation of conceptual tools and their accompanying grammars and logics, the risking of hypotheses, the approximation of control, the impact of observation, the level of error admissible, the impact of prediction on future behaviour, selectivity in communication, and the attitude we take regarding the application of findings – all either demand or imply a value commitment that transcends the empirically given.' See also E. Nagel, *The Structure of Science* (Routledge & Kegan Paul, 1961), pp. 485–502.

[37] J. L. Mackie, 'Can there be a philosophy of education', *Forum of Education*, Vol. 23 (1964), p. 41. Cf. E. Nagel in Volume II, p. 14 who says 'philosophers *qua* philosophers are not in a privileged position to make warranted pronouncements about human nature and the proper goals of human effort.' Cf. K. Thompson, 'Philosophy of education and educational practice', *Proceedings of the Philosophy of Education Society of Great Britain*, Vol. IV, Annual Conference, January 1970, pp. 45–60. See particularly pp. 45 and 46. See also P. King, 'An ideological fallacy', in P. King and B. C. Parekh, eds., *Politics and Experience* op. cit., particularly page 385 onwards.

the right people to do it.'[38] Gewirth argues for the return of the moral philosopher 'to his traditional role of clarifying and criticising men's moral ideals within the context of on-going moral practices and institutions' and for 'the reinstatement of philosophical ethics as a normative discipline'.[39]

There are in any case those who would subscribe to the view that philosophy is second order and who, at the same time, attempt to establish normative views by arguments that are not unreasonably called philosophical. R. F. Dearden produces two arguments to justify 'as a basic or minimal ideal' that of 'personal autonomy based on reason'.[40] This ideal is held to give rise to a number of educational aims. One of Dearden's arguments in particular is, in our view, philosophical. It is not the sort of argument that is likely to be found outside philosophical books or discussions. Another example is provided by R. S. Peters' discussion of worth-while activities.[41] Here Peters attempts to show both that some

[38] C. H. Whiteley, 'Rationality in morals', *Proceedings of the Aristotelian Society*, Vol. L (1949), p. 14. (See also Vol. I for Hampshire's views.)

[39] A. Gewirth, 'Positive ethics and normative science', *Philosophical Review*, Vol. 69 (1960), p. 330. The whole of this article together with A. Gewirth, op. cit., *Mind*, Vol. 69 (1960), is relevant here.

[40] R. F. Dearden, *The Philosophy of Primary Education* (Routledge & Kegan Paul, 1968), pp. 46–9. For a similar argument see P. W. Taylor, *Normative Discourse* (New Jersey: Prentice-Hall, 1961), pp. 175–88. For Dearden's view of philosophy as a second-order activity see R. F. Dearden, in J. W. Tibble, ed., (1971) op. cit., p. 85.

[41] R. S. Peters, *Ethics and Education* (Allen & Unwin, 1966), Chapter 5. Peters writes (p. 17) that 'What is distinctive of ethics as a branch of philosophy is that it is concerned with the analysis and justification of answers to practical questions where "practical" is contrasted with "theoretical".' In *Social Principles and the Democratic State* (Allen & Unwin, 1959), S. I. Benn and R. S. Peters are admittedly defending a normative position, that of 'a cautious Utilitarianism which takes full account of the principle of impartiality' (p. 5). The book is described as a book on 'social philosophy'. In 'Philosophy and education', *Proceedings of the International Seminar, March 23–25, 1966* (Ontario Institute for Studies in Education, Monograph Series No. 3, 1967), pp. 15–16, Peters writes:
'I think that it is possible to produce arguments to show both why some sorts of pursuits are more worth while than others and why some principles rather than others are justifiable in dealing with children. In other words, I think it possible for a philosopher of education to produce some kind of ethical foundations for education, the guiding lines for which are provided by the above analysis of "aims of education". But what I think a philosopher cannot do, *qua* philosopher, is to pronounce on the relative weight to be attached to such principles, to proclaim that, for example, literature is more important than science, or that a principle of options in a curriculum should be stressed rather than "wholeness", which might involve a greater element of compulsion. The justification of principles is one thing; their application in concrete circumstances is another. It is one thing to give arguments for general aims; it is quite another to say which particular one should be emphasized in contingent circumstances. Philosophy has an important contribution to make to practical wisdom; but it is no substitute for it.'
These quotations are usefully compared with Peters' claim in *Ethics and Education* (p. 7) that to expect philosophy 'to provide answers to substantive questions, is to fail to understand what sort of inquiry philosophy is and the part it can play as a contributory element in educational theory.' It seems misleading to imply, as these last quotations do, that the

things are worth while and others not, and that some are more worth while than others. The arguments employed seem to be philosophical. To establish such views about what is worth while is to establish a normative position and one which, given Peters' account of 'education', logically commits him to normative judgements of a general kind about educational practice. For these two instances however to constitute conclusive examples against a view of philosophy such as Mackie's, the following three things need to be established, independently of each other: (*i*) that the conclusions are in fact normative; (*ii*) that the arguments offered in support of the conclusions can be reasonably called philosophical; and (*iii*) that the arguments are cogent. It is not open to anyone to deny that the arguments can be philosophical, on the grounds that the conclusions are normative, even if he admits that the arguments are cogent, in that the incompatibility of the predicates 'philosophical' and 'normative' is the very point at issue. We are not concerned here, however, to argue the point one way or the other. We merely suggest that there are conceptions of philosophy as a normative discipline,[42] that they may be explicitly acknowledged or merely be implicit in philosophical work, and that there is also a conception of philosophy as value free. There is, that is to say, variety within the discipline.

(Ftn. 41 cont.)

issue about what is worth while or more worth while is not a substantive issue. Also compare this additional quotation from J. L. Mackie, op. cit., p. 40, who writes, 'Philosophy is popularly regarded as being especially concerned with evaluation, with ends or goals, and so Philosophy of Education is thought of as a subject which studies and determines, in some abstract and *a priori* way, what is right or good or valuable in education, which lays down aims which education should pursue or standards by which educational policies should be judged. But there is, and can be, no such subject. There is no way in which philosophy, or any other genuine study, can determine *a priori* what ends should be pursued or what achievement or activities are to be valued more highly than others.'

It might be argued that it is not easy to see how philosophy could be value free, in so far as it is concerned with issues of justification. If this is true, then it would seem that the theses that philosophers as philosophers cannot make value judgements, and that when philosophers of education make value judgements they do so not as philosophers of education but as educational theorists, cannot be maintained. The last two roles might not be mutually exclusive. Value judgements might be made in either capacity. Further, the notion of 'second order' seems now to be ambiguous as between (*i*) where it entails being value free, as A. R. White uses it; and (*ii*) where it does not – and this appears to be the sense that Peters' discussions of philosophy requires. One useful task would be to look in detail at some of the vocabulary used to explain and justify the distinction between doing philosophy and making value judgements. A. Gewirth, op. cit., *Mind,* Vol. LXIX, (1960), pp. 187–8 lists some of it.

[42] It might well be argued that both Peters and Dearden offer what Frankena calls a 'normative philosophy of education'. See W. K. Frankena, *Three Historical Philosophies of Education* (Glenview, Illinois: Scott, Foresman, 1965), Chapter 1; W. K. Frankena, *Philosophy of Education* (New York: Macmillan, 1965), pp. 1–10; W. K. Frankena, 'Philosophical inquiry', in J. I. Goodlad, ed., *The Changing American School,* NSEE 65th Year Book, Part II (Chicago University Press, 1966) pp. 243–65; W. K. Frankena, 'A model for analysing a philosophy of education', in J. R. Martin, ed., *Readings in Philosophy of Education: a Study of Curriculum* (Boston: Allyn & Bacon, 1970), pp. 15–22.

If this is true, then 'doing philosophy' might mean different things to different people and more particularly it might be understood sometimes as entailing 'able to make value judgements' and sometimes as entailing 'not able to make value judgements'. If this is not understood, some philosophers might be asked, in their professional capacity, for advice of a kind which they feel they cannot give, and part of the contribution of others might consist of value judgements, and these be not recognized for what they are. But whether or not we agree with King who suggests (though 'tentatively') that 'as a matter of fact and as a matter of appropriateness, normative discussion insinuates itself both into scientific and philosophical discourse',[43] it is important, as he goes on to say, 'to be clear about when we are recommending and when we are explaining (or at least that we try to be clear).'[44] The question about whether philosophy is value free is not simply a verbal one on which little turns, as some might be tempted to argue, but has implications for the way the role of philosophy is understood in education and elsewhere.[45]

4. Some reasons for the existence of different definitions of philosophy and sociology

We have suggested there might be a number of plausible and competing accounts of philosophy and sociology. Here we indicate some of the considerations that might lead individuals to adopt one or other of them.[46] We discuss philosophy mainly, but similar points may well apply to sociology. We pick out, in particular, three sorts of consideration, which in practice are likely to be closely interrelated: (i) individuals' views about what is worth doing; (ii) individuals' philosophical and sociological views; (iii) institutional factors.

(i) Some philosophers may hold, as a matter of definition, that philosophy is entirely concerned with discovering some class of truths whose

---

[43] P. King, in King and Parekh, eds., op. cit., p. 388. A comment of S. Körner is relevant here. In his book, *Fundamental Questions in Philosophy* (Allen Lane, Penguin Press, 1969), p. 2, he writes 'Sharp demarcation lines may also lead to barren demarcation disputes and to the impression that it is less important to solve a problem than to decide to which theoretical discipline it belongs.'

[44] P. King, in King and Parekh eds,. op. cit. p. 388.

[45] Cf. K. Nielsen, in K. Nielsen, op. cit. (1971), p. 3, who writes that he is concerned 'to characterise philosophy so that "consumers" of philosophy may have a clearer idea of what they may *legitimately* expect from philosophy and what they may find there that is of value.'

[46] It should be noted, here and elsewhere, that while we use some perspectives from the sociology of knowledge and from epistemology, we do not in any sense adequately cover the enormous range of philosophical and sociological problems which cohabit in that area. We attempt to explore some of these, as they relate to education, in Anthony Hartnett and Michael Naish, eds., *Knowledge, Ideology, and Educational Practice* (in preparation).

discovery is important.[47] They may deny that certain questions, methods, or approaches are philosophical at all, on the grounds that the answers to such questions are unimportant and that the methods and approaches allow only trivial conclusions to be established. The unqualified equation of philosophy with conceptual analysis of one sort or another might be ruled out on the grounds that some of the results of such analysis are trivial and unimportant.[48] If such analysis is defended on the grounds that it leads to clarity, then it might be claimed with Passmore that 'to insist upon clarity at the outset, a clarity independent of the needs of a particular enquiry, is in the pejorative sense of that phrase the essence of scholasticism', and that scholasticism is not philosophy.[49] What is important to discover and establish is a normative matter, and what individuals' normative views are might well affect the account they give of philosophy. Persuasive definitions of philosophy will almost certainly embody views about what is important and worth doing.

(ii) O'Connor, discussing what he calls 'maps of the universe' offered by philosophers such as Aquinas and Spinoza, says that 'At the present day, philosophers would state their aims very much more modestly though, naturally enough, a philosopher's view of the scope of his discipline will depend on his own philosophical opinions.'[50] An example of this is Ayer's extrusion (in 1936) of metaphysics from philosophy, which depended on an assumption that philosophy was a 'genuine branch of knowledge', and on philosophical views about the nature of meaning and of metaphysical statements.[51] So, too, today the extrusion by some of

---

[47] They will argue, to use Ayer's words, that philosophy is by definition a 'worth-while cognitive discipline'. See A. J. Ayer in J. Bobick, ed., op. cit., p. 103. He notes here that this assumption is not shared by all contemporary philosophers. If, with Danto, 'What is philosophy?' is taken to be a philosophical question, considerations under (i) are a special class of considerations under (ii) and they could be subsumed there.

[48] Cf. P. H. Hirst and R. S. Peters, The Logic of Education, op. cit., p. 9, who suggest that conceptual analysis is likely to be pointless, 'unless some further philosophical issue is thereby made more manageable.'

[49] J. A. Passmore, 'Towards an analytical philosophy of education', Melbourne Studies in Education (Carlton, Victoria: Melbourne University Press, 1966), p. 64. A. J. Ayer, in Ayer, ed., op. cit., p. 9, suggests that the charge of scholasticism brought against 'Oxford philosophy' is 'not entirely baseless'. He also suggests that some of the work there carries 'interest in ordinary use of language to a point where it might be thought that philosophical analysis has given way to the study of philology.'

[50] D. J. O'Connor, An Introduction to the Philosophy of Education (Routledge & Kegan Paul, 1957), pp. 16–17.

[51] A. J. Ayer, Language Truth and Logic, (2nd edn, Gollancz, 1946), p. 41. Remarks of A. Quinton suggest that in some cases it was not only philosophical argument that made people reject metaphysics and espouse analysis. In 'Linguistic analysis', in R. Klibansky, ed., Philosophy in the Mid-Century, Vol. II, Metaphysics and Analysis, International Institute of Philosophy (Firenze: La Nuova Italia Editrice, 1958), Quinton writes that 'Temperament is as important as argument in bringing about the rejection of metaphysics, and analytic philosophy was eagerly supported by those who were emotionally repelled by the loose, subjective and self-indulgent qualities of much metaphysical speculation' (p. 149).

moral judgements from moral philosophy might be defended, at least in part, by an appeal to a distinction between conceptual issues, and substantive and evaluatory ones, where the existence of the distinction and its nature is held to be a philosophical issue.[52]

In social science, views which might be said to fall within the area of 'theory and methods of sociology'[53] may well affect social scientists' views of what are appropriate methods and modes of explanation within their area of investigation, and in consequence affect their conception of their discipline.

(*iii*) We suggest here that institutional factors are likely to have a strong bearing on what subjects are taken to be. Bourdieu comments on the interaction between institutional contexts, and the way disciplines are seen by individuals. He draws attention to the link between the content of an area of knowledge and the manner used to impart it and suggests that what distinguishes graduates from different universities and departments is 'quite as much as the nature of the knowledge they have acquired, the way in which that knowledge has been acquired, i.e., the nature of the exercises they have had to do, of the examinations they have taken, the criteria by which they have been judged and by reference to which they have organised their studies ... all teaching practices implicitly furnish a model of the "right" mode of intellectual activity.'[54] Hudson

[52] See our discussion on page 141.

[53] We take this phrase from B. Williams, in M. Yudkin, ed., op. cit., p. 153, who suggests that 'for a number of issues, it would be arbitrary whether they were regarded as belonging to "Theory and Methods of Sociology" or to the "philosophy of sociology". For a discussion of the relationship of philosophy to sociology see A. MacIntyre, 'Rationality and the explanation of action', in A. MacIntyre, *Against the Self-images of the Age* (Duckworth, 1971), pp. 244–59. For philosophy of sociology in general see P. Winch, *The idea of a Social Science*, op. cit.; P. Winch, 'Social science', *British Journal of Sociology* (1956), pp. 18–33; A. R. Louch, 'The very idea of a social science', *Inquiry*, Vol. 6 (1963), pp. 273–86; P. Winch, 'Mr. Louch's idea of a social science', *Inquiry*, Vol. 7 (1964), pp. 202–8; A. R. Louch, 'On misunderstanding Mr Winch', *Inquiry*, Vol. 8 (1965), pp. 212–16; A. R. Louch, *Explanation and Human Action* (Blackwell, 1966); R. Rudner, *Philosophy of Social Science* (New Jersey: Prentice Hall, 1966); A. J. Ayer, 'Man as a subject for science', reprinted in P. Laslett and W. G. Runciman, eds., *Philosophy, Politics and Society*, Third Series (Blackwell, 1967); A. MacIntyre and D. R. Bell, 'The idea of a social science', *Proceedings of the Aristotelian Society*, Supplementary Volume XLI (1967), pp. 95–132; D. Milligan, 'Philosophy and the social sciences', *Proceedings of the Aristotelian Society*, Vol. LXIX (1968–69), pp. 51–72; A Ryan, *The Philosophy of the Social Sciences* (Macmillan, 1970); D. Emmet and A. MacIntyre, eds., *Sociological Theory and Philosophical Analysis* (Macmillan, 1970); C. Bryant, 'In defence of sociology; a reply to some contemporary philosophical criticisms', *British Journal of Sociology*, Vol. 21 (1970), pp. 95–106; D. Jary and J. Phillips, 'The philosophical critique of a scientific sociology: some remarks on Bryant's defence', *British Journal of Sociology*, Vol. 22 (1971), pp. 183–92. For a philosophical discussion of a specific sociological methodology see M. Black, 'Some questions about Parsons' theories', in M. Black, ed., *The Social Theories of Talcott Parsons* (New Jersey: Prentice Hall, 1961), pp. 268–89.

[54] P. Bourdieu, 'Systems of education and systems of thought', *International Social Science Journal*, Vol. XIX, No. 3 (1967), p. 350. The entire article is relevant to our discussion.

makes a similar point when he says that his suspicion 'is that every generation of students is susceptible to its teachers' presuppositions, and that
these presuppositions are potent just to the extent that they are unspoken.
It is assumptions, prejudices and implicit metaphors that are the true burden of what passes between teacher and taught. Facts, skills, details are in
comparison ephemeral, in the sciences especially, but in the arts as well.
They are also identifiable – and rejectable. What the teacher spells out, the
pupil can question. What he assumes, especially from a position of unchal-
lenged legitimacy, his pupils will tend to swallow whole and unawares.'[55]

The greater the variety in the factors that Bourdieu and Hudson mention, the more likely are there to be different and competing accounts
of what a subject is.[56] For example, if there are considerable differences
in degrees which claim to be 'sociological' or 'psychological' in different
universities (compared with, say, courses in physics) then there is likely
to be greater dispute among sociologists and psychologists about the
nature of their discipline.[57]

The following factors may also influence what a subject is taken to be:
the various organizations which make up higher education, in particular,
universities and polytechnics; professional associations, such as the
British Sociological Association; the editorial boards of professional
journals; introductory textbooks, and readers for publishing houses;
higher degree committees and external examiners; selection committees
for university chairs. These factors may result in a number of 'academic
communities',[58] with related career opportunities for those who are
members, or who are invited to become members, of such communities.
For example 'the sociology of education' or 'the philosophy of education'
in the UK at the present time, might be considered as academic communities. Within each community there might be a number of sub-com-
munities which interlock, co-operate, or are in conflict with each other.[59]

[55] Liam Hudson, *The Cult of the Fact* (Jonathan Cape, 1972), p. 43. Cf. Hudson's comment
on page 93 that 'in any educational establishment worthy of the name, malleable youth is
coerced to think in ways of which their teachers approve.'
[56] The criteria by which *individual* students select and choose from what is offered
in any particular organizational context, is a social-psychological question of considerable
importance and difficulty.
[57] For a classic sociological approach to the boundaries of knowledge see B. Bernstein,
'On the classification and framing of educational knowledge', in B. Bernstein, *Class,
Codes, and Control*, op. cit. See also review by M. Douglas, 'Speech, class and Basil
Bernstein', *Listener* (9 March 1972), pp. 312–13.
[58] The term 'community' is taken from Michael W. Apple, 'Community, knowledge,
and the structure of disciplines', *The Educational Forum*, Vol. XXXVII, No. 1 (November
1972), pp. 75–82. Note the comment on page 81, 'Within and among disciplines, as our
lenses differ, so too do the phenomena.' See also M. D. Shipman, *The Limitations of Social
Research* (Longmans, 1972), especially pp. 160–2, and the footnotes to these pages.
[59] It is a matter of empirical inquiry to establish: how many subcommunities exist (if any)
in the philosophy or sociology of education in the UK; how such communities relate to
each other; and the sort of career mobility membership of one (or more) of these communities carries. As Apple, op. cit., points out (p. 79) the social structure of disciplines
may play a critical role in maintaining and distributing knowledge.

One area that might be examined, as an example, is the editorship of professional journals. Jackson,[60] referring to educational psychology, suggests that the beliefs of editors can have a determining effect on the definition of the field. He argues that the style, structure, and procedures used may also be laid down. He writes, 'These implicit admonitions do more than define the format of a successful article – i.e., one that is accepted for publication – they also indirectly sanction a particular style of working and thinking about problems in educational psychology. Not only is the non-quantifiable left out in the cold, but form overpowers content, and technique is left to rule the roost. The result is a plethora of technically adequate but trivial exercises, lacking in cumulative significance, and unconnected, except by the wildest stretch of imagination, to the concerns of the practitioner. A sure way of arousing laughter from an audience of teachers is to say, "Here are the problems that keep educational psychologists awake at night", and then read aloud from the table of contents of any recent issue of an educational research journal.'

These points about institutional factors are likely to apply no less to philosophy and philosophy of education. Two points about philosophy of education illustrate this. Firstly, there are grounds for thinking that philosophy of education is to some extent isolated from mainstream philosophy (even though one prevalent account of philosophy of education depends on an account of the main discipline). For philosophers of education tend to be appointed to education departments whereas all other kinds of philosophers, at least in universities, will be appointed almost always to philosophy departments.[61] Further, though philosophers pure have contributed to journals and collections of articles in philosophy of education, comparatively little work in philosophy of education by philosophers of education has been published in, say, *Mind*, *Philosophical Quarterly, Philosophy, Proceedings of the Aristotelian Society, Analysis* and so on, though the philosophical range of the journals is

---

[60] P. W. Jackson, 'Stalking beasts and swatting flies', in J. Herbert and D. Ausubel, eds, *Psychology in Teacher Preparation*, Monograph Series No. 5, (Ontario Institute for Studies in Education, 1969), p. 68. Cf. also W. H. Walsh, 'Knowledge in its social setting', *Mind*, Vol. LXXX (1971), p. 329, who writes, 'There is a variety of ways of doing literary criticism or of philosophising, a circumstance which finds its most extreme expression in countries where every literary and philosophical coterie has its own journal in which it prints only work which meets with the approval of its own members.' Hudson, op. cit., makes interesting comments on this area. 'Students who wish to question the prevailing orthodoxy tend in practice to receive poor degrees. And those who get good degrees, but still wish to question, are edged – indeed move of their own volition – towards peripheral positions in their profession' (p. 101). 'Both department and examiner . . . can ensure that a radical challenge to their conception of the subject is unlikely to occur from within it. The persuasive, and if necessary the coercive, resources of such university teachers are formidable' (p. 102).

[61] Not that working in the same department, or university, guarantees knowledge of others' work. See G. Ryle's comments on his comparative ignorance of J. L. Austin's ideas, before these were published posthumously, in *Ryle: a Collection of Critical Essays* ed., O. P. Wood and G. Pitcher (Macmillan, 1971), paperback edn, p. 14.

fairly wide.[62] A second, and equally important point, is that in some cases the audiences of philosophy and philosophy of education are likely to differ. S. Cavell in a discussion of analytical philosophy and existentialism states, 'For the analyst, philosophy has become a profession, its problems technical; a non-professional audience is of no more relevance to him than it is to the scientist.'[63] Yet for some philosophers of education, the intended audience for their work might be not merely (and not even primarily in some cases) professional philosophers or philosophers of education, but student teachers, qualified teachers, administrators and so on. The dilemma this gives rise to can be seen in some remarks of Peters[64] in a paper he gave in 1966. He writes, 'The conditions under which my paper was read and discussed were scarcely ideal from the point of view of the philosopher. To start with, it was the opening paper of the International Seminar, which had to be addressed to the general public and not simply to members of the Seminar. It had, therefore, to be a talk fit for philosopher kings and yet one that preserved the common touch. This, by the way, is the usual predicament of anyone working in the philosophy of education. If he gets too technical, he loses touch with most teachers, whose activities he is trying to clarify, criticize, or justify. If, on the other hand, he succeeds in communicating with teachers, he is

---

[62] The American journal, *Journal of Philosophy*, publishes work in philosophy of education. We limit our remarks here to the UK though to judge from some of the work in philosophy of education published in the USA, there is a case for suspecting that philosophy of education as practised by some philosophers there is by no means closely in touch with the main discipline. R. D. Archambault, in *Philosophical Analysis and Education*, ed. Archambault (Routledge & Kegan Paul, 1965), states that 'interest in education by competent non-educationist philosophers has been relatively sparse.' This localization may perhaps be surprising in the light of the claim that there are no problems in philosophy of education that are *sui generis* unlike, say, those of the philosophy of science, which as a consequence are likely to be discussed in specialized philosophy of science journals. The localization may perhaps be evidence that some philosophers do regard at least some of the problems in philosophy of education as *sui generis*, or perhaps as not philosophical problems at all. D. W. Hamlyn, for example, in his review (*Philosophy*, Vol. 41 (1966), pp. 283–5) of the Archambault collection suggests that L. R. Perry's paper 'What is an educational situation?' is not genuinely philosophical. To deny that a paper is philosophical seems to us to say nothing about its value. See also R. F. Atkinson's comments in the Archambault volume (p. 171) – 'There is too little communication between academic moral philosophy and the philosophy of education. They are separate countries, and a citizen of the one finds himself an alien in the other. The language change is confusing, and it is hard to feel altogether confident of one's judgement of what is and is not worth saying when one has crossed the frontier. So, at any rate, it has come to seem to me.' The comparative localization of issues in philosophy of education can be seen to some extent from the fact that Peters' discussion of worth-while activities seems, in spite of its general importance, to have had very little discussion in other than journals in philosophy of education by philosophers of education.

[63] S. Cavell, 'Existentialism and analytical philosophy', *Daedalos* (Summer 1964), p. 947.

[64] R. S. Peters, op. cit., (Ontario; 1967), p. 24.

in danger of being criticized by philosophers for being too crude or superficial, even though they may pay him a back-handed compliment by remarking that what he says is wise!'

The dilemma is discussed again in *Ethics and Education* where Peters answers a possible criticism from philosophers to the effect that his views are not argued in sufficient detail. He states that 'the treatment of philosophical issues is simplified' but not, he hopes, 'superficial'. He goes on to say that his views can be and in some cases have been 'defended elsewhere in more detail in publications designed exclusively for students of philosophy.'[65]

Both these points may have a bearing on the accounts given of philosophy of education. The first might mean that accounts of philosophy of education might not reflect the complexity of the issues concerning the nature of philosophy and that there might be, as a matter of empirical fact, fewer competing accounts of philosophy of education than there are of philosophy.[66] The second point may mean that some philosophers of education might see themselves, in part, as simplifiers and interpreters of current philosophy to teachers and administrators and so on.[67] Consequently, because of a demand that philosophy of education should be practically relevant (perhaps in a very restricted sense) and intelligible to non-specialists, on one conception[68] it might be at least partially distinguished from say, philosophy of religion, or of history, or of science by a criterion of a kind unlikely to be used in distinguishing these or other areas of philosophy from each other.

The status of knowledge claims in philosophy and sociology

Those who intend to use statements and theories from social science, philosophy, and other disciplines to justify solutions to practical pro-

[65] R. S. Peters, op. cit. (1966), p. 7.

[66] The isolation may also affect views about what is and is not securely established in philosophy. See the coming discussion, pp. 157–64.

[67] See the discussion of 'link-men' on pp. 164–7, though the audience of these are policy makers. It is an open question whether many philosophers of education would admit to such a conception of philosophy of education. But it might be argued that there is such a conception, in practice. To what extent does some current philosophy of education reflect the complexity and uncertainty of much current philosophy? Who, for example, after reading recent philosophy of education would discover that the whole issue of ethical and non-ethical naturalism is at present hotly disputed? K. R. Minogue, op. cit., Chapter 4, is particularly relevant here.

[68] Given this conception, a distinction could be made between educational philosophy and philosophy of education roughly analogous to the one noted by McNamara (page 118 of this book) between educational sociology and the sociology of education.

blems in education need to consider how far claims made in the disciplines can be taken to be securely established.[69]

In discussing what could count as securely established E. Nagel writes, 'I would say that it is one of the marks of having a securely established proposition in any of the positive sciences that you have a consensus among those who have acquired an obvious competence in handling that kind of material. And that as long as there are divergences in any area of positive sciences about some proposition, then it seems to me you have to say, well, we have to suspend judgement.'[70] W. H. Walsh attempts to establish a similar but more general claim, and writes, 'My object in this paper is to point out a feature of the situation in which knowledge is pursued which in my opinion has not been sufficiently stressed in previous accounts. I refer to the social context in which claims to knowledge are advanced and accepted, and I wish to argue that so far from being irrelevant to the question whether such claims succeed, it is vital to their correct adjudication.'[71] The thesis he defends is 'that claims to knowledge are presented within a social framework and have to win a certain kind of public approval to succeed'.[72] and he discusses the role of recognized experts and professional journals in the adjudication of such claims.[73] Neither Nagel's nor Walsh's remarks commit them to the view that mere consensus is sufficient for saying that a claim is securely established.[74] The consensus has to be among those who are competent[75] to assess the claim and the force of the objections and counter objections to it, and who have done so in an unbiased and unprejudiced way. The consensus must be a result of assessing the claim on its merits.

Now, if the accounts of Nagel and Walsh are accepted for philosophy, there is at least a *prima facie* case for the truth of Ayer's claim about the lack of accredited facts in philosophy[76] – though to establish it fully

---

[69] Our discussion of the remaining issues raised in this part of the book can be very usefully read in conjunction with M. D. Shipman, *The Limitations of Social Research*, (Longman, 1972).

[70] E. Nagel, 'Philosophy of science and educational theory', (1969) op. cit., p. 18.

[71] W. H. Walsh, op. cit. (1971), p. 321.

[72] W. H. Walsh, op. cit. (1971), p. 326.

[73] Ibid., pp. 328–30.

[74] Cf. A. G. N. Flew, *An Introduction to Western Philosophy* (Thames & Hudson, 1971), pp. 18–23.

[75] Two important difficulties are what this term means and how the competent are to be identified.

[76] A. J. Ayer, op. cit. (1970), p. 102. Cf. G. Langford, *Philosophy and Education* (Macmillan, 1968), p. 126, who also claims that in philosophy there is 'very little which does count as established knowledge'. We are not advocating here an *a priori* scepticism about philosophical statements. Such scepticism usually manifests itself in a denial that there can be progress in philosophy or in the sort of definition of 'philosophical question' implied, for example, by the following comments of K. Thompson, in *Education and Philosophy: a Practical Approach* (Blackwell, 1972): 'It must be noted that it is, in a peculiar sense, un-

would be a lengthy task. Walsh offers support for a view similar to that of Ayer. He draws attention to the 'plurality of warring authorities'[77] in philosophy and goes on to say, 'What Hume said at the beginning of the *Treatise* about the endless disputes and disorder within the portals of philosophy is still taken, rightly, as damning criticism, though the situation is not quite as Hume described it, for philosophers tend to cling together in sets, and inside these a certain sort of order prevails, an order which is by no means incompatible with healthy controversy. That philosophers band together in this way is evidence of their desire for scientific respectability; that there are many such groups, evidence of their failure to achieve their aim.'[78]

There are then grounds for thinking that there is much in philosophy that is still disputed and little that can count as securely established. At any given time, there is likely to be little consensus of the required sort but rather a number of different views both about the nature of the philosophical issues and of the solutions to them, and these views will be advocated and defended against each other. As a consequence, it is likely in many cases to be a mistake to look to philosophy and philosophers as sources of knowledge that can be applied in solving educational problems, practical or otherwise.

(Ftn. 76 cont.)
fair to complain that philosophy does not give firm and unequivocal answers. This is because if a firm and unequivocal answer can be given to a question then, *ipso facto*, it is not a philosophical question' (p. 17). This statement gives rise to a number of questions. (*i*) In so far as Thompson's book is philosophical, what is the point of reading it since on his account it can neither contain any philosophical knowledge nor even be a means to acquiring any? (*ii*) What is the point, on Thompson's account, of teaching philosophy to student and experienced teachers? It cannot even be to demonstrate the truth of his (unargued) view of a philosophical question since, in so far as it is a philosophical view, its truth cannot in principle be known. Thompson's view which, in Ayer's words (see page 152 footnote 47 implies that philosophy is not 'a worth-while cognitive discipline' is, even so, one shared by some contemporary philosophers. An opposing view is expressed by S. Hampshire in 'The progress of philosophy', *Polemic*, No. 5 (1946), pp. 22–32. He argues (p. 24) 'that there are philosophical conclusions which we know to be true, and which were not known to philosophers of earlier periods; and that there are many propositions believed by the most respected philosophers in the past which we now know to be false or meaningless.' See also the reference in Flew's discussion given in footnote 74, page 158, and J. L. Mackie, op. cit. (1964), p. 42.

[77] W. H. Walsh, op. cit. (1971), p. 330.

[78] Ibid. See also W. B. Gallie, *Philosophy and the Historical Understanding* (Chatto & Windus, 1964), Chapter 7, and J. F. Bannan, 'The philosopher and his peers – community and freedom', *Metaphilosophy*, Vol. 2 (1971), pp. 316–30. Whether it would be true to say that there are different schools of philosophy or sociology as Nagel (p. 19) implies there are of psychology – though not of physics – will depend on the criteria by which schools are to be identified and distinguished. Nevertheless, just as the existence of different schools of psychology may make it more difficult to say that something is securely established in that field, so too might the existence of different approaches to or perspectives on sociology and philosophy. Disputes within and without disciplines about

Similar issues arise about the status of the knowledge claims made in social science. Dahrendorf makes the general point when he states, 'Critics of an empirical science of sociology often describe it as a gigantic body of applicable social knowledge that is available to any interested party. It is more rarely asked whether this empirical science of sociology even exists.' He goes on to say that sociology is 'still largely at the program stage, a matter of prospective knowledge'.[79] Hudson raises similar questions about psychology when he argues that 'it is a subject, or series of subjects, in which one research fashion succeeds another, leaving surprisingly little behind it as a residue of re-usable knowledge. In this respect, even the most experimental forms of psychology resemble much more closely an art form, modern painting for instance, than they do an established science.'[80] Bernstein makes the same sort of comment about the sociology of education. He states, 'In a subject where theories and methods are weak, intellectual shifts are likely to arise out of conflict between *approaches* rather than conflict between explanations, for by definition most explanations will be weak and often non-comparable, because they are approach-specific. The weakness of the explanation is likely to be attributed to the approach, which is analysed in terms of its

(Ftn. 78 cont.)
what is or is not securely established may have important consèquences for careers. See M. Polanyi, 'The potential theory of adsorption', reprinted in M. Grene, ed., *Knowing and Being* (Routledge & Kegan Paul, 1969), pp. 87–96. See for example Polanyi's comments on pages 89 and 93–4. He also notes on page 94 how such disputes place constraints on what can be examined. C. W. K. Mundle, 'Examining in philosophy', *Universities Quarterly*, Vol 22 (1967–8), pp. 302–6, implies that such disputes may affect grades given to examination papers in philosophy. What effect would an expressed and even tentative adherence to Ausubel's views on discovery methods, and Sullivan's on Piaget, have in an interview for a post in certain sorts of primary school? For references see Volume II, p. 76.

[79] Dahrendorf in 'The impact of sociology', op. cit., pp. 163–4 and 170.
[80] L. Hudson, 'The cult of the fact', op. cit., p. 55. Note also his statement (p. 111) about academic psychology – 'it has failed to produce a coherent body of scientific law; and its fruits, unmistakably, have about them an air of triviality . . . There is little that we have produced in the last 50 years that is, in any sense of that complex word, "relevant": the eleven-plus examination, behaviour therapy, motivational research for advertising, automatic landing devices for aircraft – the list is short, and, to say that least, ideologically fragile.' See also E. Nagel, op. cit. (1961), pp. 447–50 and A. J. Ayer, 'Man as a subject for science', in P. Laslett and W. G. Runciman, eds., op. cit. (1967), pp. 6–24. Note also the comments of Jackson when he asks what would happen if the knowledge on which educational psychology is based, 'were suddenly eliminated from the minds and books in which it is contained. How far back toward a caveman status would such a catastrophe push us? I hate to admit it, but I doubt that we would have lost much ground as humans or that the state of teaching would suffer terribly in the wake of ignorance that followed.' Jackson, 'Stalking beasts and swatting flies', op. cit., p. 70. Similar questions might usefully be asked about sociology, philosophy, and teacher training. For other approaches see H.S.N. McFarland, *Psychological Theory and Educational Practice* (Routledge & Kegan Paul, 1971). See especially pages 1–30 and 298–302. See also E. Stones, 'Educational Objectives and the Teaching of Educational Psychology', op. cit.

ideological stance. Once the ideological stance is exposed, then all the work may be written off. Every new approach becomes a social movement or sect which immediately defines the nature of the subject by redefining what is to be admitted, and what is beyond the pale, so that with every new approach the subject almost starts from scratch ... What may be talked about and how it is to be talked about has changed ... A power struggle develops over the need to institutionalize the new approach by obtaining control over the means of transmission and evaluation.'[81]

The issues implicit in these quotations include:

(*i*) The validity of the views expressed, and how far they are representative of general opinion within the disciplines from which they are taken.

(*ii*) The special complexity of the phenomena which social science has to attempt to explain.

(*iii*) The relevance of the procedures and techniques of quantification (as seen in the physical sciences) to such phenomena.[82] This may be particularly important for aspects of educational psychology and sociology, where a simplified notion of scientific method may determine the choice of problems, the methods of investigation, and the view of what is to be taken to be securely established knowledge.

(*iv*) The relationship between ideology and social science (and philosophy).[83] This may be especially important in education because of

[81] Bernstein, pp. 105–6 of Unit 17 of the Open University Course E. 282, op. cit. Noam Chomsky makes similar points in 'Psychology and ideology', *Cognition*, Vol. I, No. 1 (1972) pp. 11–46. 'At the moment, we have virtually no scientific evidence and not the germs of an interesting hypothesis as to how human behavior is determined. Consequently, we can only express our hopes and guesses as to what some future science may demonstrate' (p. 14). 'A person who claims that he has a behavioral technology that will solve the world's problems and a science of behavior that supports it and reveals the factors that determine human behavior is required to demonstrate nothing. *One waits in vain for psychologists to make clear to the general public the actual limits of what is known.* (p. 46). Our italics. Merton's distinction between frivolous and specified ignorance is germane here. See R. Merton, 'The precarious foundations of detachment in sociology', in Tiryakian, ed., op. cit., p. 191. Ignorance is frivolous where a person pretends 'to have knowledge where it is in fact absent'. Specified ignorance 'defines the boundaries of a certain part of knowledge in order to specify what next needs to be known. The express recognition of what is not yet known but needs to be known in order to lay the foundation of still more knowledge' is specified ignorance. Chomsky's remarks are a plea for the specified ignorance of psychology to be made public. His remarks might well apply to philosophy and sociology, and to educational practitioners and policy-makers.

[82] For some of the literature see page 153.

[83] This seems to us to be an area of difficulty, i.e. the relationship between positions adopted within academic disciplines and wider questions of ideology. Particularly interesting here is the role of psychology and sociology in the debate in the UK over the structure of secondary education, between about 1955 and the present time. Some of the debate seems to presuppose a link between each of these subjects and the political issues. See: D. Ingleby, 'Ideology and the human sciences: some comments on the role of reification in psychology and psychiatry' in T. Pateman, ed., *Counter Course*, op. cit.; footnote 18, on page 263 of R. Horton, 'African traditional thought and Western science', in M. F. D. Young, ed., op. cit.; M. Scriven, 'The values of the academy', op. cit. (1970);

the complexity of interaction between value issues and empirical findings.

(v) The consequences of the *internal* social organization of social science, and the social and political contexts within which social science operates,[84] for the sort of knowledge which is made available. As we suggest below,[85] the fragmentation of sociology, psychology, and anthropology may have had serious consequences for the quality and relevance of *educational* research.

(vi) The implication of these questions for the role that social science ought to play in policy making in education, and the education of teachers.

What implications does our discussion so far have for anyone who wishes to use work from theoretical disciplines in solving practical problems in education, whether at the level of the classroom, school, or educational system? Firstly, such a person needs to be able to distinguish mere consensus from a consensus based upon a competent and unbiased scrutiny of the issues. It is by no means true that complete consensus, or even widespread but not complete agreement, indicates that a claim has been assessed on its merits. Claims might be accepted or rejected by experts on all sorts of irrelevant grounds. Membership of an academic community does not bring with it immunity to the temptations of irrationality. One well-known example of this is what is known as 'the Velikovsky affair',[86] where claims made by I. Velikovsky in his book, *Worlds in Collision*, appear to have been rejected on anything but their merits by a good many scientists. Some even subjected Velikovsky's work to adverse criticism without having read it.[87] De Grazia in his own article in the book he edited described a number of models of 'the scientific reception system'[88] which could be used to explain how claims come to be assessed other than on their merits.[89] As Polanyi states in his own

---

(Ftn. 83 cont.)

K. Nielsen, 'Is empiricism an ideology?', *Metaphilosophy*, Vol. 3 (1972), pp. 265–73; K. R. Minogue, op. cit. (1973), Chapters 7 and 8; for some applications to education see A. Hartnett and M. Naish, 'Academic disciplines, ideology and education' forthcoming.

[84] See A. Gouldner, *The Coming Crisis of Western Sociology*, op. cit., p. 512. For the now classic statement of the relationship between social context and research see I. L. Horowitz, *Professing Sociology: Studies in the Life Cycle of Social Science* (Aldine, 1968), Chapter 18, 'The life and death of Project Camelot', pp. 287–304.

[85] See pp. 170–4. See also Michael Apple, op. cit.

[86] See A. de Grazia, ed., *The Velikovsky Affair* (Sidgwick & Jackson, 1966).

[87] See ibid., p. 179.

[88] See A. de Grazia, ed., op. cit. (1966), p. 171, where de Grazia writes, 'There is, in every social order a reception system. In the sub-order of scientific behaviour, the reception system consists of the criteria whereby scientists, their beliefs, and practices are adjudged by scientists as a community to be worthy, true, and effective.'

[89] See A. de Grazia, 'The scientific reception system', in A. de Grazia, ed., op. cit. (1966). This article is important for our discussion here, and is usefully read in conjunction with: B. Barber, 'Resistance by Scientists to scientific discovery', *Science*, Vol. 134,

discussion of 'the Velikovsky affair', de Grazia's article suggests 'that the acceptance of a new contribution by science may not depend on the evidence of its truth, but takes place either at random, or in the service of ruling powers, or in response to economic or political interests, or simply as dictated by accepted dogma.'[90] This may be true in areas other than science, since there is no reason to assume that the social mechanisms outlined by de Grazia are likely to operate in that area only.

Secondly, where there is no consensus of the required sort and so where nothing can be taken as securely established, anyone wishing to use work from a theoretical discipline needs to come to some conclusion about what view, given the state of the dispute in the discipline, is the least unreliable, and so the most reasonable one for him to act upon. He has, as it were, to decide who is most likely to win the war while it is still in progress. The difficulty of doing this or of determining the nature of the consensus, if there is one, gives rise to complex issues. Combining studies in social sciences or trying to draw some general inferences from them will require fairly sophisticated techniques and will presuppose detailed knowledge and expertise in the discipline, and might be said to be a form of research in itself.[91] It is unlikely that teachers or educational policy-makers, will have the time or the expertise to undertake such work. They will have to rely upon others to interpret the implications of the studies, and this view of the studies may itself be only one professional view of them among others.

Thirdly, a further consequence of the lack of securely established knowledge claims in philosophy and sociology is that the justification for using philosophy and sociology to support views about educational

(Ftn. 89 cont.)
No. 3479 (1961), pp. 596–602; M. Mulkay, 'Some aspects of cultural growth in the natural sciences', *Social Research*, Vol. XXXVI, No. 1 (1969) pp. 22–52; M. Polanyi, 'The potential theory of adsorption', and 'The growth of science in society', both reprinted in M. Grene, ed., *Knowing and Being*, op. cit., pp. 87–96 and 73–86 respectively; S. B. Barnes, 'On the reception of scientific beliefs', in B. Barness, ed., *Sociology of Science* (Penguin Books, 1972), pp. 269–91; M. W. Apple, 'Community, knowledge, and the structure of disciplines', op. cit.; E. Thorpe, 'The taken for granted reference: an empirical examination', *Sociology*, Vol. 7, No. 3 (1973), pp. 361–76. More generally see: J. Ziman, *Public Knowledge: the Social Dimension of Science* (Cambridge University Press, 1968); T. S. Kuhn, *The Structure of Scientific Revolutions*, op. cit. I. Lakatos and A. Musgrave, eds., *Criticism and the Growth of Knowledge*, op. cit. Some points arising from these books and articles are dealt with in A. Hartnett and M. Naish, eds., *Ideology, Knowledge and Educational Practice*, op. cit.
[90] M. Polanyi, in M. Grene, ed., op. cit. (1969), p. 76.
[91] See, for example, R. J. Light and P. V. Smith, 'Accumulating evidence: procedures for resolving contradictions among different research studies', *Harvard Educational Review*, Vol. 41 (1971), pp. 429–71, and K. A. Feldman, 'Using the work of others: some observations on reviewing and integrating', *Sociology of Education*, Vol. 44 (1971), pp. 86–102. See also M. D. Shipman, *The Limitations of Social Research*, op. cit., especially pp. 147–57.

practice and policy is not that in this way an initially tentative practical judgement is alchemized into an ideal and unshakeable solution to a practical problem. Rather, it will have to be argued that, inadequate as the philosophical and sociological views are, they are the best available, and are better than nothing. As Gouldner puts it, 'The issue . . . is not whether we know enough; the real questions are whether we have the courage to say and use what we do know and whether anyone knows more.'[92] Further, it does not follow from the fact that there is a consensus of the required kind, that the claims which can be taken as securely established are true. Even what is widely and justifiably taken as knowledge may, at a later date and in the light of further advances in the discipline, turn out to be of uncertain status or even false.[93]

It can be seen from this that it is very important how people concerned with issues of educational policy and practice acquire their beliefs about the reliability of philosophical and sociological views. Unless particular care is taken, the status given to such views by those outside the disciplines may bear very little, if any, relationship to what the state of the disciplines warrants at the time.

The use made of theoretical disciplines to support educational practice and policy

In this section we wish to raise one or two issues about the way in which work in theoretical disciplines is transmitted to, and received and used by policy makers, trainers of teachers, teachers, and student teachers, to support educational practice and policy. We make some general comments about this problem and then take some of Bernstein's work as a case study.

We suggested in the preceding discussion[94] that to determine the relevance of sociological and philosophical views to education, the extent to which they are securely established, and in general the degree of their reliability, competence is required in the discipline concerned. Further,

---

[92] A. Gouldner, 'Anti-minotaur: the myth of a value-free sociology', in J. Douglas, ed., *The Relevance of Sociology*, (Appleton Century Crofts, 1970)., p. 73.

[93] Cf. G. Langford, op. cit. (1968), p. 103. For a philosophical example see Bertrand Russell, *My Philosophical Development* (Allen & Unwin, 1959), p. 83. Russell writes there that, 'the theory of descriptions . . . was first set forth in my article "On Denoting" in *Mind*, 1905. This doctrine struck the then editor as so preposterous that he begged me to reconsider it and not to demand its publication as it stood. I, however, was persuaded of its soundness and refused to give way. It was afterwards generally accepted, and came to be thought my most important contribution to logic. It is true that there is now a reaction against it on the part of those who do not believe in the distinction between names and other words.'

[94] See page 163.

since many educational problems cut across a *number* of theoretical disciplines, assessment of relevance and reliability will require competence in more than one such discipline.[95]

Some of those who have to make decisions in education are unlikely to possess the competence to judge or criticize aspects of social science or philosophy at the level required.[96] They, among many others, are even more unlikely to be able to evaluate knowledge from more than one field of inquiry.[97]

As a result there are likely to be individuals who could be called 'link-men'.[98] Link-men advise those concerned with educational policy and

---

[95] See page 168.

[96] As examples of the kind of competence we mean see the following. (*i*) E. V. Sullivan, *Piaget and the School Curriculum – a Critical Appraisal*, Bulletin No. 2 (Ontario Institute for Studies in Education, 1967) – see, in particular, the foreword to this monograph by D. P. Ausubel. (Note also Hudson, op. cit., where he comments on Piaget, who he says 'has encased his brilliant studies of problem-solving in small children in a system of logico-mathematical symbolism that few if any of his admirers read, that has no detectable explanatory point, and that only logicians can disentangle' (p. 55).) (*ii*) D. P. Ausubel, 'Learning by discovery: rationale and mystique', op. cit. (*iii*) N. Friedman, 'Cultural deprivation; a commentary in the sociology of knowledge', *Journal of Educational Thought*, Vol. 1, No. 2 (1967). See also G. Eastman, 'The ideologizing of theories: John Dewey's educational theory, a case in point', *Educational Theory*, Vol. 17, no. 2 (April 1967); W. H. Burston, 'The influence of John Dewey in English official reports', *International Review of Education*, Vol. 7 (1961), pp. 311–23; D. Adelstein, 'The wisdom and wit of R. S. Peters – "The philosophy of education"', Union Society, University of London, Institute of Education (1971), now also in T. Pateman, ed., *Counter Course* (Penguin Books, 1972), pp. 115–39. Each of these statements represents one view, among many others, of a particular aspect of theoretical knowledge which is believed to relate to educational practice.

[97] The general point is that the educational system can be held to constitute 'a reception system' (to use de Grazia's term) for the work of certain theoretical disciplines, but it is a reception system which is extraneous to the disciplines in question for the most part, and consists to a very large extent of individuals who may have neither the time nor competence to assess the relevance and, in particular, the epistemological status, of the theoretical work.

[98] For example one could take all the professors of education and social science in the UK at any particular time. Those of them who are link-men would be those who advise the Secretary of State for Education and Science and who sit on committees at the Department of Education and Science on a regular basis. There may be only one or two such professors during the time of a particular Secretary of State. See M. Kogan, *The Politics of Education* (Penguin Books, 1971), especially pp. 184–5. Some academics might even act as their own link-men: they may be the ones whose names are most well known in education. In their role as link-men, academics may be under pressure to underemphasize the disputed nature of their subject and its claims since their clients may expect theoretical disciplines to supply what might be described as hard data – that is well-established and undisputed knowledge claims. See also S. B. Barnes, in B. Barnes, op. cit., pp. 284–95 where he discusses the issues of smoking and health, and fluoridation, and examines some of the consequences of making disagreements among experts explicit. See also T. Husén, 'Educational research and the state', in *Educational Research and Policy Making* (Slough: NFER, 1968), pp. 13–22 and H. Waitzkin, 'Truth's search for power: the dilemmas of the social sciences', *Social Problems*, Vol. 15, No. 4 (1968), pp. 408–19.

practice on what the various theoretical disciplines have to offer education, and even on what recommendations data from them might justify.
Link-men are likely to be thought competent to assess the epistemological status of such data and their relevance to education.[99]

Further, because of the difficulties involved in assessing the relevance
of the totality of available theoretical work, and its status, decisions may
be made about educational practice and policy without reference to such
work. Then *after* a decision has been taken, link-men may be found to
provide support from theoretical disciplines for it. Theoretical work may
be misrepresented to support such decisions,[100] and in some cases, it might
be irrelevant to them. Chomsky states that 'the question of the validity
and scientific status of a particular point of view is of course logically
independent from the question of its social function; each is a legitimate
topic of inquiry, and the latter becomes of particular interest when the
point of view in question is revealed to be seriously deficient, on empirical
or logical grounds.'[101] We speculate that in education theoretical work

[99]Some able (and no doubt some of the most able) of those professionally engaged in
theoretical disciplines may not be interested in how the educational system uses their
theoretical work or in being link-men. In these cases, there is unlikely to be any first-
hand check on whether it is misused (cf. McNamara's comment on page 119).

Few sociologists or psychologists for example who are not primarily interested in
education would be professionally concerned with the contents of recent government
reports on education or with the publications of the Department of Education and
Science, or the Schools Council. *Teachers'* perceptions of social science may be significantly related to what they read about social science in these publications. For a general
sociological approach see Hazel Sumner, MSc. Essay (1970), London School of Economics
and Political Science (unpublished). This essay 'considers the pattern of development of
psychology, and the use made of its findings and theories by those who shaped British
Education Policy, in the period from the mid-nineteenth century to the Second World
War.' Note the comments of S. B. Barnes, op. cit., p. 289, 'Necessarily then scientific
knowledge reaches the lay audience via a translation process'; and cf. L. Hudson, op.
cit., p. 130, 'A man's reputation depends on whether his research helps the able, influential but technically uninformed – vice-chancellors, politicians, civil servants – to make
sense of ideas that changes in *Zeitgeist* and social circumstance are bringing just within
their grasp.' See also our discussion of the Velikovsky affair (page 162–3). Hudson's notion of
'reputation' could usefully be applied to 'link-men'. 'Reputation' would mean how they
were regarded by policy makers and those with power. It would *not* necessarily cover how
they were regarded by their professional colleague group.

[100]See Maurice Kogan, 'The politics of education', op. cit., pp. 149–99. In that section
(Conversation with Anthony Crosland) reference is made to 'the radical sociology of the
1950s and 1960s' (p. 174). It is not clear: (*i*) what is meant by this phrase – the only
sociological advisor to the Secretary of State mentioned is A. H. Halsey (p. 185). It may
mean Halsey's perceptions of sociology; (*ii*) how this 'radical sociology' supports circular
10/65; (*iii*) whether sociology ought to play a part in research about the *consequences* of
circular 10/65. Crosland's view of research appears to be that it 'can help you to achieve
your objectives' (p. 190). The naiveté of this can easily be demonstrated, in that the
worth of the objectives is partly determined by what has to be done to achieve them. See
Nagel, page 21).

[101]Chomsky, op. cit., p. 41.

from social science (and from philosophy
simply because it performs the social fun
what policy makers want to do, or hav
appears to support the conventional wisⁱ
In other words, social function and valid

We now turn to Bernstein's work on la
There appears to be a disparity betwee
ceived, judged, and utilized by: (*i*) Berr
especially those areas of it concerned wi
educational system, in particular in the ⁱ
justification of various educational pra
education programmes'.[104] We have s
high expectations about what education can achieve, and yet no...
about how these expectations might be fulfilled.[105] Any contribution
which appears to offer help is likely to be seized upon, publicized, and
become part of the conventional wisdom of education.[106] Jackson, commenting on the sorts of degree courses that are available, makes relevant
points about this. He writes, 'Not every degree one might like to have can
at present be constructed. Sometimes this is because there are not enough
teachers, books and so on of the right kind. Sometimes it is because
human knowledge simply does not extend so far ... It is interesting to
consider what usually takes place, when a subject unfortunately does not
happen to exist, but would be important if it did. What happens as a
rule is that the subject is treated rather like God: if it does not exist, it
is invented, and it is then given a gaseous body and a very high status,
and declared to be immanent in everything ... One is tempted to think of

[102] For a discussion relevant to this issue see I. L. Horowitz, 'Social science mandarins: policy making as a political formula', *Policy Sciences*, Vol. 1 (1970), pp. 339–60.
[103] See also M. D. Shipman, *The Limitations of Social Research*, op. cit. See in particular
the discussion on Piaget, pp. 47–9; on ITA, pp. 88–92; on streaming, pp. 117–20; and on
class size, pp. 144–6.
[104] Our discussion makes only very general points. There is a need for detailed
case studies of how and why particular academics have been 'taken over' by educational
systems. For an example of a case study which raises interesting questions see David
Barratt, *An Analysis of the Use Made of the Work of Basil Bernstein in Studies on the
Language of Culturally Deprived Children*, Master of Education dissertation (unpublished),
University of Liverpool, 1974. It is important to note that Bernstein's current work
raises much more general issues in the sociology of knowledge, than his previous work
on language. For current work see 'On the classification and framing of educational
knowledge', op. cit.; and 'Sociology and the sociology of education: some aspects',
pp. 49–108 of Unit 17 of the Open University Course E.282, op. cit.
[105] See above, Vol. 1, Section 2, pp. 190–204.
[106] Note Bernstein's comments in 'Class, codes, and control', op. cit., p. 18, about how
'ritual references' to his work came up even in O level. For a discussion on 'The
conventional wisdom of education and sociology', see Marvin Bressler, pp. 76–114
in Charles H. Page, ed., *Sociology and Contemporary Education* (New York: Random
House, 1963).

way ... the sweeping, exciting generalizations about float so far above any empirical data exhibited; and are used now as an all-purpose kit to explain differences in [107] How Bernstein's work became 'an all purpose kit', if that d happen, raises questions about the processes through which earch was 'given its various meanings by receiving social con- , [108] especially colleges of education. Students attending such colleges might be attempting to master psychology, philosophy, main subjects, and other areas, in addition to sociology. They (and the staff) may well lack knowledge of the theoretical disciplines required for a reasoned judgement about Bernstein's contribution to the study of language.[109] Such a judgement would need competence in linguistics, aspects of psychology, and certain specialized areas of sociology.[110]

The issues Bernstein's work raises about educability derive from the interactions between cultural symbols, language, thought, forms of social control, boundaries, ideology and power.[111] This is an area of great difficulty and Bernstein's work reflects this.[112] He comments that his papers 'are obscure, lack precision and probably abound with ambiguities'.[113] Further, during the 1960s very little of the work of the research unit (under his direction at the London Institute of Education) was available in *published* form. Discussion of the research, except among those involved in it, tended to be based on hearsay. This may have had important consequences for the way in which the work was received by those concerned with the training of teachers.

[107] L. Jackson, 'Radical conceptual change and the design of honours degrees', Open University Reader, *School and Society*, op. cit., p. 212.

[108] B. Bernstein, 'Class, codes, and control', op. cit., p. 18. On this area see also J. David Colfax, 'Knowledge for whom?', *Sociological Inquiry*, Vol. 40, No. 1 (Winter 1970).

[109] See above for our discussion on competence, page 163, and issues contained in the article by McNamara, pp. 125–6. This whole area of using the work of others raises difficulties. See for example K. A. Feldman, op. cit. (1971); and R. J. Light and P. V. Smith, op. cit. (1971).

[110] Thus even the theoretical problems raised by Bernstein's work cross subject boundaries, let alone the practical problems in education which it might be used, along with other theoretical work, to answer.

[111] See M. Douglas, 'Speech, class, and Basil Bernstein', *The Listener*, 9 March, 1972, p. 312.

[112] Compare, for example, B. Bernstein, 'A socio-linguistic approach to social learning', in *Penguin Survey of the Social Sciences* (1966), and his 'Education cannot compensate for society', *New Society*, 26 February, 1970, with the statement of his views in Schools Council Working Paper 27, *'Cross'd with Adversity:' the Education of Socially Disadvantaged Children in Secondary Schools* (Evans/Methuen Educational, 1970), particularly pp. 17–18. Note also the comments made by J. Gould, *The Listener* (9 March, 1972), p. 302, on Bernstein's work: 'I sense in his work an attunement to the diversities of culture – and to the symbolic forms which culture takes – that is alien to shallow thinkers (inside and outside the teaching profession) and to dogmatists of all persuasions.'

[113] Bernstein, 'Class, codes and control', op. cit., p. 19.

As a result of these factors *apparent* relevance to educational practice may have been confused with a theoretical judgement about a particular contribution to the study of language, and notions of securely established knowledge. Because Bernstein's work was made to appear relevant to education, it was assumed to be established beyond dispute. In fact, the work was a weak interpretative frame;[114] Bernstein was doing sociology, and the teachers wanted to know how to answer the question 'What do I do Monday?'[115]

We conclude this section by noting Bernstein's own comments. He writes, 'There are few indications in the papers about changes in the curricula, pedagogy, or organizational structures of the school. This omission was deliberate. It has always seemed to me that educational institutions at secondary or primary levels are likely to absorb ideas, and try them out on a fairly large scale, provided that those subject to them are either the very young children or the so-called less able working class children, before the ideas are sufficiently worked through to be useful. I felt I did not know enough about the problem nor did I have sufficient evidence to make any recommendation to teachers. It was also the case that I was trying to develop an analysis of the social basis of knowledge made available in schools, which I considered was prior to offering suggestions to teachers of pupils of the age group five to seven years.'[116]

If Bernstein's work was misunderstood in this way, this raises questions about the *quality* of the education that teachers are given; in particular, it may be that students are 'not taught the skills, the data or the attitudes necessary for handling and acting on controversial, moral-political-

---

[114]B. Bernstein, *Class, Codes and Control*, op. cit., p. 20. See our previous reference to this quotation, page 144.

[115]The phrase is taken from the title of one of John Holt's books published by Pitman, 1971. Note the comments of Donald A. Hansen, 'The uncomfortable relation of sociology and education', in D. A. Hansen and J. E. Gerstl, eds, *On Education: Sociological Perspectives* (New York: John Wiley, 1967), p. 15, where he writes, 'sociology is by nature an abstracting and generalizing discipline, while education is oriented toward predictive statements required in diagnosis and planning ... the educator may be frustrated in his efforts to interpret the sociologist's findings in ways useful in application. And it means that the sociologist, unused to the pressures of practicalities, may be frustrated as he realizes that educators fail to properly evaluate his work: that which seems to the sociologist his least worthy effort may win the greatest applause, while his most serious work is greeted with shaking heads.' See also pp. 156–7 for similar comments by R. S. Peters.

[116]B. Bernstein, *Class, Codes and Control*, op. cit., p. 19. A further point can also be made about Bernstein's work. It is that it can apparently be converted into *psychology*, and used to provide labels for, and explanations of, the 'failure' of *individual* children. This raises a series of further questions about the relationships between levels of analysis, teacher education, and educational policy. On this see Donald Swift, 'Status systems and education', part one of Block 5, Open University course, *Education, Economy, and Politics*, E. 352 (Open University Press, 1973).

scientific issues.'[117] They are confused about the relationships between theoretical knowledge, values, and action.

Social factors affecting the production of theoretical work in education

We have suggested that educational problems are likely to raise issues which cut across subject boundaries.[118] In this section we discuss briefly some of the relationships between the institutional structures of academic disciplines (particularly sociology and psychology) and the theoretical work on which the educational system can draw. The development of interdisciplinary work, which may be necessary for increasing that knowledge which can be directly applied to educational problems and practice, raises questions within and between disciplines, and about their structure and the modes of professional socialization they employ.[119]

The disciplines of psychology and sociology appear to be relatively separate 'academic communities'[120] with their own career structures,

[117] M. Scriven, 'The values of the academy (moral issues for American education and educational research arising from the Jensen case)', *Review of Educational Research*, Vol. 40, No. 4 (1970), p. 546. See also Hudson, op. cit., pp. 114–25 and A. G. N. Flew, 'The Jensen uproar', *Philosophy*, Vol. 48 (1973), pp. 63–9.

[118] Examples would be: (*i*) the area surrounding the notion of intelligence, in which the disciplines involved would include genetics, biology, psychology, sociology, anthropology and others – the Jensen case provides a good example of some of the difficulties involved; (*ii*) the study of language which involves a number of disciplines, see above, page 168; (*iii*) educability and related issues; (*iv*) discovering the consequences of educational policies and practices – as we have suggested this would *necessarily* involve raising questions at the level of individuals, groups, organizations and systems, and one could speculate that the crucial issues would concern interactions between levels, especially between individuals, groups and organizations. See Vol. I, Section 2, pp. 188–90.

The above is not an adequate statement. More needs to be said about why educational problems, in general, may be better served by interdisciplinary approaches. Detailed argument is required about particular areas/problems which may be especially suitable for this kind of treatment. On this see Muzafer Sherif and Carolyn W. Sherif, eds, *Interdisciplinary Relationships in the Social Sciences* (Chicago: Aldine, 1969). See especially papers by Donald T. Campbell, Robert B. MacLeaod, and Murray L. Wax.

[119] For a discussion of the possibilities of cooperative research in philosophy see J. L. Thompson, 'Philosophy – practice and theory: a venture into the sociology of philosophy', *Metaphilosophy*, Vol. 3 (1972), pp. 274–82.

[120] See above, page 154, and the paper by M. Apple, op. cit. An advert from the British Sociological Association suggests that a 'study group in Social Psychology should be set up in order to stimulate interest in the subject *as a branch of sociology*.' (Our italics.) *B.S.A. News and Notes*, No. 2 (January 1972). On this area see D. Wilkinson, 'Sociological imperialism: a brief comment on the field', *Sociological Quarterly*, Vol. 9, No. 3 (Summer, 1968). The belief that one's own discipline has more to offer than other disciplines may form an important part of the socialization process into academic disciplines. On this

journals, professional associations, and forms and modes of professional socialization.[121] Some sociologists and psychologists will have simplistic views of each other's disciplines.[122] The consequence of this may be that educational problems are arbitrarily fragmented to accommodate them to the existing structure of academic disciplines. This problem is unlikely to be resolved by assembling together a group of specialists and calling the result 'interdisciplinary inquiry'. If educational research involves developing theoretical schemas, methodologies, etc., which cut across various levels of analysis, is such research possible, given the sort of training which social scientists appear to receive before they enter the area of education?

There are other factors that might impede the production of theoretical work of the required kind. In particular there are constraints from outside the disciplines on the sort of research undertaken in education. Firstly, the conditions upon which research funds are granted will have

<hr/>

(Ftn. 120 cont.)

see J. Matthiasson, 'My discipline is better than your discipline: some barriers to interdisciplinary research', *Canadian Review of Sociology and Anthropology*, Vol. 5, No. 4 (November, 1968), especially pp. 268–9. It is also important to appreciate that the reference group of sociologists, philosophers, sociologists of education, philosophers of education, and others involved in training teachers, or involved in producing work that might appear on college of education curricula, or be used in education, is likely to be their professional colleague group and *not* trainee teachers or qualified teachers. This is likely to be true even where the *audience* for the theoretical work is by intention trainee teachers or teachers. Note Jackson's comment, 'In my more cynical moods this state of affairs leads me to conclude that the major function of research in education is to advance the careers of educational researchers', P. W. Jackson, 'Stalking beasts and swatting flies' in J. Herbert and D. Ausubel, eds., *Psychology in Teacher Preparation*, op. cit., p. 68. Hansen, 'The uncomfortable relation of sociology and education', op. cit., p. 6 says of the sociologist who is interested in education that there is little prestige to be borrowed from education and 'there is also a strong possibility that his research will be confused with that of the educator (risking offhand rejection of his publications by many in his own field, and even by some in education), and that he himself may be mistaken for "an educationist" by his fellow sociologists.'

[121] On careers within universities see Q. D. Leavis, 'The Cambridge tradition', in F. R. Leavis, ed., *A Selection from Scrutiny*, Volume I (Cambridge University Press, 1968), pp. 1–46. See, in particular, the footnote on pages 3–5. Note also the comment on page 20, 'Raleigh wrote to D. Nichol Smith from Oxford (1904): "They told me in Liverpool that it was all-important to spend weary hours on diminishing the incapacity of dull students. I did not contradict them, but I didn't do it: I wrote a book. No one who understands the real thing cares twopence about the dull student, expect as a man and a brother. Drink with him; pray with him; don't read with him, except for money."' Note Q. D. Leavis' comments on this quotation. See also our previous quotation from L. Hudson, page 155 (Hudson, p. 102). For some American evidence see G. S. Kirk, 'Impressions from America', *Didaskolos*, Vol. 3 (1971), pp. 600–13. On page 603 Kirk says, 'A successful professor must have as many graduate students as possible ... so that he can place them in strategic posts across the country and use them as sources of information, admiration, and, if necessary, intrigue.'

[122] See pp. 153–7.

important implications for the kind of theoretical work produced.[123] Secondly, research may be set up so as to provide data to support decisions which have already been taken, and equally may *not* be set up where it is thought it might not do this.[124] Thirdly, certain sorts of research may be directed away from high status groups and organizations within the educational system, and towards low status groups (like teachers and children) and low status organizations (like schools). For example, there appears to be little empirical work on such groups as advisers to local education committees, directors of education, principals of colleges of education,[125] civil servants in the Department of Education and Science, or Her Majesty's Inspectorate.[126] These groups are likely to be involved

[123] B. Bernstein, *Class, Codes and Control*, op. cit., p. 10, writes 'From the spring of 1962 until almost the end of the year, continuous discussions took place at the Department of Education which eventually resulted in a very different research proposal. The Department considered the original proposal to be too academic, and pressed me towards an applied study which would involve an attempt to design a programme for infant school children which would enhance their contextual use of speech. I felt very unhappy about this proposal. I knew nothing about infant school children, and even less about the infant school . . . In the end I accepted the focus of the research required by the Department of Education.' See also Colfax, 'Knowledge for whom?', op. cit. It might also be said that the educational and political system may demand theoretical work of a kind which enables solutions to educational problems to be immediate and simple. Relevant theoretical work, whether or not it is interdisciplinary, is unlikely to be of this kind.

[124] It would be interesting to know the reasons why, for example, Joan Barker Lunn's supplementary research proposal on the effects of streaming on gifted children was turned down by the DES. See the part of her letter quoted in C. Burt, The Organisation of Schools, in Black Paper Three, Critical Quarterly Society, p. 23. See also the letter from J. M. Morris and M. Power, *The Times*, 25 May, 1972, p. 19. They argue that a local education authority stopped research into the links between delinquency rates and school attended. Note also the reply from Irene Chaplin, *The Times*, 31 May, 1972, p. 15. The whole area of the criteria by which research proposals are allowed, or not allowed, in schools and colleges of education would be a fruitful one for study. The crucial control exercised by the education system is over funds, and *access* to the organizations.

[125] See W. Taylor, 'The training college principal', *Sociological Review*, Vol. 12, No. 2 (1964), pp. 185–201. Note also Taylor's comments in the *Colston Papers, No. 20*, W. Taylor, ed. (Butterworth, 1969), p. 227. He writes, 'The creation of a policy implies the activity of policy makers, and it is clearly of importance to identify who these are in the field with which we are concerned. Again, we come up against a lack of hard research.' Academics (especially link-men) might also be another relevant group for study.

[126] On HMIs, for example, it would be useful to have some research evidence on: the sort of advice that they offer to teachers and the Secretary of State; what the 'knowledge base' of that advice is; by whom, and by what processes, they are trained; what kind of career structure exists for them at the DES; how (if at all) advancement relates to what advice they offer; how, and by what criteria, they are selected. One possible way of characterizing HMIs is as 'contact men'. The term is taken from Harold L. Wilensky, *Organizational Intelligence: Knowledge and Policy in Government and Industry* (New York: Basic Books, 1967). Wilensky defines the contact man as someone who 'supplies political and ideological intelligence the leader needs in order to find his way around modern society, he mediates the relations of the organization and the outside world. His primary concern and skill is with facts about and techniques of changing the thoughts, feelings,

in decisions which radically affect the contexts in which teachers and children work. It is therefore particularly important to discover how these groups are made up and how they function. The tendency for research to be concentrated in low status areas is not only to be found in education. Brown draws attention to it in the mass media. He suggests that mass media managers have been able to emphasize the importance of what 'Lazarsfeld early on referred to as purely "administrative" research, in which media problems (in a rather literal sense) are tackled in terms dictated by the "interests" of media managers themselves' and that this emphasis 'is also a consequence of the difficulty of access to media practitioners, particularly at the higher levels. It is worth suggesting that the response to this latter *impasse*, particularly on the part of empirical researchers in the United States, has been to study the lower echelons of the media hierarchy (the small town press rather than the metropolitan press, the reporter rather than the owner).' Brown goes on to say that 'to work

---

(Ftn. 126 cont.)

and conduct of men through persuasion and manipulation. He is valued for his knowledge of the political and social topography of the containing society – the kind of realistic political intelligence that tells him who can make what decisions or who has what information and how and when to reach him' (p. 10). The importance of the inspectorate is made clear in Kogan, op. cit., where Crosland, talking about implementing Circular 10/65, says that, 'the detail of the options was mainly a product of thinking in the inspectorate' (p. 188). This presumably means that the *actual* schemes for reorganization, as distinct from general ideological stance, came from the HMIs. Further there appears to be no research evidence about how HMIs resolve their role conflicts. J. Blackie, a retired member of the inspectorate, writes in his book, *Inspecting and the Inspectorate* (Routledge & Kegan Paul, 1970), p. 53, that, 'the Department could not tolerate a situation in which one of its employees was openly and explicitly hostile to a policy which it was implementing at the behest of Parliament. At the same time an inspector is not expected to preach any particular doctrine. That is the job of politicians, not of civil servants.' Given the changes in secondary education policies in recent years, these views must present difficulties for HMIs. Blackie makes high claims for the inspectorate. He notes, for example, that inspectors run courses 'usually with success' (p. 50) and that 'they do know, between them, more about English education than any one other body in the country' (p. 69). These claims are unsupported. His book gives rise to various issues. It reads very often like a defence of the inspectorate rather than an account or explanation of what it does. It may, in fact, be part of the inspectorate's reply to the Select Committee of 1968 and as such, an attempt to influence the implementation of its recommendations. Nevertheless, it appears in a series designed for 'students of Education at Colleges of Education and at University Institutes and Departments'. Blackie's professed main target group appears to be students. Further, J. W. Tibble, the editor of the series, states that the book will help the young teacher 'to distinguish between reality and fantasy in his relationship with the Inspectorate' (p. vi) and Blackie hopes 'that the book will provide the young student with the material necessary for making his own assessment of the inspectorate' (p. 3). Yet there is no reference to any up-to-date empirical work on the inspectorate in the book. The first part of the bibliography is almost entirely concerned with the 1968 Select Committee. Apart from this, the most recent reference is to the Plowden Report (1967). A 1963 reference to Ball concerns the inspectorate from 1839 to 1849. The reference to Edmonds (1962) is also historical. Given this, how are the tasks Tibble and Blackie set for student teachers to be undertaken?

"from the top down", although more difficult, may in the end be more revealing.'[127] This may also be true in education.[128]

Some comments on the justification of philosophy and sociology in teacher education[129]

The question of the justification of philosophy, sociology, and of theoretical disciplines in general in teacher education is a complex one, as the readings by McNamara and Scheffler, and our own discussion of philosophy and sociology suggest.[130] Firstly, as Scheffler makes clear, it in-

[127] R. Brown, 'Mass media ideologies', in P. Halmos, ed., *Sociological Review*, Monograph No. 13 (January 1969), University of Keele, p. 166. See also I. Weinberg, 'Some methodological and field problems of social research in elite secondary schools', *Sociology of Education* (Spring 1968).

[128] The effects of research into how societies, institutions, educational systems and so on work is itself a matter for empirical investigation. Some comments of Barnes suggest that they might not be entirely beneficial. He says that it seems to him that, 'any human community relies on ignorance of itself for its smooth working; that there are all sorts of things that go on in the community which everybody knows about but nobody likes to see in cold print; they don't like having to deal with it at a conscious level. There are two problems here. First, the extent to which a community can face up to itself in this way ... Secondly, the problem of whether a society which is fully self-conscious can operate, or at least can operate in quite the same way as most of the societies that we deal with'. J. Barnes in *The Listener* (5 August 1971), p. 175.

[129] For some relevant discussions see: L. A. Reid, *Philosophy and Education* (Heinemann Educational Books, 1962), Chapter 13; M. L. Borrowman, 'Liberal education and the professional preparation of teachers', in M. L. Borrowman, ed., *Teacher Education in America: a Documentary History* (Columbia: Teachers College Press, 1965), pp. 1–53; P. Renshaw, 'A re-appraisal of the college of education curriculum', *Education for Teaching*, No. 75 (1968), pp. 28–34; P. Renshaw, 'The objectives and structure of the college curriculum', in J. W. Tibble, ed., *The Future of Teacher Education* (Routledge & Kegan Paul, 1971), pp. 53–67; P. Renshaw, 'A curriculum for teacher education', in T. Burgess, ed., *Dear Lord James – a Critique of Teacher Education* (Penguin Books, 1971), pp. 78–105; P. Renshaw, 'A flexible curriculum for teacher education', in D. Lomax, ed., *The Education of Teachers in Britain* (New York: John Wiley, 1973), Chapter 12; D. Aspin, 'On the "educated" person and the problem of values in teacher education and training', in D. E. Lomax, op. cit.; D. Sharples, 'Towards a concept of college', *Education for Teaching*, No. 79 (1969), pp. 29–34; P. J. Higginbotham, 'The concepts of professional and academic studies in relation to courses in institutions of higher education (particularly colleges of education)', *British Journal of Educational Studies*, Vol. 17 (1969), pp. 54–65; B. R. Joyce, M. Weil and R. Wald, 'The training of educators: a structure for pluralism', *Teachers College Record*, Vol. 73 (1972), pp. 371–91. For a survey of labels used on sociology courses in colleges of education see P. Chambers, 'The sociology of education in education courses: an analysis', and references pp. 18–19, in 'Conference on the Sociology of Education', DES, September 1969, held at West Midlands College of Education; and the ATCDE publication 'Sociology in the education of teachers' (1969). See also D. F. Swift and H. Acland, 'The sociology of education in Britain, 1960–1968: a bibliographical review', *Social Science Information*, Vol. 8, No. 4, pp. 31–64, note especially the comments on pp. 31–4.

[130] See pages 117–38 and 139–57.

volves a normative question about teachers' roles – normative in that it is a question about the sorts of attitudes and practical and intellectual abilities that teachers ought to have. Ought teachers, for example, to be taught to be effective and competent classroom performers and no more, or to occupy the wider role described by Scheffler and so to be able to raise questions about the nature and context of the enterprise in which they are engaged? Secondly, if what we have said about philosophy and sociology is true, there may be no very determinate answers to questions about what philosophy and sociology are. As a consequence, the question about justification might take a number of different senses depending on what philosophy and sociology, and what philosophy of education and sociology of education, are taken to be. We raise here two other issues which further indicate the complexity of the question of justification.

1. Justification and outcomes

Questions about justifying philosophy, sociology, theoretical disciplines, and indeed anything in the education of teachers, can be asked at two levels. One level is what might be called the general and context-free level. Here the questions are discussed largely without reference to information about institutions, resources, teachers, students, outcomes of the teaching, and so on. This is the level of McNamara's and Scheffler's discussions. The second level is one at which these factors are taken into account, and at which policy decisions of all sorts, and not only those about teacher education, ought to be taken.[131] Though first-level discussions may be valuable, it is important to notice that to make out a first-level justification is not the same as making out a second-level one. The former will only be a prima facie justification which might not hold for the specific contexts in which the decision would be implemented.

It follows that even if there were agreement on teachers' roles, and agreement on what was, in the context of teacher education, to count as doing philosophy and sociology, a second-level justification cannot be properly undertaken in advance of the sort of empirical information mentioned above. For one thing, merely teaching philosophy and sociology to trainee or qualified teachers, or to anyone at all, does not ipso facto make them more able or willing to question the purposes and contexts of whatever activity they are engaged in.[132] Some students might be unable

---

[131] This argument is relevant to decisions about the organizational structure of education at primary, middle- and secondary-school levels. See the paper by Naish et al., pp. 55–117.

[132] Cf. W. Taylor, *Society and the Education of Teachers*, op. cit. for evidence on this. For a discussion relevant to the issues here see M. Scriven, op. cit. (1970). Cf. the comments of M. L. J. Abercrombie, *The Anatomy of Judgement* (Penguin Books, 1969), pp. 15–16. Mrs Abercrombie writes, 'As a teacher of zoology I had been disappointed in the effects that learning about science seemed to have on habits of thinking ... It was found that

to cope with the subjects at all; others may be able to but, because of a narrow conception of their role, be indifferent to such questions or be unwilling, perhaps because of the psychological stress involved, to bring these disciplines to bear on questions which affect their own values; others may simply take over what they are offered from the disciplines quite uncritically. Again, some sorts of teaching might not promote, but even militate against, fundamental questioning. Students might become not merely indifferent but hostile to the disciplines and to the issues raised by them. What, in philosophy or sociology, is to be said, at least prima facie, of large formal lectures with little or no seminar work, or of seminars conducted by teachers brought in from other disciplines? It might even be the case that, given the variety of the human input into the teacher training process, the apparent variety of the tasks for which teachers are trained, the enormous diversity in the institutional contexts in which teachers work and the relative paucity of easily usable and relevant work from theoretical disciplines, some teachers need not be *trained*, in any formal sense, at all.[133]

What the consequences are of teaching sociology and philosophy of education is a research problem of great complexity upon which we have little data of quality.[134] The apparent failure of the James Report[135]

(Ftn. 132 cont.)

students who had satisfied the examiners for the Higher School Certificate ... were well grounded in the facts of biology, physics and chemistry' but 'did not necessarily use scientific ways of thinking to solve problems presented in slightly new ways. They might be able, for example, to recite all the lines of evidence for the theory of evolution but yet be unable to use this material to defend the theory in an argument with an anti-evolutionist. They might know what the function of a certain organ is believed to be, but did not always know why, nor did they clearly understand on what kind of evidence a belief of that sort was based. When asked to describe what they saw in dissecting an animal, they often did not distinguish sufficiently sharply between what was there and what they had been taught "ought" to be there.'

[133] It may also be the case that some teachers are not trained formally now, in as much as they develop their 'professional capital' on the job, and that training is merely an attempt to win status, and to preserve a belief that teachers (and schools) can be, and are being, radically changed through teacher training.

[134] R. S. Peters, for example, writes, in 'Reply to A. Thompson and E. A. Martin', *Education for Teaching*, No. 81 (1970), p. 28, that 'It is ... a hunch and not just a hope that philosophy of education might contribute something to the quality of teachers' lives and teaching as well as to the quality of their arguments.' By the use of 'hunch' he appears to acknowledge the lack of empirical data about the consequences of teaching philosophy to teachers. See also L. A. Reid, 'Philosophy and the theory and practice of education', in R. D. Archambault, ed., *Philosophical Analysis and Education* (Routledge & Kegan Paul, 1965), particularly pp. 34–5, and F. H. Hilliard, 'Theory and practice in teacher education', in F. H. Hilliard, ed., *Teaching the Teachers* (Allen & Unwin, 1971), pp. 33–54. Besides examining the consequences of teaching philosophy and sociology of education, it would also be useful to know how the disciplines came to play the part they do in teacher education, and what particular perspectives have been adopted. This might be usefully done by comparing England and Wales with Scotland where psychology appears to play a major part in teacher education and philosophy very little – at least what might be described as philosophical analysis, in one or other of its senses.

[135] *Teacher Education and Training*, op. cit. On this report, it would be useful to know:

to commission any research[136] into the consequences of teaching theoretical disciplines such as philosophy, psychology, sociology and so on,
though recommending fairly extensive change in the structure of teacher
education, may be an important political sign that decisions about teacher
education are likely to continue to be taken on the basis of hunches.

2. Justification and practical relevance

But for the question of justification to be answered at the second level it
is not enough to have some idea of the consequences of teaching philosophy, sociology and other disciplines to students. Criteria are needed
by which the worth of the consequences is to be assessed. One notion
commonly used in attempts to provide such criteria is that of 'practical
relevance'. It is often argued that only if a discipline or the consequences
of teaching it are practically relevant can its inclusion in teacher education be justified.[137]

An appeal to practical relevance, in the context of teacher education,
embodies an appeal to some role definition or other of a teacher. Arguments about practical relevance will, therefore, unavoidably involve normative issues. Further, to claim that something has practical relevance is to
claim that it is necessary for an adequate or improved performance in that
role. To show therefore that something is practically relevant, it must be
shown that the role definition is justified and that what is said to be necessary for the role performance is in fact so. Rebuttals of claims to practical
relevance can be made either by denying the adequacy of the role definition
or by denying the necessity, or by denying both of these together.[138]

It follows that where there are competing role definitions, as in the
case of teachers, there are likely to be no fixed and uncontested criteria
for what is and is not practically relevant. Arguments which turn on
appeals to practical relevance are likely to contain implicit paradigms of

(Ftn. 135 cont.)
what criteria were used for selecting members of the Committee; how many people were
asked to serve on the Committee and declined and what reasons they offered for declin-
ing; why the Committee had to report within a fixed period; why research was not commissioned.
[136] We are not suggesting that research by itself would provide answers: only a contribution to an answer. Note the comments of F. Musgrove, (1966) op. cit., p. 12, on research:
'Even research must be treated cautiously, with a full awareness of what it can do and
what it cannot. It can too easily breed a false self-confidence and sense of security: it
can even be used as a substitute for hard thinking, and, most dangerous of all, as an
evasion of the proper exercise of judgement. Research may tell us something about the
possible; it will tell us nothing about the desirable.' See also our discussion on practical
reasoning, in Vol. 1, Section 1, pp. 94–107.
[137] In so far as the outcomes of teaching anything to teachers are unknown, it is also
unknown whether what was taught had in fact any practical relevance for them – that
is to say affected, for better, their teaching and their views about education.
[138] 'Practical relevance' can be seen to have some similarities with 'need', and may,
too, often obscure rather than clarify issues. For 'need' see R. F. Dearden, op. cit. (1968),
Chapter 2.

the practically relevant and implicit role definitions, both of which need to be brought into the open and assessed. In the case of a student teacher, for example, the paradigm of the practically relevant may be teaching practice, and possibly method lectures. Whatever does not offer results in terms of effective teaching or good discipline (however these are understood) may be held to be practically irrelevant. Academics and others concerned with the training and education of teachers may appeal to a paradigm of the practically relevant which is determined by their own theoretical discipline, or by their own courses, or by their own work and their own role. They may, that is, work with a definition of a teacher's role which is set no wider than to include the capacities, abilities, and skills which they believe their own subject and teaching can impart. In such cases, the various definitions of the practically relevant, and of a teacher's role that go with them, may reflect much more the competition within an institution for additional resources and time than any disinterested attempt to arrive at a justifiable definition of such a role.

It can be seen that appeals to practical relevance do not (as some might have hoped) avoid the normative issues about teachers' roles, though they might obscure them. For the very criteria of what is to be taken as practically relevant will be in dispute where, for example, one party assumes that a teacher's role is that of an 'intellectual technician'[139] whose job is simply to carry out, unquestioningly and as effectively as possible, the tasks set for him, and another party assumes a definition corresponding to the wider role that Scheffler describes.[140]

[139] See the reading by I. Scheffler pp. 137–8. The issue about these two conceptions of the role of a teacher can be seen to concern the distinction between an educated teacher and a trained one and whether educated teachers are to be preferred to trained ones. For 'educated' see our discussion in Vol. 1 Section 1 pp. 73–94, and for 'training' and 'education' see R. S. Peters, 'What is an educational process', in R. S. Peters, ed. *The Concept of Education* (Routledge & Kegan Paul, 1967), particularly pp. 14–16; and L. R. Perry, 'Training and education', *Proceedings of the Philosophy of Education Society of Great Britain*, Annual Conference, Vol. VI, No. 1 (January 1972), pp. 7–29. The issue about role definitions can be raised in a very similar way in the context of training and educating, say, lawyers, policemen, surgeons, and nurses. On a narrow conception of their role, surgeons, for example, might need mastery of nothing more than a number of diagnostic, surgical, and post-operative skills. On the wider conception, they might need to have some informed understanding of the moral issues raised by medical or surgical practice – that is, to take two areas of recent moral controversy, they might need not only to know how to carry out abortions and heart-transplants but to have some understanding of how and under what circumstances they might be justified. On the first conception of the role, moral philosophy or sociology are unlikely to be said to be practically relevant but might well be on the second. The distinction, roughly, is between teaching people how to do tasks, and how to raise issues about the nature and justification of the tasks themselves. Thus the claim by R. M. Hare in his *Applications of Moral Philosophy* (Macmillan, 1972), p. x, that 'philosophical thought can help us towards the solution of practical problems' is better understood as referring to issues about justifying the tasks rather than to learning how to do them. For a historical comment on the narrow role definition of teachers in elementary schools, see R. F. Dearden, op. cit. (1968), p. 5, and the reference there to W. A. L. Blyth, *English Primary Education* (Routledge & Kegan Paul, 1965).

[140] It might be argued that some teachers are not capable of, or do not want, the

Further, appeals to practical relevance may embody an epistemological requirement, as it might be called. Arguments about role definitions might be combined with arguments to the effect that neither philosophy nor sociology nor other theoretical disciplines that teachers might study can provide statements or theories of sufficient reliability to be of use to teachers, and that therefore they are not practically relevant.[141] This objection might perhaps be met in a number of ways. It might be said, as we have suggested,[142] that such statements and theories, though unreliable, are better than none, or that some acquaintance with theoretical disciplines is needed if the complexity of educational issues, and the limits of current knowledge and so the extent of current ignorance, are to be adequately understood. The objection might, perhaps, be true. Whatever the case, attempts to meet it can only make issues about what is practically relevant more complex.

But it might even be argued that to rest the entire justification of curricula in teacher education on the notion of practical relevance is, from the start, to prejudge the issue against theoretical disciplines, such as philosophy, sociology, or psychology, and is to obscure the fact (as it might be) that different things in such curricula might be justified in different ways. It might be argued, that is, that there are grounds against using the notion of practical relevance to justify everything in teacher education. Scheffler's article might even be held to support such a view.[143]

What all this suggests is that the notion of practical relevance, certainly in the context of teacher education, is not a straightforward one, and that arguments about what to teach to teachers which depend upon unexamined notions of the practically relevant are not satisfactory.

(Ftn. 140 cont.)
wider role described by Scheffler. Whether this is so, is an empirical matter. In any case, this has no bearing on the issue of justifying such a role definition for those who are prepared to adopt it. Our own view, which for reasons of space must remain unargued here, is that the more an activity or enterprise involves complex value disputes about serious issues, the more important it is that those who engage in it adopt the wider conception of their role.

[141] For what appears to be a variant on this argument see pp. 121–4 of the reading by McNamara. For a discussion of the distinction between the academic and the practical that can be usefully read in conjunction with the reading by McNamara and Scheffler and with our discussion of teacher education, see K. R. Minogue, op. cit. (1973), Chapter 4.

[142] See page 164.

[143] See pp. 128–38 of this book. See, too, R. S. Peters, who writes in 'The place of philosophy in the training of teachers', *Paedagogica Europaea*, Vol. III (1967), p. 153, 'It could well be agreed that though the main emphasis at the level of initial training must be on the *training* of teachers, we cannot altogether neglect our duty as educators to educate them as persons.' This suggests that there are at least two kinds of justification that might be used in answering questions about curricular content in teacher education. It might be asked here whether if you *start* by training someone it is possible to educate them at some later date, or whether it makes education difficult. See the comments of Dewey quoted in Vol. 1 Section 1, pp. 118–19. For a further relevant discussion see M. Naish and A. Hartnett, 'What theory cannot do for teachers', *Education for Teaching*, No. **96**, Spring 1975, pp. 12–19.

Bibliography

(Included here are the main references in Volumes I and II to be found in: the editor's introductions to the readings, the discussion of issues arising from the readings, and in the paper in Volume II by Michael Naish, Anthony Hartnett, and Douglas Finlayson, 'Ideological documents in education: some suggestions towards a definition')

Abercrombie, M. L. J. *The Anatomy of Judgement*. Penguin Books, 1969.

Apple, Michael W. 'Community, knowledge, and the structure of disciplines.' *The Educational Forum*, **XXXVII**, 1, 1972, pp. 75–82.

Archambault, R. D., ed. *Philosophical Analysis and Education*. Routledge & Kegan Paul, 1965.

Atkinson, R. F. *Conduct: an Introduction to Moral Philosophy*. Macmillan, 1969.

Ausubel, D. P. 'Learning by discovery: rationale and mystique.' *The Bulletin of the National Association of Secondary School Principals*, **45**, 1961, pp. 18–58.

Ayer, A. J., ed., *Logical Positivism*. Glencoe: Free Press, 1959.

Ayer, A. J. 'Philosophy as elucidating concepts', in J. Bobick, ed., *The Nature of Philosophical Inquiry*. Indiana: Notre Dame Press, 1970.

Baier, K. *The Moral Point of View*. Abridged edn. New York: Random House, 1967.

Banks, Olive. *The Sociology of Education*. Batsford, 1968.

Bannan, J. F. 'The philosopher and his peers – community and freedom.' *Metaphilosophy*, **2**, 1971, pp. 316–30.

Bantock, G. H. 'Conflicts of values in teacher education', in Colston Papers No. 20, *Towards A Policy for the Education of Teachers*, ed. W. Taylor, Butterworth, 1969.

Baratz, S., and Baratz, J. 'Early childhood intervention: the social science base of institutional racism.' *Harvard Educational Review*, **40**, 1, Winter 1970, pp. 29–50.

Barber, B. 'Resistance by scientists to scientific discovery.' *Science*, **134**, 3479, 1961, pp. 596–602.

Barker-Lunn, Joan C. *Streaming in the Primary School*. Slough: National Foundation for Educational Research in England and Wales, 1970.

Barnes, B., ed., *Sociology of Science*. Penguin Books, 1972.

Barratt, D. J. *An Analysis of the Use Made of the Work of Basil Bernstein in Studies on the Language of Culturally Deprived Children*. Master of Education dissertation, University of Liverpool, 1974 (unpublished).

Bealing, Deanne. 'The organization of junior school classrooms.' *Educational Research*, **14**, 3, 1971–72, pp. 231–5.

Becher, R. A. 'A lack of discipline'. *Philosophy*, **49**, No. 188, 1974, pp. 205–11.

Benyon, Lois. *An Analysis of Some of the Literature Relating to the Education of Children under Social Handicap*. Master of Education dissertation, University of Liverpool, 1973 (unpublished).

Bergmann, G. 'Ideology.' *Ethics*, **LXI**, 1951, pp. 205–18.

Bernstein, Basil. 'Education cannot compensate for society.' *New Society*, 26 February 1970, pp. 344–7.

——. 'On the classification and framing of educational knowledge', in M. F. D. Young, ed., *Knowledge and Control: New Directions for the Sociology of Education*. Collier-Macmillan, 1971, pp. 47–69.

——. *Class, Codes and Control*. Volume 1, Theoretical Studies towards a Sociology of Language. Routledge & Kegan Paul, 1971.

——. *Sociology and the Sociology of Education: Some Aspects*. Unit 17, Open University Course E.282, School and Society. Open University Press, 1972, pp. 99–109.

Best, E. 'The empty prescription in educational theory.' *Universities Quarterly*, **14**, 1960, pp. 233–42.

——. 'The suppressed premiss in educational psychology.' *Universities Quarterly*, **16**, 1962, pp. 283–95.

——. 'A failure in communication.' *Studies in Philosophy and Education*, **13**, 1964, pp. 163–84.

——. 'Common confusions in educational theory', in R. D. Archambault, ed., *Philosophical Analysis and Education*. Routledge & Kegan Paul, 1965, pp. 39–56.

Bilski, Raphaella. 'Ideology and the comprehensive schools.' *The Political Quarterly*, **44**, 2, April–June 1973, pp. 197–211.

Blackie, John. *Inspecting and the Inspectorate*. Routledge & Kegan Paul, 1970.

Black, M. *Critical Thinking*. New Jersey: Prentice Hall, 1946.

——. 'The definition of scientific method', in R. C. Stauffer, ed., *Science and Civilisation*. Madison, Wisconsin: University of Wisconsin Press, 1949, pp. 67–95.

The Labyrinth of Language. Penguin Books, 1972.

Black, M., ed. *The Social Theories of Talcott Parsons*. New Jersey: Prentice Hall, 1961.

Bohannan, P. 'Field anthropologists and classroom teachers'. *Social Education*, **32**, 2, 1968, pp. 161–6. (Reprinted in Volume I, pp. 149–58.)

Boucher, Leon. *Education in Sweden*. World Education Series (forthcoming).

Bourdieu, Pierre. 'Systems of education and systems of thought'. *International Social Science Journal*, **19**, 3, 1967, pp. 338–58.

Bressler, Marvin. 'The conventional wisdom of education and sociology', in Charles H. Page, ed., *Sociology and Contemporary Education*. New York: Random House, 1963, pp. 76–114.

Breton, R. 'Academic stratification in secondary schools and the educational plans of students'. *Canadian Review of Sociology and Social Anthropology*, 7, 1, 1970, pp. 17–34.

Broudy, H. 'Can research escape the dogma of behavioral objectives?' *School Review*, **79**, November 1970, pp. 43–56.

Brown, Roger. 'Some aspects of mass media ideologies.' *Sociological Review*, Monograph No. 13, P. Halmos, ed. University of Keele, January 1969.

Burgess, T. *Inside Comprehensive Schools*. HMSO, 1970.

Burgess, T. and Pratt, J. *Policy and Practice: the Colleges of Advanced Technology*. Allen Lane, Penguin Press, 1970.

Burgess, T., ed., *Dear Lord James–a Critique of Teacher Education*. Penguin Books, 1971.

Burke, P. R. and Howard, V. A. 'On turning the philosophy of education outside-in.' *British Journal of Educational Studies*, **XVII**, 1969, pp. 5–15.

Burns, Tom. 'Sociological explanation.' *British Journal of Sociology*, **18**, December 1967, pp. 353–69. (Reprinted in Volume II, pp. 23–39.)

Cane, B. and Smithers, J., ed. Gabriel Chanan. *The Roots of Reading: a Study of 12 Infant Schools in Deprived Areas*. Slough: National Foundation for Educational Research in England and Wales, 1971.

Care, N. S. 'On fixing social concepts.' *Ethics*, Vol. **84**, No. 1, October 1973, pp. 10–21. See also A. MacIntyre (1973).

Chomsky, Noam. 'Psychology and ideology.' *Cognition*, **1**, 1, 1972, pp. 11–46.

Cicourel, A. V. *Method and Measurement in Sociology*. New York: Free Press, 1964.

———. *The Social Organization of Juvenile Justice*. New York: John Wiley, 1968.

Cicourel, A. V. and Kitsuse, J. *The Educational Decision-Makers*. Indianapolis: Bobbs-Merrill, 1963.

———. 'The social organization of the high school and deviant adolescent careers' in E. Rubington and M. Weinberg, eds, *Deviance: the Interactionist Perspective*. New York: Macmillan Company, 1968, pp. 124–35.

Colfax, J. David. 'Knowledge for whom?' *Sociological Inquiry*, **40**, 1, Winter 1970, pp. 73–83.

Cooper, J. 'Criteria for successful teaching: or an apple for teacher.' *Philosophy of Education Society of Great Britain, Proceedings of the Annual Conference*, 1966, pp. 5–18.

Corbett, P. *Ideologies*. Hutchinson, 1965.

Cosin, B. R., Dale, I. R. et al., eds., *School and Society: a Sociological Reader*. Routledge & Kegan Paul, and the Open University Press, 1971.

Coulson, M. and Riddell, D. S. *Approaching Sociology*. Routledge & Kegan Paul, 1970.

Cox, C. B. and Dyson, A. E., eds., *Fight for Education*, A Black Paper. Critical Quarterly Society, 1969.

———. *Black Paper Two*. Critical Quarterly Society, c.1970.

———. *Black Paper Three*. Critical Quarterly Society, 1971.

Daveney, T. F. *Education – a Moral Concept*. Inaugural Lecture. University of Exeter Press, 1970.

Davies, W. Brian. *On the Contribution of Organizational Analysis to the Study of Educational Institutions*. Paper read to the 1970 Annual Conference of the British Sociological Association, Durham, England. Also in Richard Brown, ed., *Knowledge, Education and Cultural Change*. Tavistock Publications, 1973, pp. 249–95.

Dearden, R. F. *The Philosophy of Primary Education*. Routledge & Kegan Paul, 1968.

———. 'Philosophy and curriculum innovation', in *Curriculum Development*. Themes in Education, No. 21. Conference Report. University of Exeter, 1969, pp. 1–10.

———. 'The aims of primary education', in *Perspectives on Plowden*, R. S. Peters, ed., Routledge & Kegan Paul, 1969.

———. 'The philosophy of education', in J. W. Tibble, ed., *An Introduction to the Study of Education*. Routledge & Kegan Paul, 1971.

Dearden, R. F., Hirst, P. H. and Peters, R. S., eds., *Education and the Development of Reason*. Routledge & Kegan Paul, 1972.

Denby, Maeve. *Pre-School – the Cycle of Opportunity*. National Elfrida Rathbone Society, 1973.

Dewey, J. 'The relation of theory to practice in education,' in *The Third Yearbook of the National Society for the Scientific Study of Education, Part I*, ed., C. A. McMurry, Chicago Illinois: Chicago University Press, 1904, pp. 9–30.

Diggs, B. J. 'A technical ought.' *Mind*, **LXIX**, 1960, pp. 301–17.

Dixon, Keith. *Sociological Theory: Pretence and Possibility*. Routledge & Kegan Paul, 1973.

Douglas, Jack D., ed., *The Impact of Sociology*. New York: Appleton-Century-Crofts, 1970.

———. *The Relevance of Sociology*. New York: Appleton-Century-Crofts, 1970.

Dumont, R. and Wax, M. 'Cherokee school society and the intercultural classroom.' *Human Organization*, **28**, 3, Fall 1969, pp. 217–26. (Reprinted in Volume I, pp. 158–73.)

Dunlop, F. N. 'Education and human nature.' *Proceedings of the Philosophy of Education Society of Great Britain*. *Proceedings of the*

Annual Conference, January 1970. **IV**, pp. 21–44.

Eastman, George. 'The ideologizing of theories: John Dewey's educational theory, a case in point.' *Educational Theory*, **17**, 2, 1967, pp. 103–19.

Edel, A. 'Reflections on the concept of ideology.' *Praxis*, **4**, 1967, pp. 564–77.

———. 'Education and the concept of ideology.' *Proceedings of the 24th Annual Meeting of the Philosophy of Education Society of America*, 1968, pp. 70–87.

Eisner, Elliot W. 'Educational objectives help or hindrance?' *School Review*, Autumn 1967, pp. 250–60.

Elboim-Dror, Rachel, 'Some characteristics of the education policy formation system.' *Policy Sciences*, **1**, 1970, pp. 231–53.

Emmet, D. *Rules, Roles, and Relations*. Macmillan, 1966. (Chapter 9 'Living with Organisation Man' reprinted in Volume 1 pp. 51–72.)

Entwistle, H. 'Practical and theoretical learning.' *British Journal of Educational Studies*, **XVII**, 1969, pp. 117–28. (Reprinted in Volume 1 pp. 38–50.)

———. 'The relationship between theory and practice', in J. W. Tibble, ed., *An Introduction to the Study of Education*, Routledge & Kegan Paul, 1971.

Esland, G. M. 'Teaching and learning as the organization of knowledge', in M. F. D. Young, ed., *Knowledge and Control*, op. cit., pp. 70–115.

Evetts, Julia. *The Sociology of Educational Ideas*. Routledge & Kegan Paul, 1973.

Feigl, H. 'The difference between knowledge and valuation.' *The Journal of Social Issues*, **VI**, 4, 1950, pp. 39–44. (This issue of the *Journal of Social Issues* is entitled, 'Values and the Social Scientist.')

———. 'Aims of education for our age of science: reflections of a logical empiricist', in *Modern Philosophies and Education*, 54th Year Book of the National Society for the Study of Education, ed. N. B. Henry. Chicago, Illinois: NSSE, 1955, Part 1, pp. 304–41.

———. De principiis non est disputandum, in J. Hospers ed., *Readings in Introductory Philosophical Analysis*. London: Routledge and Kegan Paul, 1969, pp. 111–135.

Feldman, K. A. 'Using the work of others: some observations on reviewing and integrating.' *Sociology of Education*, **44**, 1971, pp. 86–102.

Feldman, K., ed. *College and Student: Selected Readings in the Social Psychology of Higher Education*. New York: Pergamon Press, 1972.

Flew, A. G. N. 'The Jensen uproar.' *Philosophy*, **48**, 1973, pp. 63–9.

Ford, Julienne. *Social Class and the Comprehensive School*. Routledge & Kegan Paul, 1969.

Foss, B. 'Other aspects of child psychology', in R. S. Peters, ed., *Perspectives on Plowden*. Routledge & Kegan Paul, 1969, pp. 42–54.

Frankena, W. K. *Ethics*. New Jersey: Prentice Hall, 1963.
──────. *Three Historical Philosophies of Education*. Glenview, Illinois: Scott Foresman, 1965.
Friedrichs, Robert W. *A Sociology of Sociology*. New York: Free Press 1970.
Fuchs, E. *Teachers' Talk*. New York: Anchor Books, Doubleday, 1969.
Gallie, W. B. 'Essentially contested concepts.' *Proceedings of the Aristotelian Society*, LVI, 1955–56, pp. 167–98.
──────. 'Art as an essentially contested concept.' *Philosophical Quarterly*, 6, 1956, pp. 97–114.
──────. 'What makes a subject scientific.' *British Journal for the Philosophy of Science*, 8, 1957–8, pp. 118–39.
──────. *Philosophy and the Historical Understanding*. Chatto & Windus, 1964.
──────. 'Essentially contested concepts', Chapter Eight of W. B. Gallie, *Philosophy and the Historical Understanding*, op. cit.
──────. 'The idea of practice.' *Proceedings of the Aristotelian Society*, LXVIII, 1967–68, pp. 63–86.
Gauthier, D. P. *Practical Reasoning*. Oxford University Press, 1963. (Chapter 1, 'Practical Problems', reprinted in Volume 1 pp. 18–24.)
Geer, B. 'Teaching', in D. Sills, ed., *International Encyclopedia of the Social Sciences*. New York: Free Press, 1968.
Geertz, C. 'Ideology as a cultural system', in D. E. Apter, ed., *Ideology and Discontent*. New York: Free Press, 1964, pp. 47–76.
Gellner, E. A. *Words and Things*. Penguin Books, 1968.
──────. 'The concept of a story.' *Ratio*, Vol. 9, 1967, pp. 49–66.
Gewirth, A. 'Positive "ethics" and normative "science".' *Philosophical Review*, 69, 1960, pp. 311–30.
──────. 'Meta-ethics and normative ethics.' *Mind*, LXIX, 1960, pp. 187–205.
Gotesky, R. 'The uses of inconsistency.' *Philosophy and Phenomenological Research*, 28, 1967–68, pp. 471–500.
Gouldner, A. W. 'Anti-minotaur: the myth of a value-free sociology', in Jack D. Douglas, ed., *The Relevance of Sociology*, op. cit., pp. 64–84.
──────. *The Coming Crisis of Western Sociology*. Heinemann Educational Books, 1971.
Grazia, A. de., ed., *The Velikovsky Affair*. Sidgwick & Jackson, 1966.
Gross, Neal, Giacquinta, Joseph B., Bernstein, Marilyn. *Implementing Organizational Innovations: a Sociological Analysis of Planned Educational Change*. New York: Harper & Row, 1971.
Hampshire, S. 'The progress of philosophy.' *Polemic*, 5, 1946, pp. 22–32.
──────. 'Fallacies in moral philosophy.' *Mind*, LVIII, 1949, pp. 466–82. (Reprinted in Volume 1 pp. 24–38.)
Hannam, Charles, Smyth, Pat, and Stephenson, Norman. *Young Teachers and Reluctant Learners*. Penguin Books, 1971.

Hansen, D. A., and Gerstl, J. E., eds., *On Education: Sociological Perspectives.* New York: John Wiley, 1967.

Hare, R. M. 'The practical relevance of philosophy', in R. M. Hare, *Essays on Philosophical Method.* Macmillan, 1971, pp. 98–116.

Hargreaves, D. *Social Relations in a Secondary School.* Routledge & Kegan Paul, 1967.

Hartnett, A. *Professional Ideologies in Institutions: Some Methological Problems.* University of London, Master of Arts, 1969 (unpublished).

Hartnett, A., ed., *The Sociology of Education: An Introductory Guide to the Literature.* Library Publication No. 3. University of Liverpool, School of Education, 1975. (Copies available from the School of Education Library.)

Hartnett, A. and Naish, M. 'Academic disciplines, ideology and education', (forthcoming).

Hartnett, A. and Naish M., eds., *Knowledge, Ideology and Educational Practice* (in preparation).

———. *Education, Conflict, and Values* (in preparation.)

Herbert, J. and Ausubel, D. P., eds., *Psychology in Teacher Preparation.* Monograph Series No. 5. The Ontario Institute for Studies in Education, 1969.

Hilliard, F. H. 'Theory and practice in teacher education', in F. H. Hilliard, ed., *Teaching the Teachers.* Allen and Unwin, 1971, pp. 33–54.

Hilsum, S. and Cane, B. S. *The Teacher's Day.* Slough: National Foundation for Educational Research in England and Wales, 1971. (Part reprinted in Volume 1 pp. 125–48.)

Himmelweit, H. 'The teaching of social psychology to students of education and social work', in *The Sociological Review* Monograph No. 4, ed. P. Halmos. University of Keele, July 1961, pp. 77–92.

Hirst, P. H. 'Liberal education and the nature of knowledge', in R. D. Archambault, ed., *Philosophical Analysis and Education.* Routledge & Kegan Paul, 1965, pp. 113–38.

———. 'Morals, religion, and the maintained school.' *British Journal of Educational Studies,* **14**, 1965, pp. 5–18.

———. 'Educational theory', in J. W. Tibble, ed., *The Study of Education.* Routledge & Kegan Paul, 1966, pp. 29–58.

Hirst, P. H. and Peters, R. S. *The Logic of Education.* Routledge & Kegan Paul, 1970.

Horowitz, I. L. *Professing Sociology: Studies in the Life Cycle of Social Science.* Chicago: Aldine, 1968.

———. 'Social science mandarins: policymaking as a political formula.' *Policy Sciences,* **1**, 1970, pp. 339–60.

Hospers, J. *An Introduction to Philosophical Analysis.* 2nd edn. Routledge & Kegan Paul, 1967.

Hudson, Liam. *The Cult of the Fact.* Jonathan Cape, 1972.

Husen, T. 'Educational research and the state', in W. D. Wall and T.

Husén, *Educational Research and Policy Making*. Slough: National Foundation for Educational Research in England and Wales, 1968, pp. 13–22.

Hyman, R. T. 'Means-ends reasoning and the curriculum.' *Teachers College Record*, **73**, 3, 1972, pp. 393–401.

Jackson, P. W. *Life in Classrooms*. New York: Holt, Rinehart & Winston, 1968.

———. 'Stalking beasts and swatting flies', in J. Herbert and D. P. Ausubel, eds., *Psychology in Teacher Preparation*, op. cit., pp. 65–73.

James Report, *Teacher Education and Training*, a Report by a Committee of Inquiry appointed by the Secretary of State for Education and Science, under the chairmanship of Lord James of Rusholme. HMSO, 1972.

Jencks, Christopher et al. *Inequality: a Reassessment of the Effect of Family and Schooling in America*. New York: Basic Books, 1972.

Keddie, N. 'Classroom knowledge', in M. F. D. Young, ed., *Knowledge and Control*, op. cit., pp. 133–60.

Keddie, N., ed. *Tinker Tailor: the Myth of Cultural Deprivation*. Penguin Books, 1973.

Kelvin, Peter. *The Bases of Social Behavior*. New York: Holt, Rinehart & Winston, 1970.

King, Preston. 'An ideological fallacy', in P. King and B. C. Parekh eds., *Politics and Experience, Essays Presented to Michael Oakeshott on the Occasion of his Retirement*. Cambridge University Press, 1968, pp. 341–94.

Kogan, Maurice. *The Politics of Education: Edward Boyle and Anthony Crosland in Conversation with Maurice Kogan*. Penguin Books, 1971.

Körner, S. *Fundamental Questions in Philosophy*. Penguin Books, 1971.

Krause, E. A. 'Functions of a bureaucratic ideology: "citizen participation".' *Social Problems*, **16**, 2, Fall 1968, pp. 129–43.

Kuhn, T. S. 'The function of dogma in scientific research', in A. C. Crombie, ed., *Scientific Change*. Heinemann Educational Books, 1963.

———. *The Structure of Scientific Revolutions*. 2nd edn. Chicago: University of Chicago Press, 1970.

Lacey, C. *Hightown Grammar*. Manchester: Manchester University Press, 1970.

Lakatos, Imre and Musgrave, Alan, eds., *Criticism and the Growth of Knowledge*. Cambridge University Press, 1970.

Langford, G. *Philosophy and Education*. Macmillan, 1968.

———. *Human Action*. Macmillan, 1972.

Laslett, P. and Runciman, W. G., eds., *Philosophy, Politics and Society*. Third Series. Oxford: Blackwell, 1967.

Leavis, F. R., ed. *A Selection from Scrutiny*. Volume 1. Cambridge University Press, 1968.

Light, R. J. and Smith, P. V. 'Accumulating evidence: procedures for resolving contradictions among different research studies.' *Harvard Educational Review*, **41**, 1971, pp. 429–71.

Lindblom, C. E. 'The science of "muddling through".' *Public Administration Review*, **19**, 1959. Reprinted in W. J. Gore and J. W. Dyson, eds., *The Making of Decisions*, pp. 155–69. Glencoe: Free Press, 1964.

Lunsford, T. F. 'Authority and ideology in the administered university.' *American Behavioral Scientist*, **11**, 5, 1968, pp. 5–14.

MacDonald, B. and Rudduck, J. 'Curriculum research and development projects: barriers to success.' *British Journal of Educational Psychology*, **41**, 2, 1971, pp. 148–54.

MacIntyre, A. *Against the Self-images of the Age*. Duckworth, 1971.

———. 'The essential contestability of some social concepts.' *Ethics*, **84**, 1, October 1973, pp. 1–9. (See also N. S. Care 1973).

Mackie, J. L. 'Can there be a philosophy of education?' *Forum of Education*, **23**, 1964, pp. 40–7.

MacRae, D. G. *Ideology and Society*. Heinemann Educational Books, 1961.

Magee, B., ed., *Modern British Philosophy*. Secker & Warburg, 1971.

Mannheim, K. *Ideology and Utopia*. Routledge & Kegan Paul, 1936.

Martin, Bernice. 'Progressive education versus the working classes.' *Critical Quarterly*, **13**, 4, Winter 1971, pp. 297–320.

McNamara, D. R. 'Sociology of education and the education of teachers.' *British Journal of Educational Studies*, **20**, 2, 1972, pp. 137–47. (Reprinted in Volume II pp. 117–28.)

Melden, A. I. 'Reasons for action and matters of fact,' *Proceedings and Addresses of the American Philosophical Association*, **XXXV**, 1961–2, pp. 45–60.

Minogue, K. R. *The Concept of a University*. Weidenfeld & Nicolson, 1973.

Moore, A. *Realities of the Urban Classroom: Observations in Elementary Schools*. New York: Anchor Books, Doubleday, 1967.

Mundle, C. W. K. 'Examining in philosophy.' *Universities Quarterly*, **22**, 1967–68, pp. 302–6.

Musgrove, F. *Faith and Scepticism in English Education*. Inaugural Lecture, Bradford Institute of Technology, 1966.

Nagel, E. 'Philosophy in Educational Research', Chapter 5 in F. W. Banghart, ed., *Educational Research: Phi Delta Kappa First Annual Symposium*, USA, 1960, pp. 71–84. (Reprinted in Volume II, pp. 13–23.)

———. *The Structure of Science*. Routledge & Kegan Paul, 1961.

———. 'Philosophy of science and educational theory.' *Studies in Philosophy and Education*, **7**, Fall 1969, pp. 5–27.

Naish, M., Hartnett, A., and Finlayson, D., 'Ideological documents in education: some suggestions towards a definition.' Published for the first time in Volume II pp. 55–117.

Naish, M. and Hartnett, A. 'What theory cannot do for teachers'. *Education for Teaching*, No. 96, Spring 1975, pp. 12–19.

Newsom Report, *Half Our Future*. A report of the Central Advisory Council for Education (England). HMSO, 1963.

Oakeshott, M. 'Political education', in M. Oakeshott, *Rationalism in Politics and other essays*. Paperback edn. Methuen, 1967, pp. 111–36.
———. 'Learning and teaching', in R. S. Peters, ed., *The Concept of Education*. Routledge & Kegan Paul, 1967, pp. 156–76.
O'Connor, D. J. *An Introduction to the Philosophy of Education*. Routledge & Kegan Paul, 1957.
O'Connor, D. J. and Hirst, P. H. 'The nature of educational theory, a symposium.' *Proceedings of the Philosophy of Education Society of Great Britain*, VI, 1, 1972, pp. 97–118.
Ormell, C. P. 'Ideology and the reform of school mathematics.' *Philosophy of Education Society of Great Britain, Proceedings of the Annual Conference*, III, January 1969, pp. 37–54.
Page, Charles H., ed., *Sociology and Contemporary Education*. New York: Random House, 1963.
Passmore, J. A., 'Towards an analytical philosophy of education.' *Melbourne Studies in Education 1965*. Carlton, Victoria: Melbourne University Press, 1966, pp. 61–79. See also essay three by J. A. Passmore, 'Analytical criticisms of traditional philosophies of education,' pp. 41–60.
Perry, L. R., 'Training and education.' *Proceedings of the Philosophy of Education Society of Great Britain, Annual Conference*, VI, I, 1972, pp. 7–29.
Peters, R. S., *Authority, Responsibility and Education*. Allen & Unwin, 1959.
———. *Education as Initiation*. Inaugural Lecture. Harrap, for the University of London Institute of Education, 1964.
———. 'Education as initiation', in R. D. Archambault, ed., *Philosophical Analysis and Education*. Routledge & Kegan Paul, 1965, pp. 87–111.
———. 'The philosophy of education', in J. W. Tibble, ed., *The Study of Education*. Routledge & Kegan Paul, 1966, pp. 59–89.
———. *Ethics and Education*. Allen & Unwin, 1966.
———. 'Aims of education, a conceptual inquiry', in *Philosophy and Education*. Proceedings of the International Seminar, March 23–25, 1966. Monograph Series No. 3. The Ontario Institute for Studies in Education, 1967, pp. 1–32.
———. 'What is an educational process', in R. S. Peters, ed., *The Concept of Education*, op. cit., pp. 1–23.
———, ed., *The Concept of Education*. Routledge & Kegan Paul, 1967.
———. 'Michael Oakeshott's philosophy of education', in P. King and B. C. Parekh, eds., *Politics and Experience*. Cambridge University Press, 1968, pp. 43–63.
———. 'Theory and practice in teacher training.' *Trends in Education*, 9, 1968, pp. 3–9.

————, ed., *Perspectives on Plowden*. Routledge & Kegan Paul, 1969.

————. '"A recognisable philosophy of education": a constructive critique', in *Perspectives on Plowden*, R. S. Peters, ed., op. cit., pp. 1–20.

————. 'Education and the educated man.' *Philosophy of Education Society of Great Britain, Proceedings of the Annual Conference*, **IV**, January 1970.

————. 'A reply to A. Thompson and E. A. Martin.' *Education for Teaching*, **81**, 1970, pp. 23–9.

Plamenatz, J. *Ideology*. Pall Mall Press, 1970.

Plowden Report, *Children and their Primary Schools*. A report of the Central Advisory Council for Education (England). Volume 1: Report. HMSO, 1967.

Polanyi, M. *Personal Knowledge*. Routledge & Kegan Paul, 1958.

————. 'Knowing and being.' *Mind*, **LXX**, 1961, pp. 458–70.

————. *Knowing and Being: Essays by Michael Polanyi*, M. Grene, ed., Routledge & Kegan Paul, 1969.

————. 'The potential theory of adsorption', in *Knowing and Being*, M. Grene, ed., op. cit., pp. 87–96.

————. 'The growth of science in society', in *Knowing and Being*, M. Grene, ed., op. cit., pp. 73–86.

Popper, K. R. *Conjectures and Refutations*. 3rd edn, paperback. Routledge & Kegan Paul, 1969.

————. *The Poverty of Historicism*. Paperback edn. Routledge & Kegan Paul, 1961.

Pugh, D. S. 'Modern organizational theory: a psychological and sociological study.' *Psychological Bulletin*, **66**, 1966, pp. 235–51. Also in F. Carver and T. Stergiouanni, eds., *Organizations and Human Behavior: Focus on Schools*. New York: McGraw Hill, 1969, pp. 111–29.

Reddiford, G. 'Conceptual analysis and education.' *Proceedings of the Philosophy of Education Society of Great Britain*, Supplementary Issue, **VI**, 2, 1972, pp. 193–215.

Rée, H. A. *The Essential Grammar School*. Harrap, 1956.

Rhees, R. *Without Answers*. Routledge & Kegan Paul, 1969.

Riesman, D. 'Teachers amid changing expectations.' *Harvard Educational Review*, **XXIV**, 2, Spring 1954, pp. 106–17.

Rorty, A. O. 'Naturalism, paradigms, and ideology.' *Review of Metaphysics*, **XXIV**, 1971, pp. 637–67.

Rouceck, J. S. 'A history of the concept of ideology.' *Journal of the History of Ideas*, **5**, 1944, pp. 479–88.

Ryan, A. *The Philosophy of the Social Sciences*. Macmillan, 1970.

————. 'An essentially contested concept.' *The Times Higher Educational Supplement*, No. 120, 1 February 1974, p. 13.

Ryle, G. 'Knowing how and knowing that.' *Proceedings of the Aristotelian Society*, **XLVI**, 1945–46, pp. 1–16.

————. *The Concept of Mind*. Hutchinson, 1949.

Sagarin, E. 'Ideology as a factor in deviance.' *Journal of Sex Research*, **4**, 2, 1968, pp. 84–94.

Scheffler, I. 'Justifying curriculum decisions.' *School Review*, **66**, 1958, pp. 461–72.

———. *The Language of Education*. Springfield, Illinois: Charles C. Thomas, 1960.

———. *Conditions of Knowledge*. Glenview, Illinois: Scott Foreman, 1965.

———. 'University scholarship and the education of teachers.' *The Record*, **70**, 1968–69, pp. 1–12. (Reprinted in Volume II pp. 128–38.)

———. *Reason and Teaching*. Routledge & Kegan Paul, 1973.

Schools Council Working Paper 27. '*Cross'd with Adversity': the Education of Socially Disadvantaged Children in Secondary Schools*. Evans/Methuen Educational, 1970.

Scott, Robert A. 'The construction of conceptions of stigma by professional experts', in Jack D. Douglas, ed., *Deviance and Respectability, the Social Construction of Moral Meanings*. New York: Basic Books, 1970, pp. 255–90.

Scriven, M. 'The values of the academy (moral issues for American education and educational research arising from the Jensen Case).' *Review of Educational Research*, **40**, 4, 1970, pp. 541–9.

Searle, J. R. *Speech Acts*. Cambridge University Press, 1969.

Sherif, Muzafer and Sherif, Carolyn, W., eds., *Interdisciplinary Relationships in the Social Sciences*. Chicago: Aldine, 1969.

Shipman, M. D. *The Role of the Teacher in Innovating Schools*. Paper read to Organization for Economic Cooperation and Development. Paris: OECD, 1971.

———. *The Limitations of Social Research*. Longman, 1972.

Smith, D. 'Power, ideology, and the transmission of knowledge: an exploratory essay', in E. Hopper, ed., *Readings in the Theory of Educational Systems*. Hutchinson University Library, 1971, pp. 240–61.

Smith, G. and Stockman, N., 'Some suggestions for a sociological approach to the study of government reports.' *Sociological Review*, **20**, 1, 1972, pp. 59–77. (Reprinted in Volume II pp. 39–55.)

Stebbins, Robert A. 'The meaning of disorderly behavior: teacher definitions of a classroom situation.' *Sociology of Education*, **44**, Spring 1970, pp. 217–36.

Stenhouse, L. 'Some limitations of the use of objectives in curriculum research and planning.' *Paedagogica Europaea*, **6**, 1970–71, pp. 73–83.

Stevenson, L. 'Applied philosophy', *Metaphilosophy*, **1**, 1970, pp. 258–67.

Stones, E. and Anderson, D. *Educational Objectives and the Teaching of Educational Psychology*. Methuen, 1972.

Strauss, A. et al. *Psychiatric Ideologies and Institutions*. New York: Free Press, 1964.

Struthers, M. 'Educational theory: a critical discussion of the O'Connor-Hirst debate.' *Scottish Educational Studies*, **3**, 2, 1971, pp. 71–8.

Sullivan, E. V. *Piaget and the School Curriculum – a Critical Appraisal.* Bulletin No. 2. Ontario Institute for Studies in Education, 1967.

Swift, D. F. *The Sociology of Education.* Routledge & Kegan Paul, 1969.

Swift, D. F. *Recent Research in the Sociology of Education.* DES/ATCDE Conference, 'The sociology of education in colleges of education', West Midlands College of Education, September 1969. Department of Education and Science, 1969.

Swift, David W. *Ideology and Change in the Public Schools: Latent Functions of Progressive Education.* Columbus, Ohio: Charles E. Merrill, 1971.

Taylor, W. *Society and the Education of Teachers.* Faber, 1969.

——, ed., *Towards a Policy for the Education of Teachers.* Colston Papers No. 20. Butterworth, 1969.

Thompson, J. L. 'Philosophy – practice and theory: a venture into the sociology of philosophy.' *Metaphilosophy*, 3, 1972, pp. 274–82.

Thompson, K. 'Philosophy of education and educational practice.' *Proceedings of the Philosophy of Education Society of Great Britain*, IV, Annual Conference, January 1970, pp. 45–60.

Thorpe. E. 'The taken for granted reference: an empirical examination.' *Sociology*, 7, 3, 1973, pp. 361–76.

Tibble, J. W., ed. *The Study of Education.* Routledge & Kegan Paul, 1966.

——. *An Introduction to the Study of Education.* Routledge & Kegan Paul, 1971.

Tiryakian, E., ed., *The Phenomenon of Sociology.* New York: Appleton-Century-Crofts, 1971.

Vaughan, J. E. and Argles, Michael. *British Government Publications Concerning Education: an Introductory Guide.* School of Education, University of Liverpool, 1969. (Copies available from School of Education Library).

Waitzkin, Howard. 'Truth's search for power: the dilemmas of the social sciences.' *Social Problems*, 15, 4, Spring 1968, pp. 408–19.

Walker, Rob. 'The sociology of education and life in school classrooms.' *International Review of Education*, Special Number, 18, 1, 1972, pp, 32–41.

Waller, W. *The Sociology of Teaching.* New York: Russell & Russell, 1961.

Walsh, W: H. 'Knowledge in its social setting.' *Mind*, LXXX, 1971, pp. 321–36.

Walton, J. and Kuethe, J. L., eds., *The Discipline of Education.* Madison, Wisconsin: University of Wisconsin Press, 1963.

Warnock, G. *Contemporary Moral Philosophy.* Macmillan, 1967.

Webb, J. 'The Sociology of a school.' *British Journal of Sociology*, 13, 3, 1962, pp. 264–72.

Weingartner, R. H. 'The meaning of "of" in "Philosophy of . . .".' *Journal of Value Inquiry*, 2, 1968, pp. 79–94.

Wheatley, J. 'Reasons for acting.' *Dialogue: Canadian Philosophical Review*, **VII**, 1969, pp. 553–67.

White, J. 'The concept of curriculum evaluation.' *Journal of Curriculum Studies*, **3**, 2, 1971, pp. 101–12.

Wilensky, Harold L. *Organizational Intelligence: Knowledge and Policy in Government and Industry*. New York: Basic Books, 1967.

Wilkinson, D. 'Sociological imperialism: a brief comment on the field.' *Sociological Quarterly*, **9**, 3, Summer 1968, pp. 397–400.

Williams, B. 'Philosophy', in M. Yudkin, ed., *General Education*. Allen Lane, Penguin Press, 1969.

———. 'Conversations with philosophers – Bernard Williams talks to Bryan Magee about philosophy and morals.' *The Listener*, **85**, 2184, 4 February 1971, pp. 136–40. Reprinted in B. Magee, ed., *Modern British Philosophy*. Secker & Warburg, 1971.

———. 'Philosophy and imagination.' *Times Educational Supplement*, 28 April 1972, p. 19.

Winch, P. 'The universities and the state.' *Universities Quarterly*, **12**, 1957, pp. 14–23.

———. *The Idea of a Social Science*. Routledge & Kegan Paul, 1958.

Wollheim, R. 'Philosophie analytique at pensée politique.' *Revue Française de Science Politique*, 2, 1961, pp. 295–308.

Woods, R. G., ed., *Education and its Disciplines*. University of London Press, 1972.

Young, M. F. D., ed., *Knowledge and Control: New Directions for the Sociology of Education*. Collier-Macmillan, 1971.

Ziff, P. 'The task of defining a work of art.' *Philosophical Review*, **62**, 1953, pp. 58–79.